I0810709

What Others Are Say[ing]

Terry Ruscin's Hidden History *endows future generations with historical facts versus lore, exposing the evolution of Henderson County's places and telling of its world-famous and local personalities. The diverse material proffers a heart-warming, nostalgic glance into the past.*

I loved it!

—*Gayle Hamilton Stepp, seventh-generation native and director of music, Hendersonville First Presbyterian Church*

The past few years I have had the great pleasure of serving with Terry Ruscin on the Design Review Advisory Committee for the Hendersonville Historic Preservation Commission. Terry has always shown an unceasing interest and genuine affection, not only for the historic places and events of our county, but even more so for the people and families from whom these places and events sprang. His unconcealed delight in the region is wonderfully evident in Hidden History of Henderson County, *where stories and descriptions long unrevealed are finally given the attention they deserve.*

—*John Horton, historic preservation architect/chair of the Hendersonville Design Review Advisory Committee*

This presentation represents tireless research and a multitude of interviews with longtime and lifelong residents—the result, a splendid documentary of the land and its people—a most worthwhile read.

—*Wick Andrews, seventh-generation native and publisher of books by Louise H. Bailey, Kermit Edney and Frank L. FitzSimons*

Over the past two years Terry Ruscin has frequently—sometimes daily—spent time at the Henderson County Genealogical and Historical Society reading old deed books and seeking the assistance of the volunteers in searching early documents and photographs as one source in his determination to accurately relate previously untold history of Henderson County and some of its people. The result of this endeavor, Hidden History of Henderson County, *is a most intriguing and interesting book focusing on some of the not-so-well-known early homes, churches, businesses and families of the county and concluding with an in-depth tour of Crab Creek Road, which will make you want to jump in your car and explore for yourself!*

—*Virginia Thompson, president, Henderson County Genealogical and Historical Society, Inc.*

HIDDEN HISTORY *of* HENDERSON COUNTY, NORTH CAROLINA

Terry Ruscin

THE History PRESS

Published by The History Press
Charleston, SC 29403
www.historypress.net

Unless otherwise credited, photographs are by Terry Ruscin.

Back cover: A distillery operation in Cathead with, from left to right, "Mr. Corn," Tyler Drake, Rufus Brown and John Bates Brown. *Photo courtesy of Betty Lakey and Henderson County Genealogical and Historical Society, Inc.*

First published 2013
Second printing 2013
Third printing 2014

Manufactured in the United States

ISBN 978.1.62619.129.7

Library of Congress Cataloging-in-Publication Data

Ruscin, Terry, 1951-
Hidden history of Henderson County, North Carolina / Terry Ruscin ; [foreword by] William "Wick" Andrews.
pages cm. -- (Hidden history)
Includes bibliographical references and index.
ISBN 978-1-62619-129-7 (pbk.)
1. Henderson County (N.C.)--History. 2. Henderson County (N.C.)--Biography. I. Title.
F262.H47R87 2013
975.6'92--dc23
2013027078

Notice: The information in this book is true and complete to the best of our knowledge. It is offered without guarantee on the part of the author or The History Press. The author and The History Press disclaim all liability in connection with the use of this book.

Dedicated to the memory of Chester "Chat" Jones (1949–2012),

and to our farmers and millers, past and present—the backbone of Henderson County.

Contents

Contents

Foreword

Kudos to Terry Ruscin for his wonderful new book, *Hidden History of Henderson County, North Carolina*. This presentation represents tireless research and a multitude of interviews with longtime and lifelong residents. The result, a splendid documentary of the land and its people—a most worthwhile read.

In my past experience in the printing business, I was happy to have published for several local authors, including:

- Frank L. FitzSimons—*From the Banks of the Oklawaha*. Frank submitted all copy to us in "somewhat readable" handwriting, which required four different proofs for each of his three volumes.
- Kermit Edney—*The Kermit Edney Weather Book* and *Things I Remember*—also handwritten, albeit not quite as legible as Frank's scrawl.
- Bush Laughter—*Tales from the Bush*. Louise Bailey, Terry's and my close personal friend and one of Terry's local history mentors, introduced me to Bush. God bless you, Louise.
- Louise Howe Bailey—four of her books, including *Draw Up a Chair*, each of the manuscripts meticulously presented in typed copy. We would sit on her front porch to discuss the production of the books—what a joy!

Terry Ruscin, thank you, Sir, for letting me participate in another fine book about Henderson County's heritage. I learned a lot.

WICK ANDREWS

Preface

Gazing at an aged building, a nostalgic voyeur might fancy flashbacks to architectural styles and life-ways of bygone eras. Some of us even find ourselves contemplating the figures that passed through, of historic events that may have occurred upon the grounds or within the walls of these venerable edifices. Particularly for the latter group—those who might wonder about the historic structures and sites and notable people of North Carolina's Henderson County—I tackled this book project.

Ever wondered who lived in those long-abandoned homesteads alongside our backcountry roads or who carved their farms from the wilderness, amending the rambling acreage now girded by ghostly gray fenceposts and rusted barbed wire? Imagine the human stories these places could tell! And what of all the homespun distilleries obscured deeply within the hollows—those secreted family enterprises so closely guarded or wholly overlooked by our former keepers of history and heritage?

And why did our earlier chroniclers touch only lightly—if at all—on the southwest sector of Henderson County known as Crab Creek Valley? Surely its legacy and people are worthy of print.

What about the provenance of our campgrounds and recreational forests? Who settled in those places long before the arrival of camp directors and forest rangers? How did steel magnate Andrew Carnegie impact the cultural milieu of Hendersonville? What of those august domiciles screened by thickets and wooded buffers off Kanuga Road, and who lived in the stately mansions up the lanky driveways beyond the granite pillars, gatehouses and security signs?

If you, too, are inquisitive, join me now as a fellow sojourner to discover and rediscover some of the wonders and mysteries of historic Henderson County, North Carolina.

The spirit of a place takes its color and shape
from the dreams of the dead no less than
from the thoughts of the living.
—*Francis Brett Young*

Note: In researching proper names through genealogical, census, birth, delayed-birth, marriage and death records, one encounters variations in the spellings of given names and surnames. In the case of this work, I used the more popular spellings.

Acknowledgements

History does not take the writer-researcher down the same lonesome path the field of fiction may propose to its scribes. Contrarily, the researcher spends much time away from the writing pad and keyboard, meeting with kindred parties intrigued with history and heritage and genealogy—which has surely been the case for yours truly, and not in the least "a lonely art," as some have described the practice of writing. Most importantly, friendships blossom during the process of sharing history as we probe its complex layers, striving to prove or refute its lateral folklore.

I extend special appreciation and indebtedness for the magnanimous gifts of knowledge, time and resources granted by V. Leon Pace, Jean Lance Pace and Gayle Hamilton Stepp. Without their undying and selfless assistance, this work would have been even more challenging than it proved to be.

Neicee Stepp Johnson, Mike Stepp, Sonya Stepp Hollingsworth and other descendants of the J.H. Stepps added to the enjoyment of exploring aspects of Henderson County, as did William "Wick" Andrews, Swann Burnitte Babb Jr., Joseph Bailey Jr., Larry Ball, Becky Sherman Banadyga, Dr. Michael Beckerman, Barbara Blaine, Brigadier General Frank Blazey, Everett Camp III, Betty Jean Carswell, Archie Case, Baynard Chamberlain, Tim Culberson of Aerial Photo Professionals, Nancy Harden Dotson, Dennis Dunlap, JoAnn Fain, Dr. Jack Frisch, Gem Stepp Garren, Carol Mantinband Ginsburg, Martha Connell Grose, Sindy Drake Hamilton, Oscar Harbin, genealogist-extraordinaire Janet Goad Hill, Louise Jackson Hill, Trudy Hill, John Horton, Sally Walker Hughes, James Johnson, Susan

Johnson, Chester "Chat" Jones, Frederick B. Jones, John Paul Jones, Bobby Justus, Carolyn King Justus, Nancy Kussrow, Janet Strider Link, Melinda Pilgrim Lowrance, David S. Mallett, Reverend Harold and Lois McKinnish, Dessie Orr, Jean Osteen Orr, Edgar Dwight Osteen, the dear Enie McCrary Pace, Donnie Parks, Ronnie Pepper, E. Hortence Potts, Reverend Danny Pridmore, Reverend Jonathan Rackley, Scott Reese, Linda and Sam Riddle, Susan Shepherd Sneeringer, Reverend D. Lewis Staton, Dennis Stepp, Chuck and Linda Stewart, Elmer Suttles, Sallie Thompson, Todd Thompson, Martha Justus Todd, Jim Toms, Patricia Walker, Lu Ann Welter, Kathleen Featherstone Williams and that prince among men, Sammy Williams.

I shall never forget, and am eternally grateful for, the road tours with Bobby and Robin Neill McGraw, V. Leon Pace, Gayle Hamilton Stepp, Ted Hamilton, Sam Sosebee, Carolyn King Justus, Clifford Bishop and Bobby Justus. And many thanks to the eminent Henderson County genealogist, scholar and historian Jennifer "Jennie" Jones Giles for her insight and her superb history courses at Blue Ridge Community College.

To be highly commended would be the unstinting assistance of Henderson County Genealogical and Historical Society volunteers Bill Barnwell, Sally Berger, Jeannie Taylor Lindsey, Stella Mace, V. Leon Pace, Margaret Payne and the society's president, Virginia Thompson, and director emeritus and co-founder Dr. George Alexander Jones. We in Henderson County are blessed to have at our disposal the society, its archives and its staff of dedicated volunteers and board members.

Thank you most kindly, one and all.

Part I
Historic Log Structures

Hold to the now, the here, through which all future plunges to the past.
—*James Joyce,* Ulysses

A Primer: Appalachian Pioneer Architecture

Many of us commonly refer to small—or even large—log structures as cabins, although technically the *cabin* would be of rudimentary construction, built with whole logs retaining all or most of their bark; and the log *house* would be a more finished edifice, constructed of logs hewn with an adze and broadaxe. In principle, a cabin would be hastily erected of un-hewn logs and then serve as temporary quarters on its builder's homestead. Such a structure generally lacked windows, and at best, its roof would have been covered with lanky hewn boards rather than shingles. The building would have in lieu of a stone chimney one constructed of logs or sticks and mud and daubed on its interior facing. Whether of logs or weatherboarded, slave dwellings were oftentimes referred to as cabins. Travel writer Thaddeus Harris wrote in an 1803 account, "If the logs be hewed; if the interstices be stopped with stone, and neatly plastered; and the roof covered with shingles neatly laid on, it is called a log house."

As settlers cleared their newly claimed land for home sites and fields, felling trees with axes or girdling them (cutting a ring through the bark to kill the tree), they laid in a natural supply of building materials from which they could erect their preliminary dwellings and outbuildings.

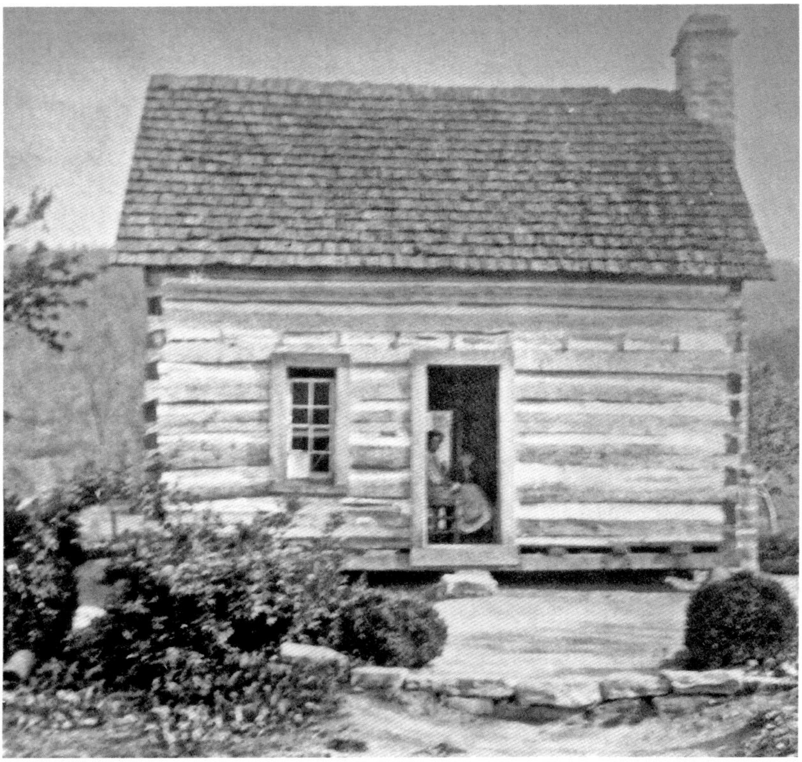

In their early married years, Reverend Jesse and Emma Osteen lived in this log home, which Jesse expanded and sheathed in weatherboarding. Family descendants believe the woman inside to be Emma and the builder to have been Jesse's father, Montiville F. Osteen. *Photo courtesy of the Osteen/Orr family.*

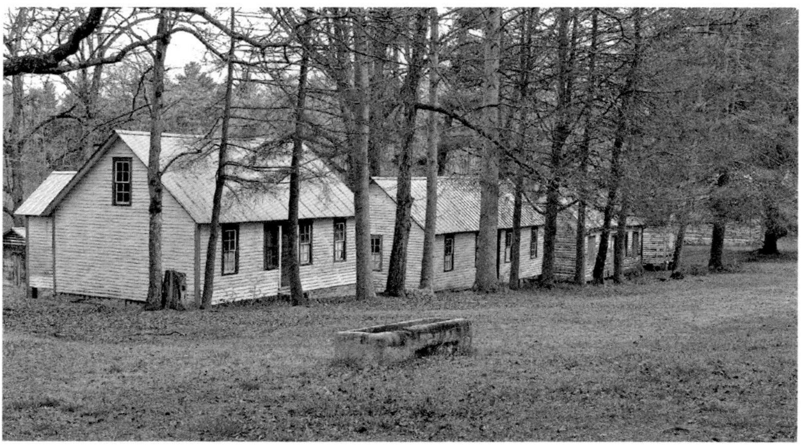

A row of slave cabins at Many Pines, Flat Rock, North Carolina.

Log structures ranged in form and style from crudely built huts or even lean-tos to elaborate plantation houses, and in days of old, builders also constructed city dwellings, schoolhouses, churches, jails, forts and courthouses of logs. Scandinavians, Germans and other Continental Europeans brought to America log-building technology, and the English, who did not build with logs in their homeland, quickly espoused the American pioneer technique of log construction.

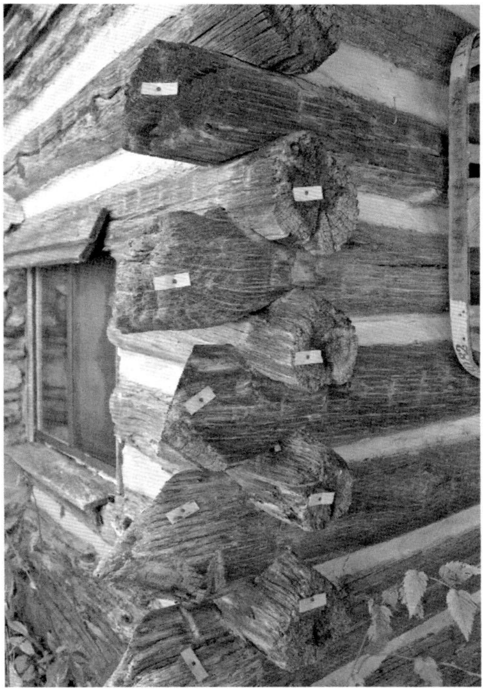

An example of saddle-notch construction: John Hiram Justice and Mary Jane King Justice home. Larry Ball numbered the logs with metal strips before dismantling the structure.

Another feature distinguishing a cabin from a house would be its foundation, the simplest of which consisted of log sills laid flat on the earth or on a single course of flat stones. Superior-quality houses sported sills raised on wooden blocks or stone piers, with wood flooring inside, lain on wood joists. The best of foundations, of continuous masonry—usually of stone, either dry laid or mortared—in some instances included a storage cellar. Taller foundations maintained a drier environment, less penetrable by pests and rot.

Builders constructed walls by stacking logs horizontally and joining them at the corners through one of several notching techniques: half-dovetail, V-notch or saddle notch. The logs ranged from large to small and from relatively unaltered, un-barked poles to carefully hewn rectangular planks. The most common surviving log buildings incorporate logs hewn flat on the interior and exterior faces, with tops and bottoms left round. The builder sealed the spaces between the logs, or interstices, with chinking—a caulking of moss, straw or animal hair—and then daubed the spaces with mud.

The crudest of cabins oftentimes had dirt floors—common as late as the Civil War—although, in accordance with the findings of Henderson

County historian Jennie Jones Giles, earthen floors were infrequent in western North Carolina due to weather conditions and/or to the building preferences of the occupants. Certain log houses featured floors of puncheon boards—long, thick, unfinished slabs of wood, riven (hand-split along the grain) and/or hewn approximately even and with gabled roofing generally of riven shingle, although clapboard may have been a common option.

Henderson County architect John Horton (1957–) explained that windows were generally protected with single board-and-batten shutters until glazed sashes could be obtained at some later date. Occasionally, sheets of oiled parchment were stopped in the openings to let in light while keeping out drafts. If iron hardware were not available, pintle-style strap hinges would have been carved from wood or fashioned from leather for the purpose of attaching doors and window covers.

Styles of log houses include single-pen, double-pen or saddlebag and dogtrot. A single-pen house, by and large consisting of one room—the "pen"—might include a chimney at one end of the structure. The saddlebag house utilizes two log pens straddling a central chimney. The dogtrot version features a room at each end, each with a fireplace, and the space between referred to as the "dogtrot." The space may have originated as an open breezeway, later framed as a central hall. Any of these styles could range in height from one and a half stories, including a loft, to two stories. And any of them could have been overlaid with weatherboarding at later dates.

JOHN JONES/GOVAN KING HOUSE (CIRCA 1835)

Some refer to the tulip tree (*Liriodendron tulipifera*) as "poplar," "yellow poplar" and even "fiddle tree," when in fact it belongs to the order and family of wild magnolia. This species, common to western North Carolina, grows quickly, straight and tall, and falls under the category of hardwood—a winning combination for the construction of log buildings.

Old-timers remember having seen it standing in its original location, off King Road across from Atlas Lane, east of Mill Creek. The sturdy dwelling, already 130 years old and sporting hewn tulip tree logs, pine roof shingles and a stone chimney emerging from the center of its roof, housed many generations before its abandonment.

John Jones (1815–1864), who built the stalwart house, was the son of Captain Robert Jones (1794–1890) and Elizabeth McGuffie Jones (1794–

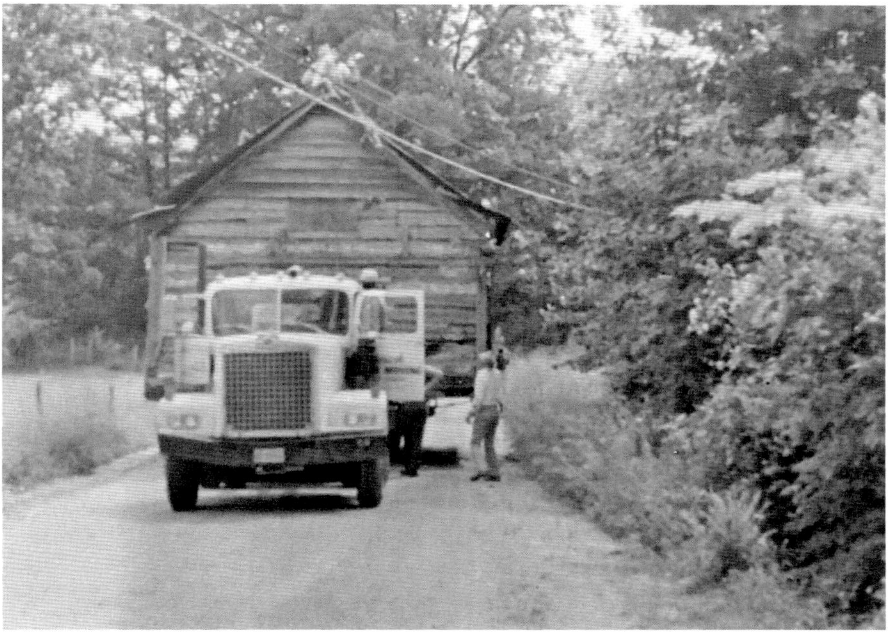

The John Jones home being moved from Dana to Flat Rock. *Photo courtesy of Elizabeth Lee.*

1889) and grandson of two of the region's earliest settlers, John Jones Sr. (1764–1860) and Mary Jane Hicks Jones (1767–1857). John Jones married Elizabeth Hamilton (1814–1894). Govan Thompson King (1879–1955) and Arminta Ellen Elizabeth Case King (1877–1960), farmers at Upward, were last to reside in the home. Govan was a son of Robert Jones King (1840–1924) and Sarah Emily A. Hill King (1838/40–1912).

In the 1960s, Dr. Lawrence Lee Jr. (1915–1999) and his wife, Elizabeth Lowndes Andrews Lee (1926–2010), moved Jones's log house to Highland Fling, their property alongside the shore of Highland Lake in Flat Rock. The Lees had the chimney dismantled and then the single-pen structure lifted in one piece and moved to Flat Rock on a flatbed truck. A mountain craftsman rebuilt the chimney at one end of the log house, dropped the ceiling, sheathed the roof in metal and attached a larger structure—with the same roofing material—to one end of the Jones home. The newer addition sports bedrooms, kitchen and laundry room with heartwood pine floors and a garage, with the original Jones home serving as the dwelling's parlor. One of the doors features a primitive bar-latch described by Frank L. FitzSimons after his visit to this log home during the tenure of Mrs. Govan

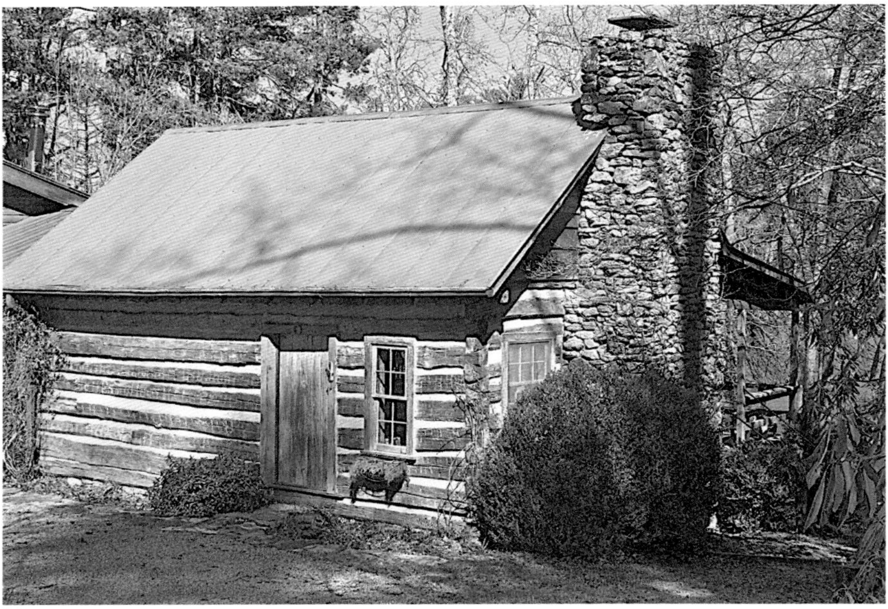

The John Jones home in its current setting alongside Highland Lake.

King. Mr. FitzSimons later told his publisher, William P. "Wick" Andrews (1929–)—Mrs. Lee's brother—about the log house, believing it should be saved. The Lees of Savannah, Georgia, and Bluffton, South Carolina, used the restored and appended log abode as a summer residence.

Betty Lee and her brother, Wick Andrews, descended from the prominent Lowndes family, whose members lived full time or during summertime in Flat Rock since the seminal days of the colony that became known as "the little Charleston of the Mountains."

HIRAM KING JONES HOME (CIRCA 1853)

Just north of Flat Rock, near the junction where Erkwood Drive T-bones the Greenville Highway, a thicket of laurels and pines masks a log house from any possible scrutiny of passersby. Owned since 1974 by Betty Jean Billingsley Carswell, this structure has been moved twice—from its original location where Hiram King Jones erected his family's domicile near the Big

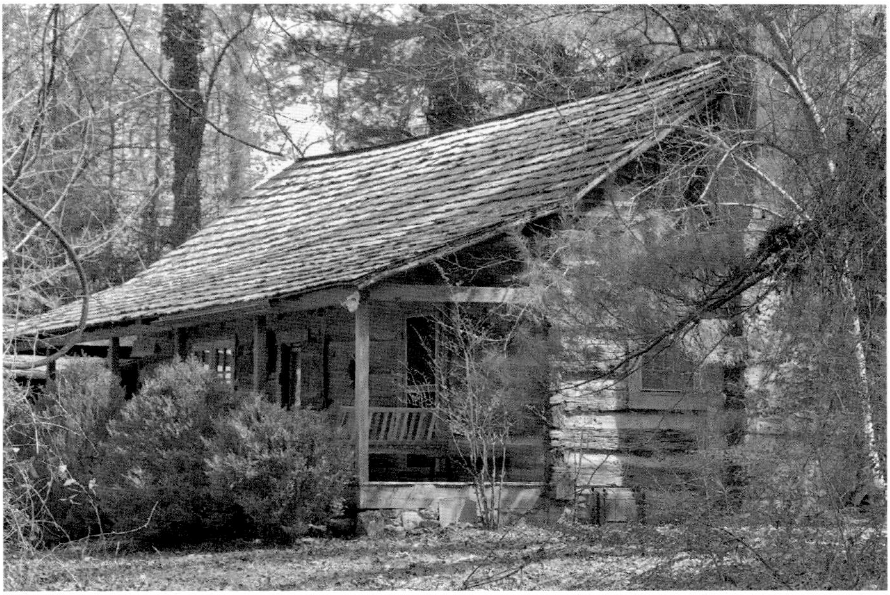

Hiram King Jones's Big Hungry home in its third and current location.

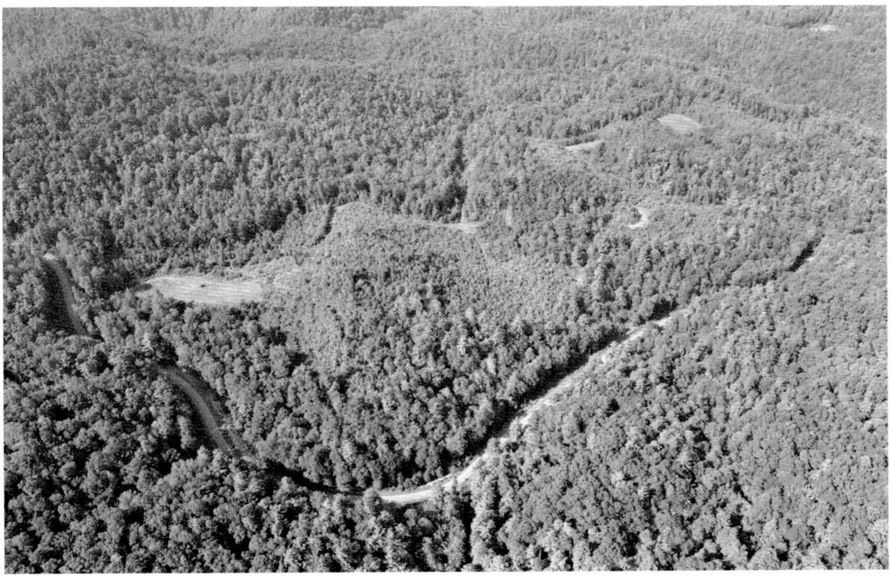

Aerial view of the Hiram King Jones home's Big Hungry location, now owned by the North Carolina Wildlife Resources Commission. *Photo courtesy of Tim Culberson of Aerial Photo Professionals.*

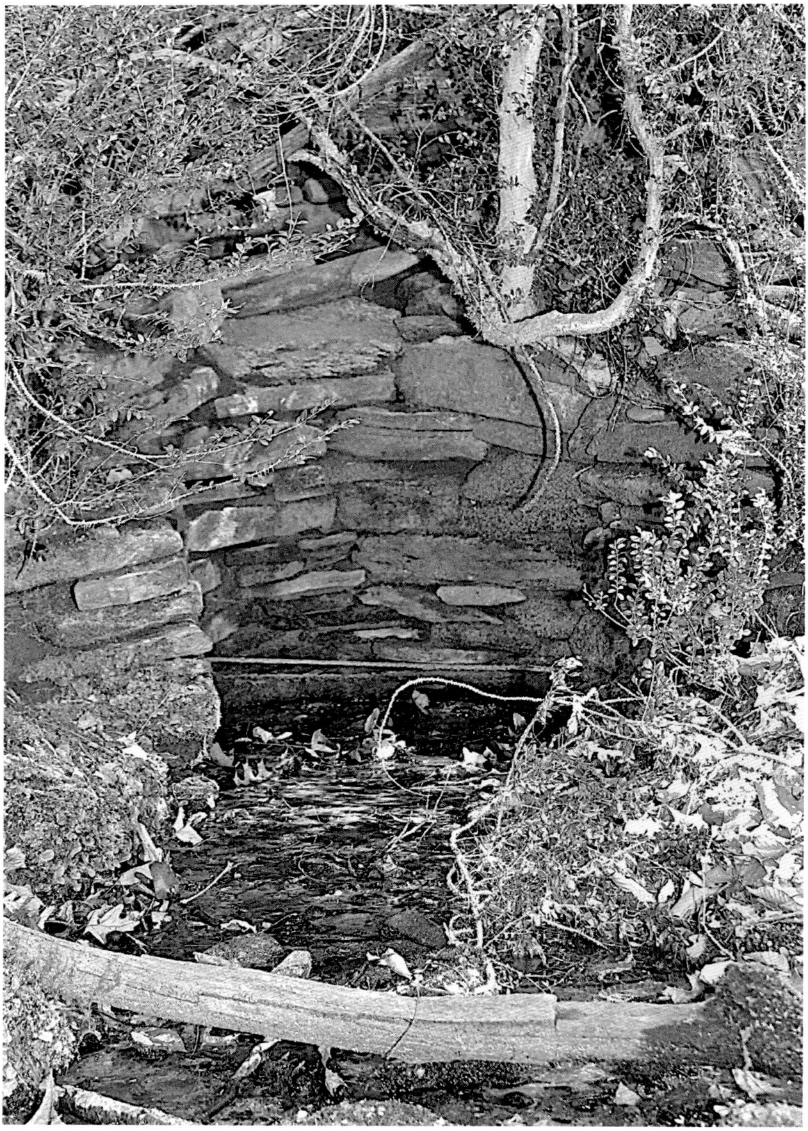

The intact springhouse at the Hiram King Jones home's Big Hungry location.

Hungry River and, subsequently, from its relocated situation alongside the Spartanburg Highway where the Upward Community Club outfitted it as Old Homestead Crafts and Gifts in the 1950s.

Named for his uncle Hiram King (1792–1891), Hiram King Jones (1820–1912) and his first wife, Mary Caroline Justus Jones (1824–1887), bore thirteen children; one, Mary Ann, died before the age of three. Born and reared in Blue Ridge, Jones spent his active years as a farmer, land speculator and trader, also involving himself in the lumbering business and working the family sawmills.

Jones kept at least two mistresses on the side, and one of them, Naomi Caroline "Oney" (sometimes spelled "Onie") Johnson (circa 1843–1887), bore three of his sons: Hiram K. Johnson (1862–1927), Andrew Jackson Johnson (1863–1940) and Grayson Leander Johnson (1867–1936). Jones kept another mistress, Sarah Elvinia Shipman Stepp (1842–1917), in a log house tucked away in the small population center known as Pink Bed within what is now the Pink Beds at Pisgah National Forest, Transylvania County.[1] An 1880 Transylvania County census listed the following "boarders" in this home: Sarah Elvinia Stepp and her child Mahulda[2] (age fifteen) and Andrew Johnson (age sixteen). After Jones's wife Mary filed an adultery case against him in the court of Henderson County in 1867, Jones contracted to indenture his illegitimate sons until they reached the ages of twenty-one—a contract witnessed by Jones's brother-in-law, Moses Heatherly (1815–1890). With at least seventeen children to his credit, one can only wonder how the man found time for any of his attributed trades.

When his wife Mary died, Jones married Sarah Elvinia Stepp. Jones sold the home to his daughter Emily Delilah King Jones Morrison (1853–1954) and her husband, Daniel Lafayette "Fate" Morrison (1855–1923), in 1887. Daniel Morrison served as the Decatur postmaster from 1899 to 1906, when a star route out of Dana took over to serve the area. Morrison, a farmer, operated the post office from his living room in the log home. When the state bought the property in the 1950s, a group of crafters moved the log house to Spartanburg Highway.

Emblematic of pioneer homes of the Blue Ridge Mountains, the Jones abode sports dovetailed log construction chinked with mortar; heart-pine floorboards; hand-adzed ceiling beams; native stone foundations, stoop and chimney; windows with single-panel, board-and-batten shutters; and an open front porch. The kitchen and dining ell, which sported a chimney, is no

1. Transylvania deed records (December 7, 1881; Book 4; pp. 175–76) show the Pink Bed/Cradle of Forestry property—349 acres running south, the headwaters of Mills River and east to the Mill Shoals, known today as Looking Glass Falls—belonged to Hiram King Jones, the nephew of Hiram King (1792–1891).
2. Mahulda Morris Jones McGraw (1864–1936).

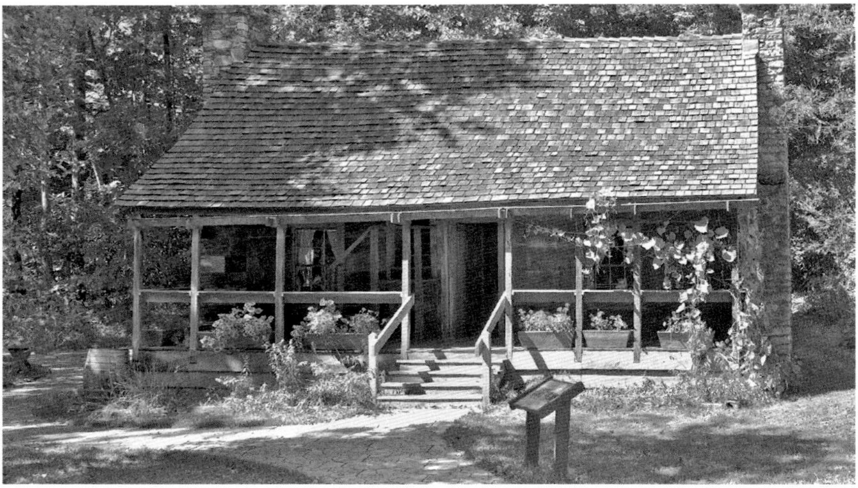

The circa 1880s home once owned by Hiram [Woodfin] King (1844–1935), Cradle of Forestry. This one-and-one-half-story, side-gabled, log-frame structure boasts an intact interior.

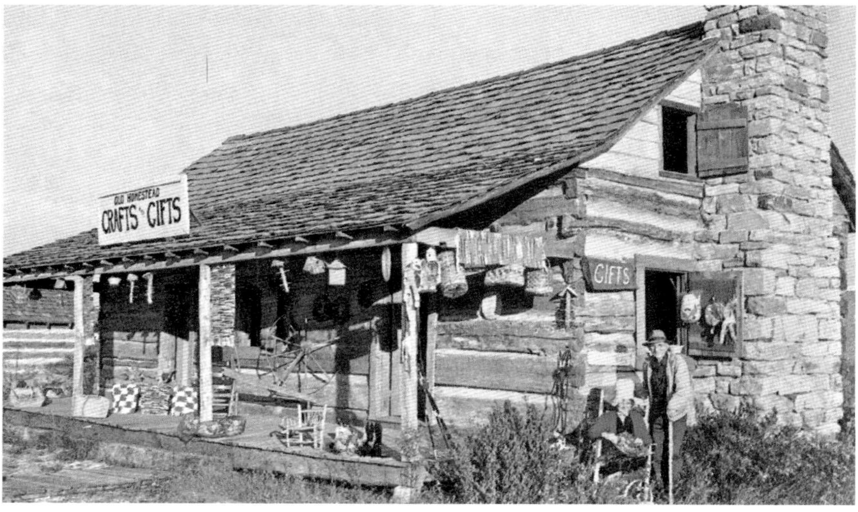

A vintage postcard showing the Hiram King Jones home in use as a folk art shop alongside Spartanburg Highway, with Mr. and Mrs. James Bradley. *Photo courtesy of John Paul Jones.*

longer extant. Another ell, still intact, incorporated a loom room. Modern enhancements such as electricity and running water add to the abode's comfort as used for vacation lodging by the Carswells' guests.

JOHN MCCARSON HOUSE (CIRCA 1830)

In the early 1800s, frontiersman John McCarson (circa 1803 or 1808–1884) acquired 140 acres of land in southwestern Buncombe County on what would become known as Long John Mountain. Son of James Andrew McCarson (1779–1863) and Martha Richardson McCarson (1786–1830) and grandson of Scottish-born John David McCarson Sr. (1752–1821)—one of the region's first white settlers—John McCarson was said to have stood at least six-foot-seven and his wife, Anne, at six-foot-five. John McCarson, "tall as a poplar and strong as an oak," was a foxhunter known to raise a little Cain. On his mountainside farm, he raised sheep and purportedly grew the first peaches in what is now Henderson County.

McCarson erected his two-room house with oak, tulip tree and pine logs on the mountain later named for him. He hewed out the logs, chinked them and set the stone in the two fireplaces and chimneys. As his

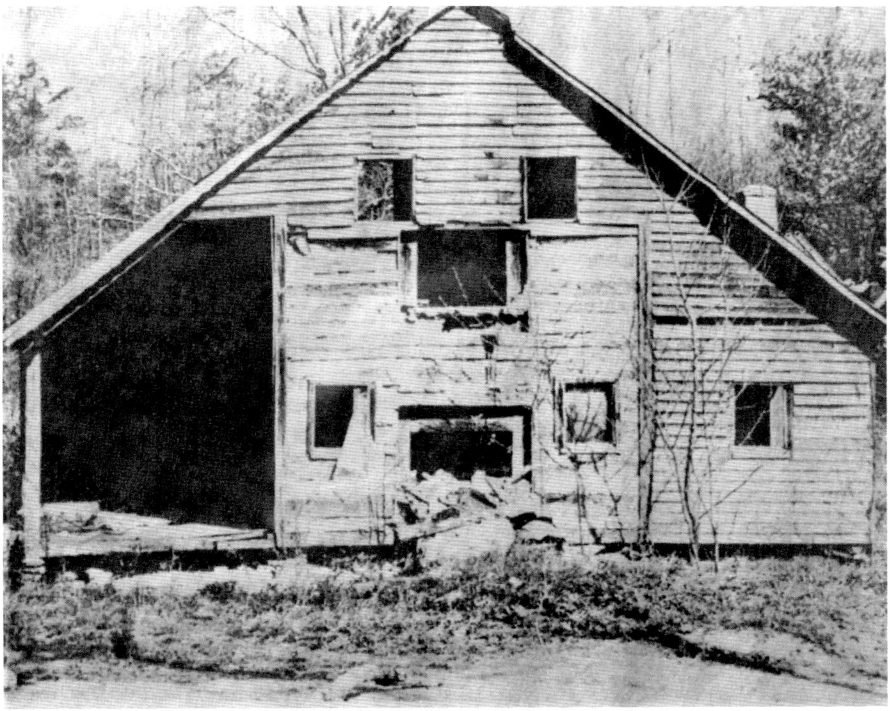

This *Times-News* photo shows the McCarsons' original log home at the center of its added wings. *Photo courtesy of Linda S. Riddle.*

family grew and more timber became available on the slope, McCarson family descendants added rooms on either side by building around the nucleus of the original log home. Luther Smith, a land planner, recalled the original site of the house, in Governor's Point—in the Carriage Park subdivision—on or near the lot of 130 Jenny Lind Drive. Smith said a springhouse stood below that point.

The industrious McCarson, said to have been honest, dependable and a man who always paid his debts, cleared land for his orchards and carved a mile-long wagon road from what is now Haywood Road up to his home on the mountain. He married Anne Frances Carver (circa 1813–circa 1880), who had a boy and a girl from a previous marriage. John and Anne had two more children. At age seventy-five, McCarson found religion and became a deacon in Shaw's Creek Baptist Church. During the Civil War, a bushwhacker purportedly shot John H. Carver (circa 1838–1864), one of the McCarsons' sons.

Decades ago, Scott Staton and Vernon Edney began dismantling the McCarson house, marking the logs so they could be reassembled on a plot farther down the mountainside as a guest lodge for local banker Forest V. "Foffie" Hunter Jr. (1901–1988), who purportedly used the log house during his hunting excursions. Staton and Edney removed the additions,

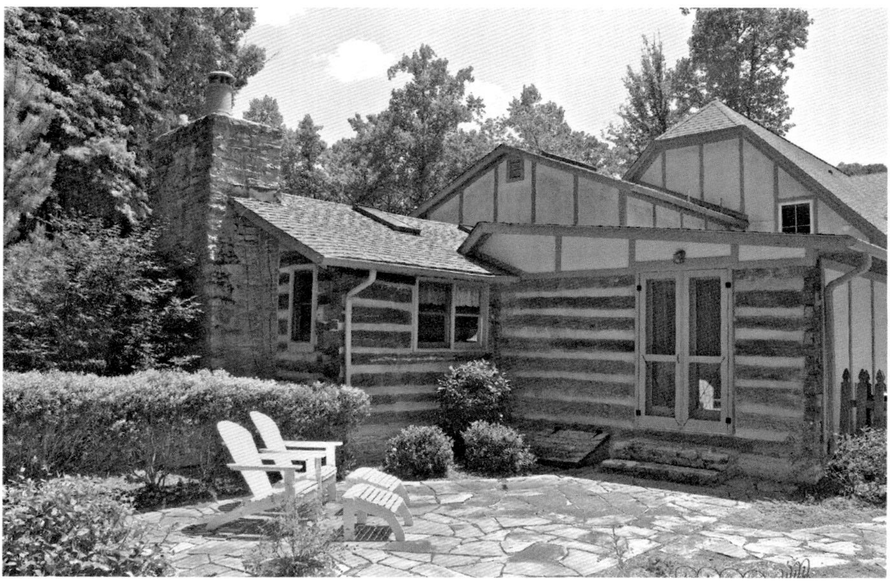

Long John McCarson's log home, now attached to the Riddles' home.

returning the structure to its original two-room-plus-loft status. The builders also rescued its stonework, including the hearths, for use in the reconstruction. Today, Samuel E. and Linda S. Riddle of Riddle Construction own the property. The Riddles updated the McCarson house, maintaining for the most part its rusticity, and built their Tudor-style mansion onto one end of it, living in the log house during construction of the larger dwelling.

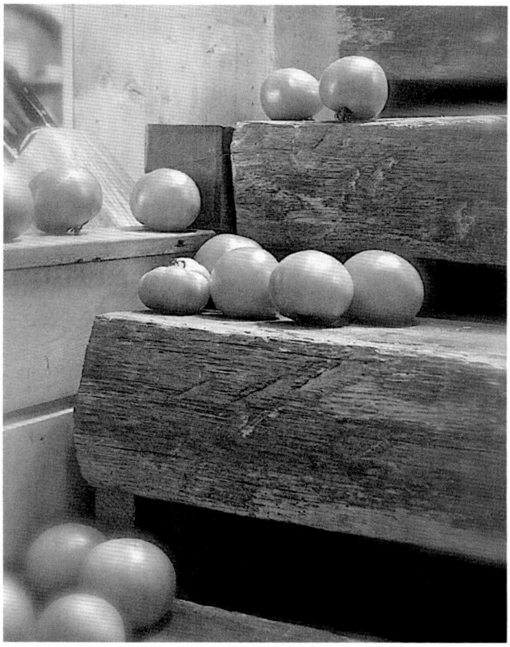

The original stair steps in Long John McCarson's log home.

The log home's parlor, incorporating original stones from one of McCarson's fireplaces, mantel and chimney, proffers a charming and cozy retreat for guests. The Riddles had the original timber stair steps reassembled and added balustrade and struts fashioned from trees on the property.

Just up the road in the Creekside subdivision, one finds the McCarson Cemetery (established 1909), the burial ground of McCarson family members. Older tombstone inscriptions have mostly eroded away, with what some have identified as Long John's monument no longer legible. Speculation suggests that McCarson's remains were reinterred here.

Old-timers in the Haywood area claimed to have heard dogs barking toward Long John Mountain after dark, alleging that the dogs were answering the calls of Long John McCarson's foxhounds baying in the past. On a more historically accurate note, John McCarson's brother Jacob Pinckney McCarson (1810–1894) owned land on Echo Mountain, where there exists another McCarson family cemetery, which was desecrated for the sake of development.

MARY JANE "POLLY" KING JUSTICE HOUSE (CIRCA 1834)

Dana farmer Larry Ball (1936–) has a penchant for pioneer structures, so much so that he built and lives in one—a two-story-plus-loft log home of massive proportions. Ball also rescued aged log structures and reconstructed them on his property, including the home of "Doctor" Mary Jane "Polly" King Justice (1819–1904), built by her husband, John.

Mary Jane King, daughter of Hiram King, married John Hiram Justice (1816–1901) in 1835, and the couple had thirteen children, three of whom died in infancy.

Polly, a "granny woman"—sometimes referred to as "granny doctor"—ranked among Henderson County's earliest midwives and medical practitioners. Many granny women, self-ordained physicians, maintained a keen sense of holistic healing passed down through generations of other granny women and Native Americans. Such "doctors" dosed their patients with purgatives and emetics and potions or elixirs composed of natural ingredients harvested from the woodlands: herbs, berries, roots, bark and honey—earning for such women the title of "yarb doctor." Backwoods doctors also coated their hands with lycopodium powder—the spores of club mosses—both water-repellant and antiseptic. If literate, granny women consulted home medicine guides and herbal handbooks. And

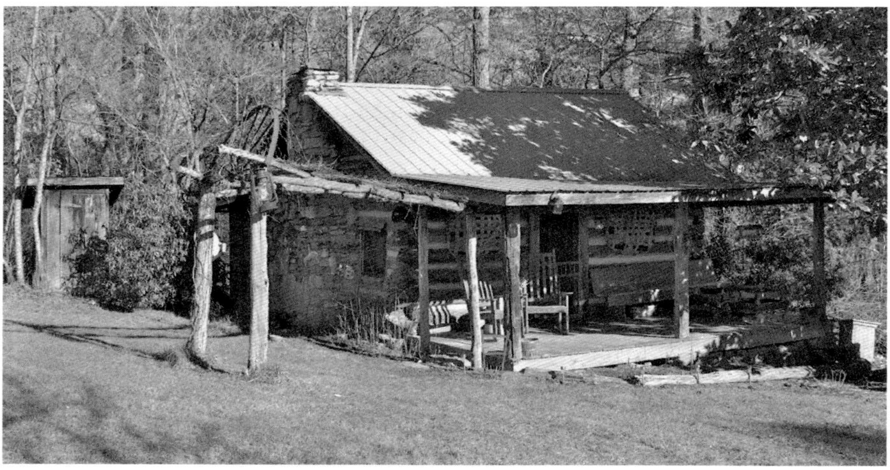

Larry Ball moved the Justice home to his property from its original site on Ridge Road near Dana Baptist Church.

when all seemed hopeless, they used the power of prayer, chanted Bible verses and employed such notions as placing a sharp knife or axe in the bed of the patient to "cut the pain." If nothing else, the services of the granny doctor alleviated the patient's symptoms.

Unlike the average granny doctor, however, Polly Justice was said to have been a licensed physician, yet no documentation exists to prove such an accreditation. She nevertheless made house calls by traveling through all manner of weather, scaling steep slopes and fording creeks, on the back of a horse through the hinterlands of the county and beyond, working—as did a number of our pioneer healers—mostly for barter or for no remuneration whatsoever.

Polly would have likely laid in a supply of laudanum, quinine and morphine when she could get to a drugstore to purchase such medications. And she surely employed homeopathic ingredients such as blackberry for dysentery, dandelion for its diuretic effect and ginseng—or "sang"—for colic, plus a pinch of superstition.

Granny women proffered much-needed services in an era when many physicians were poorly trained and inept, some folks claiming that every woman was born a doctor. These highly trusted women served not only as healers but also as midwives. Generations ahead of their time, these women realized the importance of nurturing, caring environments, much like hospitals' special birthing suites of today. Midwifery in that era included psychological support by way of the empathy another woman could offer the delivering mother. The granny woman would attend to the medical needs of her patient and also perform necessary household chores, affording the mother time to recover and recuperate. And she would stay with her patient until it was safe to leave her, thus offering preventive care during the possible onset of postpartum symptoms.

Midwives would sometimes use mother's milk or even the mother's urine to wash the newborn's eyes, in lieu of the silver nitrate or povidone iodine solutions prescribed by today's medical practitioners. And they generally performed breech deliveries by reaching into the birth canal to turn the baby rather than risking infection with the dangerous medical technique of removal by forceps. If the baby should die within the womb, the midwife sometimes performed a craniotomy as a last-resort procedure.

The Justices' log house stands today in tribute to one of Henderson County's earliest and highly regarded medical practitioners. The Justices are buried at Hiram King (King's Grove Baptist Church) Cemetery in Dana.

NATURAL PHARMACEUTICALS

A Sampler of Ingredients Employed by Granny Women in Treating Their Patients

aster (*Aster curtisii*): used to treat stomach disorders, hysteria, parasites and gout

blackberry (*Rubus species*): as a tea for its astringent qualities and to prevent hemorrhaging

bloodroot (*Sanguinaria canadensis*): for treating sores and external pre-cancerous conditions

cabbage and collard leaves: wraps for poultices and also for inflammations, sore eyes and hangovers

castor oil (*Ricinus communis*): antimicrobial (antiviral, antibacterial and antifungal), labor stimulant, anti-inflammatory and analgesic

catnip (*Nepeta cataria*): sedative and astringent qualities, for colic, teething, hives, bronchitis, colds, diarrhea, fever, chicken pox and headaches

clover (*Trifolium pratense*): an ingredient for cough syrup, menopausal symptoms, ulcers and pH balancing

cobwebs: rich in vitamin K, applied as natural bandages and for clotting blood

cod liver oil: rich in vitamins A and D, used to accelerate wound healing; prescribed to nursing mothers to increase fat content of milk

dandelion (*Taraxacum*): diuretic, bile and liver symptoms

dogwood bark (*Cornus florida*): substitute for quinine, brewed as a tea to ease fever

ginseng (*Panax trifolius*): vitality enhancement, stress reduction, insomnia and chest congestion

goldenseal (*Hydrastis canadensis*): natural antibiotic, anti-inflammatory, laxative, canker sores, cancer

honey: antibacterial; an ingredient in cough syrups and for treating certain allergies and as a balm for wounds

lady's-slipper root (*Cypripedium acaule* and *Cypripedium calceolus*): sedative, anti-depressive, nervine qualities

leeches (*Hirudo medicinalis*): primitive method of bloodletting, also for treatment of osteoarthritis and abscesses

molasses: rich in sulfides, prescribed for anxiety, constipation, edema, heart palpitations, anemia, joint pain, acne, hemorrhoids and cancer

mullein (*Verbascum*): cold and flu symptoms, coughing and earaches

myrtle (*Myrtus*): astringent, antiseptic and anticonvulsant qualities, prescribed for sinus infections, bronchitis, fatigue, depression, itching and headaches and as an expectorant

peach (*Prunus persica*): bark, kernels and leaves boiled as a tea for stomach, liver and skin complaints and to treat worms and wounds
pine tar: cough suppressant also used in treating skin conditions such as rashes, psoriasis, acne and eczema
poison ivy (*Toxicodendron radicans*): herpetic eruptions, palsy, acute rheumatism, articular stiffness and incontinence
pokeweed (*Phytolacca*): for itching, stings and cancer
rabbit tobacco (*Gnaphalium obtusifolium*): stuffed in a pillow to relieve asthma, colds and congestion and as an insect repellant
ramp (*Allium tricoccum*): "plant penicillin" rich in sulfides, used in treating ailments of winter colds and congestion and for lowering blood pressure
raspberry (*Rubus idaeus*): as a tea to relax uterine muscles during contractions
rattlesnake plantain (*Goodyera pubescens*): rash, yeast infection, headaches, bee stings and snakebites
sassafras (*Sassafras albidum*): antiseptic qualities; roots and bark steeped as a tea for treating fevers, scurvy, skin sores, kidney problems, toothaches, rheumatism, bronchitis, conjunctivitis, hypertension and dysentery
sumac (*Rhus typhina*): astringent qualities, leaves and berries prescribed for bladder, digestive, reproductive and respiratory ailments, infections, stomachaches, diabetes and hyperglycemia
sweet gum (*Liquidambar*): astringent and expectorant qualities; anti-inflammatory; incorporated into salves and administered in treating frostbite, hemorrhoids, sore throats and strokes
urine: cauterizing agent, astringent qualities; substitute for silver nitrate or povidone iodine for prevention of neonatal conjunctivitis; administered also in treatment of oral ulcers, acne and warts
wild ginger (*Asarum canadense*): ingredient in salves for burns
wild violet roots (*Viola papilionacea*): expectorant qualities, also used in herbal salves for skin irritations

ANKIE PHILLIPS HOUSE (CIRCA 1850)

Another of the log structures rescued by Larry Ball was home to Steve Anthroit "Ankie" (sometimes spelled "Anthy") Phillips (1826–1905/06), daughter of Stephen Phillips (1761–1845) and Violet Hood Phillips (1784–1870). Ankie's brother-in-law, Joe Taylor (1810–1891), built the house on the family farm for Ankie and an orphaned child named Ellen T. Morgan (1863–1927).

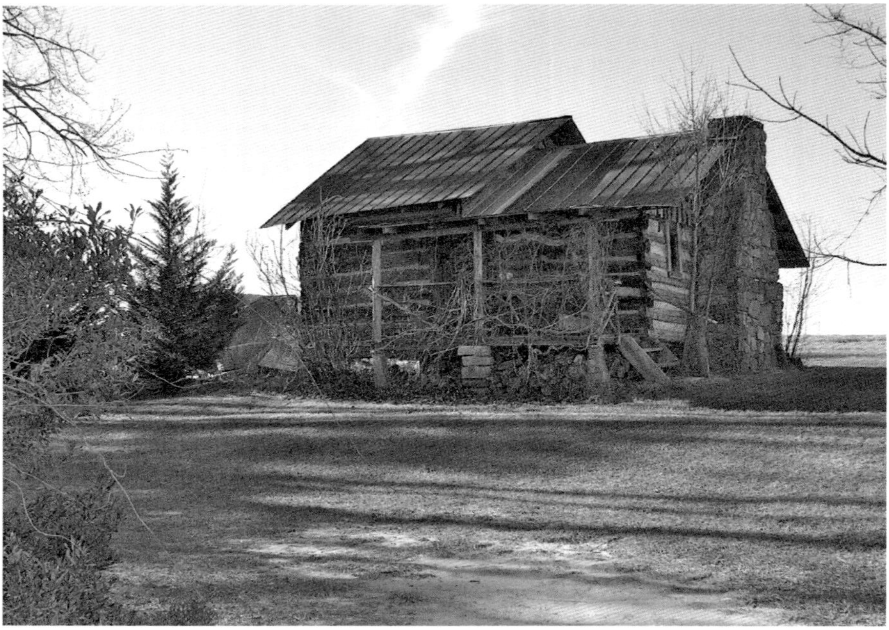

Ankie Phillips's log home.

When after her mother's burial service the little bastard child Ellen was left standing alone at the graveside, Joe Taylor rescued her, taking her to his sister-in-law for rearing. Ankie remained unmarried, caring for Ellen into adulthood and also caring for her aged mother and, according to a 1900 census record, an "insane man" named Daniel Justus. Because he was elderly at the time, it might be assumed that Mr. Justus suffered from old-age dementia.

Family members buried Ankie on the site of her home off what is now Sunset Drive near Sugarloaf Road, posing a problem for resale of the property. After potential buyers demurred, family members arranged for exhumation of the body for reburial at Ebenezer Baptist Church Cemetery.

Govan Tabor House (circa 1860)

A few of Henderson County's ninteenth-century log homes exist to this day only because interested parties moved them from their construction sites to new localities and restored them. One such example stands on

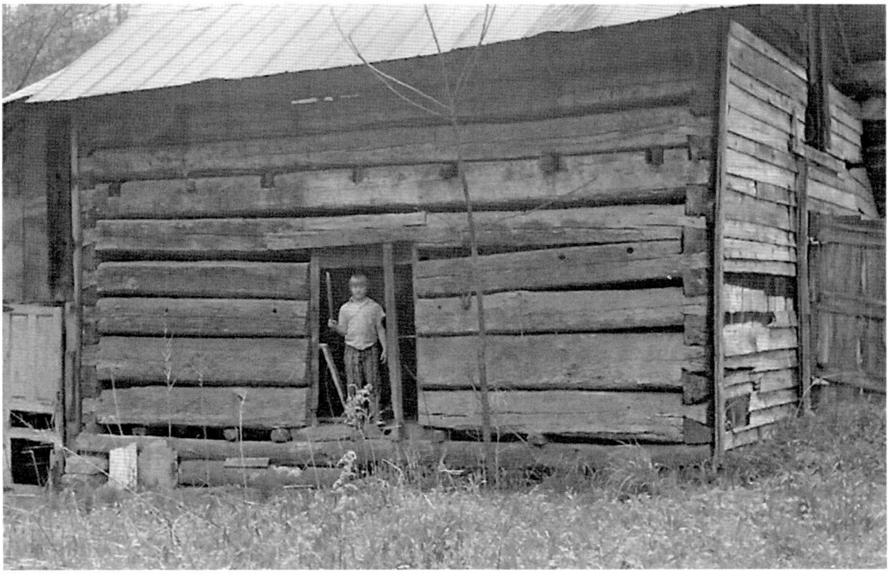

Jeff Thompson (1955–) in the doorway of Govan Tabor's log home at its Deep Gap location, 1972. *Photo courtesy of Sallie M. Thompson.*

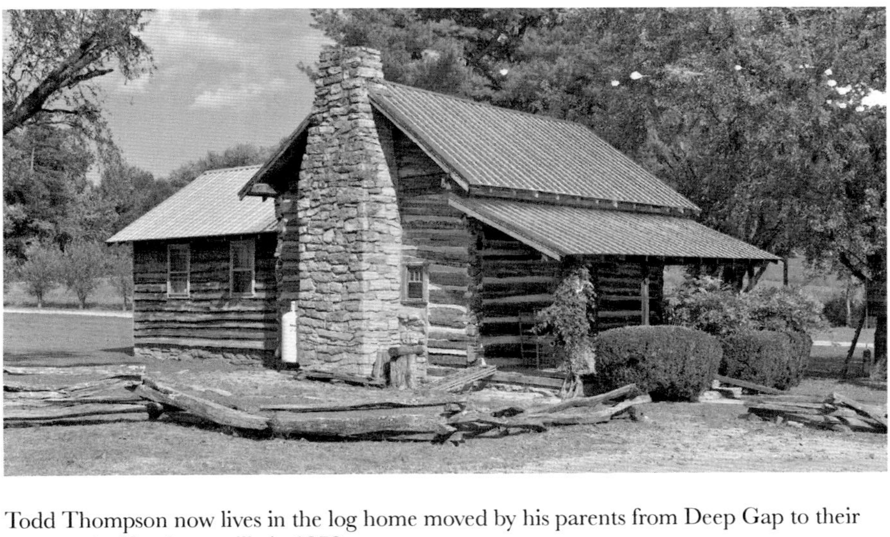

Todd Thompson now lives in the log home moved by his parents from Deep Gap to their property in Hendersonville in 1972.

the property of the late Harry Zebulon Thompson (1932–1993) and his wife, Sallie Mauldin Thompson (1934–), set back from Dana Road within a stone's throw of the Blue Ridge Mall. The Thompsons—owners of Hendersonville's Piggy's & Harry's—purchased the structure from Champion Fiber Company, which once owned the property adjacent to the Thompsons' property in Deep Gap. Champion held the land for the purposes of logging and pulpwood production.

According to Dr. Reid Sinclair, who wrote a paper on the Tabor log home in 1975, Harry Thompson and his three sons took the structure down, numbering each log so that they could put them back in place. The logs of tulip poplar likely had been cut with a broadaxe and string, and at some point someone had covered the structure with a barn, protecting it from the elements and accounting, no doubt, for its long life. Govan Tabor (1825–1897) was the last to reside in this home in its original Deep Gap location, and Harry Thompson recalled having played in the abandoned building as a child. Todd Thompson (1956–), son of Harry and Sallie, currently lives in the log home.

ZACHARY YOUNG HOUSE (CIRCA 1880)

Against a wooded backdrop alongside Marshall Road in Dana stands a clutch of log houses, a gray barn and a shed. Robert Siebold (1949–) of Naples, Florida, dismantled and relocated the structures to this site for the purpose of letting them out as guest and client cottages. Siebold moved two of the houses from McDowell County, one of them from Marion and another from the vicinity of Old Fort, and still another from Buncombe County. Perhaps the most impressive of the lot hails from about a mile away—erected in 1764 or 1771, depending on who tells the story—but more likely this house was built in the 1880s. Descendants of Zachary "Zack" Taylor Young (1860–1931) tell of his having lived there with his wife, Eliza Jane Jones Young (1850–1927). Zack was the son of William G. Young (1815–1890) and Catherine Case Young (1817–1901), who first lived there.

Zack and Eliza's daughter Florence Young Stepp (1884–1926) lived in the log home with her husband, Hiram Kimsey Stepp (1883–1947), and their daughter Georgia Stepp (1910–1994) was last to reside there before it was abandoned and then moved in 2008 to its present site from

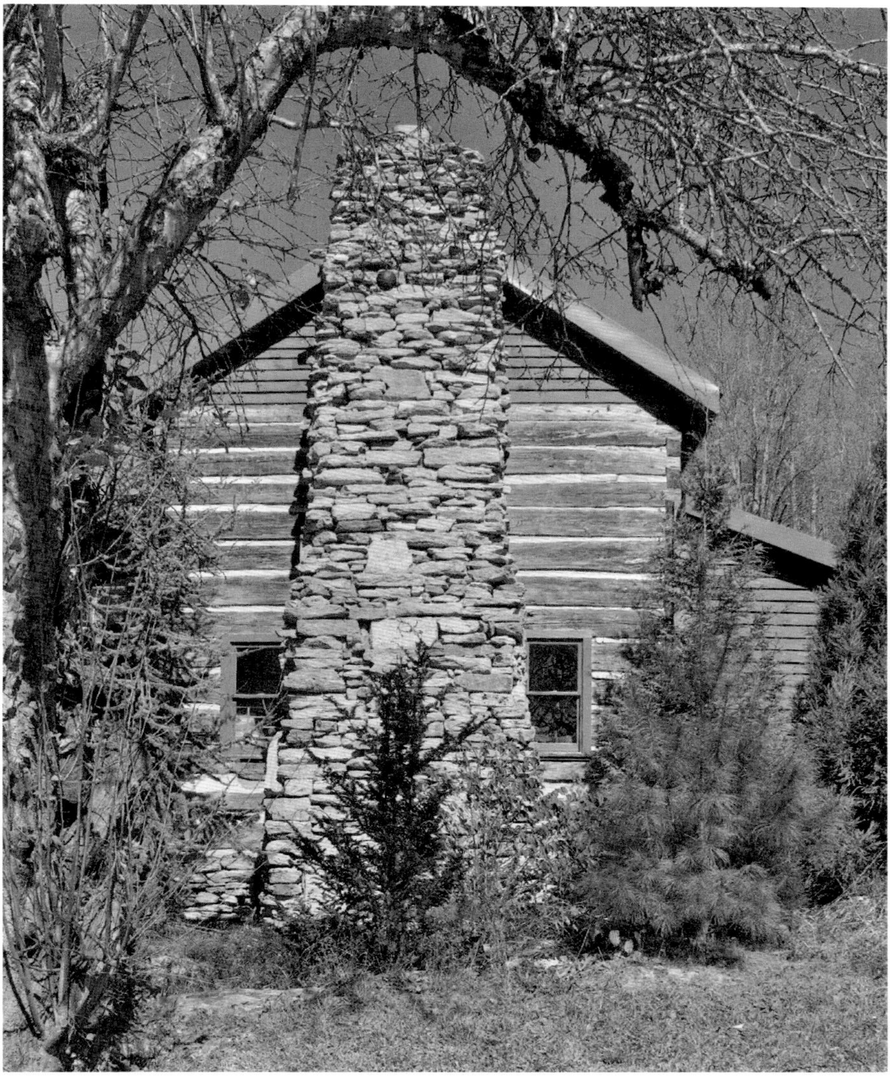

The log home of Zachary Taylor Young.

Sugarloaf Road near Pilot Mountain. Robert Siebold remarked that he did not have to dismantle the house but rather had it moved in two sections and placed on its rebuilt foundations. If this house had indeed been built in the later 1700s, it would likely be the oldest extant log structure in Henderson County.

FRANCIS ALEXANDER STEPP HOUSE (CIRCA 1850)

Alongside Stepp Road in Hoopers Creek a stone chimney leans, revealing a gap between it and a two-story log house. Surely the chimney would have tumbled by now had someone not strapped it back in place. Francis Alexander Stepp (1878–1959) and his wife, Lovdie Ann Couch Stepp (1882–1968), were the last family members to live in this dwelling. F.A. Stepp was a son of Joseph Livingston Stepp (1848–1915) and Martha Salome Corn Stepp (1847–1922). If indeed the home dates to the mid-nineteenth century, as suggested by Stepp descendants, then perhaps J.L. Stepp's father, John Jones Stepp (1822–1864), built the home for himself and his first wife, Cynthia (Charity) Elizabeth Case Stepp (circa 1825–1883). Family descendants also believe this structure or its predecessor housed an early schoolhouse.

The original frame structure, erected on this site, owes its state of preservation to its having been clad with weatherboarding for decades. About a decade ago, one of F.A. Stepp's grandsons removed the siding and secured the chimney, in hopes of restoring it one day.

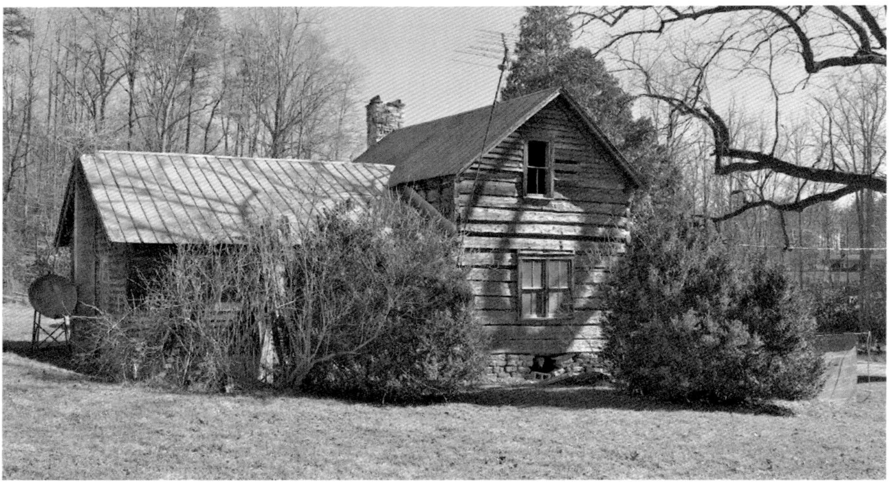

The Francis Alexander Stepp home.

Part II
What Was That?

Tuscarora

On the west side of the Greenville Highway, across from the subdivision of Brookland Manor, stands an expansive white edifice referred to as "the white Collison [*sic*] mansion" in one of Frank L. FitzSimons's books. Mr. FitzSimons also mentioned the locality as having once been the "old Hanckel estate." Within the last decade, Park Place Developers LLC raised the subdivision called Towne Place with the white mansion as its centerpiece. In 2006, the developers restored the mansion, dividing it into two upscale town homes.

In poring through Henderson County deed records dating back to the time of the county's formation, one finds this plat of land and contiguous plats having passed through the hands of many, including Shipmans, Braddocks, Ducotes, Rays, Rickmans, Drakes, Barnetts, Mileses, Barrings and Sittons. If—according to Frank L. FitzSimons—the Hanckels indeed once owned this parcel of land, it was perhaps in the days before Henderson was carved from Buncombe County.

In the 1940s, Carl Ault (1899–1968), president of the Henderson County Board of Realtors, and his wife, Dorothy Dean Ault (1897–1991), purchased the tract—under the title "Aultwood Court, Inc."—from Virginia G. Shipman (from the will of Elsie Merle Ray). Mr. Ault owned Carl Ault Realty Company in Hendersonville. The couple, originally from Ohio, also lived in Hialeah, Florida, where Mr. Ault was mayor.

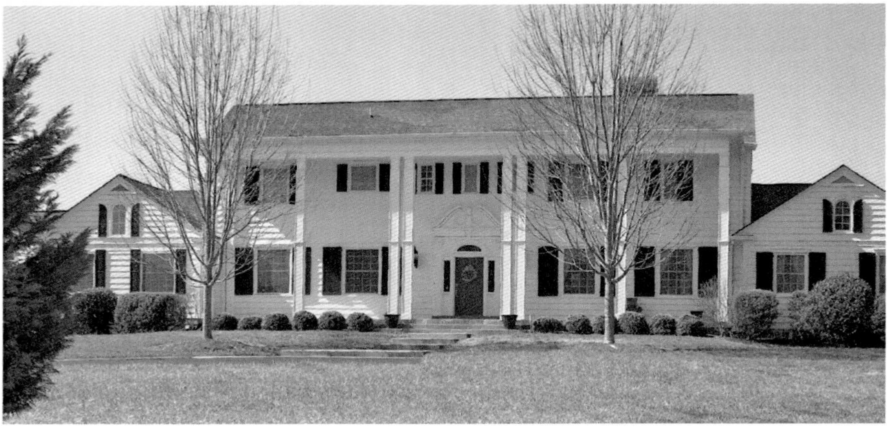

Tuscarora.

On the site, the Aults built the 6,800-square-foot mansion, which they named Tuscarora, meaning "hemp gatherers," from the Iroquoian language family. The Ault family sold to Norman Harvey Collisson (1902–1966) and his wife, Rita A. Collisson (1920–2006), in 1956. Collisson, an engineer and chairman of the board of directors of Olin Mathieson Chemical Corporation, chaired the United States economic mission to Germany after World War II. The widowed Mrs. Collisson married Lawrence Lee Hopkins (1921–1978) and sold the property to Hendersonville attorney William Harley Stepp Jr. (1934–) in 1976. Stepp described the fifty- by eighty-foot seamless, poured-concrete basement as having "been built like a bunker." This amenity likely appealed to the engineering-minded Mr. Collisson.

APPLEDORE, BONNIE BRAE AND THE MAYBANKS

Alongside the Greenville Highway (U.S. 225) at Golden Gate Drive, just one block north of Appledore Avenue, a lone granite pillar stands against a partial gate wall. There had previously been a pair of these with a set of wrought-iron gates hinged between them, limiting access to a hydrangea- and pine-flanked sweep of driveway terminating at the foot of a mansion on the distant hill. In 1948—more than half a century before the ACE Hardware store stood at the corner of U.S. 225 and Golden Gate Drive—successive owners of Appledore had two pillars

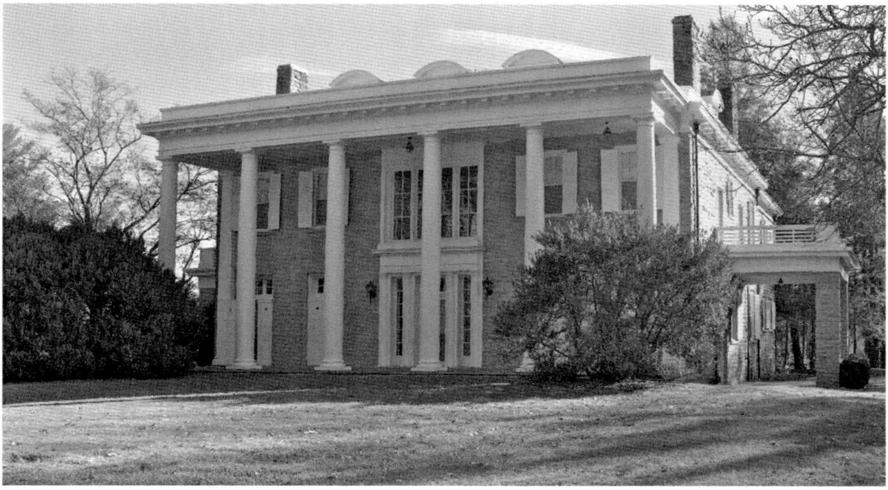

John Maybank's Appledore.

erected farther back from the highway and reattached the privacy gates at that point. Appledore Avenue leads to the service entry of the back of the mansion for which the road was named.

Henderson County's summertime residents have included the Maybanks of Charleston, South Carolina, descended from one of the oldest families who settled on the banks of the Ashley River in 1670. In 1916, John Frampton Maybank (1870–1941) hired architect Erle Gullick Stillwell (1885–1978) to design his summer home Appledore—a name derived from an ancestral home in England—to be built on a huge tract of land on the west side of the Greenville Highway. This was the first of Stillwell's major house designs.

Appledore exudes stateliness in its two-story colonnade, gray-granite exterior and overall setting amidst formal gardens and lawns. John Maybank, a cotton broker, rumored to have been exceedingly hands-on with the oversight of the construction of his summer home, attended to its every detail. The domicile features cavernous rooms with exquisite woodwork, sleeping porches and a basement kitchen with dumbwaiter. Stillwell stabilized the heavy walls of interior rooms, not with bearing walls, but with suspension trusses in the attic.

In the 1940s, the Maybank family sold much of the land at the Greenville Highway site to a developer. Leslie Eaddy Hanna (1895–1959) and his wife, Ella Maude Putnam Hanna (1897–1990), of South Carolina bought the house and its remaining acreage from Willie Allen Harter (1888–1957) and

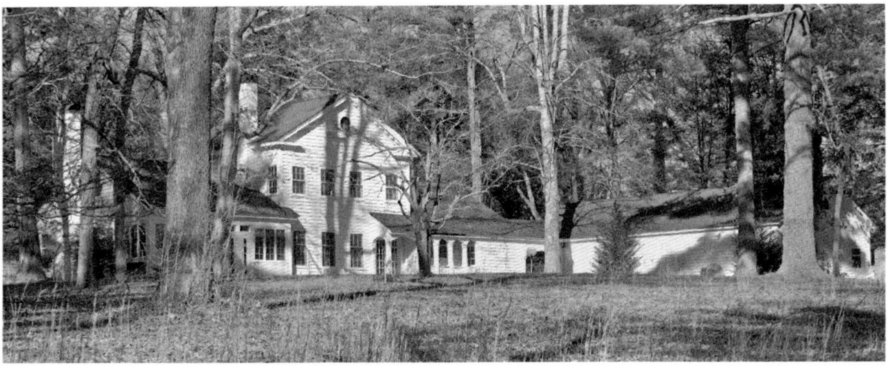

Bonnie Brae.

Katie Selena Corbin Harter (1904–1985), also of South Carolina, in 1947. The Hannas' daughter Charlotte Marie Hanna Trotter (1931–) currently owns the property.

Another mysterious stacked-stone pillar stands just off Blue Ridge Road near a large tract of land once scheduled for development as the Braewood subdivision but left unfinished. The pillar bears an iron sign pierced with the phrase "Bonnie Brae," meaning "pleasant hill" in Gaelic. Unseen from the main road and set back and to the left of the far-reaching drive stands a white mansion built in 1941 and once the summer home of Senator Burnet Rhett Maybank (1899–1954), a nephew of John Maybank of Appledore. Bonnie Brae, on Highland Lake, once belonged to Admiral Charles Purcell Cecil (1893–1944), married to Mary Randolph Pelzer (1901–1994), who in turn married Burnet R. Maybank. The Maybank couple also summered there. Maybank and his first wife, Elizabeth deRossett Myers (1901–1947), had three children. Burnet and Mary wed in 1948 and had no children.

Burnet Rhett Maybank, a powerful United States senator (1941–54), ninety-ninth governor of South Carolina (1939–41) and mayor of Charleston, South Carolina (1931–38), like his uncle John, was also a cotton broker. During his tenure in the Senate, Maybank served as chairman of the Banking and Finance Committee and also as a member of the Appropriations Committee and the Sub-Committee for Military Appropriations. After Maybank's death, J. Strom Thurmond filled his vacated seat in Congress. The Maybanks are buried at Magnolia Cemetery in Charleston.

Frank L. FitzSimons recounted a story about the Maybanks in volume three of his *From the Banks of the Oklawaha* series. John and his brother Dr. Joseph Maybank, together with Frank Hanckel and a Mr. Mullens, made a road trip from Hendersonville to Charleston in 1914. The *Charleston News and Courier* carried the story about how the threesome had made the 265-mile journey "at 19mph in just 17 hours, including layovers." The *French Broad Hustler* also carried the story under the headline, "NEW AUTOMOBILE RECORD."

THE WELSH COLONY AND BRYN AVON

Historic treasures lie tucked within the heavily wooded bluff known as Bowman's southeast of Etowah on the south side of the French Broad River—an area better known, perhaps, as Big Willow. Welsh emigrants settled this land in the early 1880s, bringing with them not only their traditions and language but also remnants and fixtures from their Anglican church, which they incorporated into their Chapel of the Gethsemane (1887) on a hill, according to Frank L. FitzSimons, above Beulah Baptist Church Cemetery. The chapel's stained-glass panels invoke a noteworthy saga, hailing as they do from a fifteenth-century Anglican church from the Isle of Anglesey off the coast of Wales.

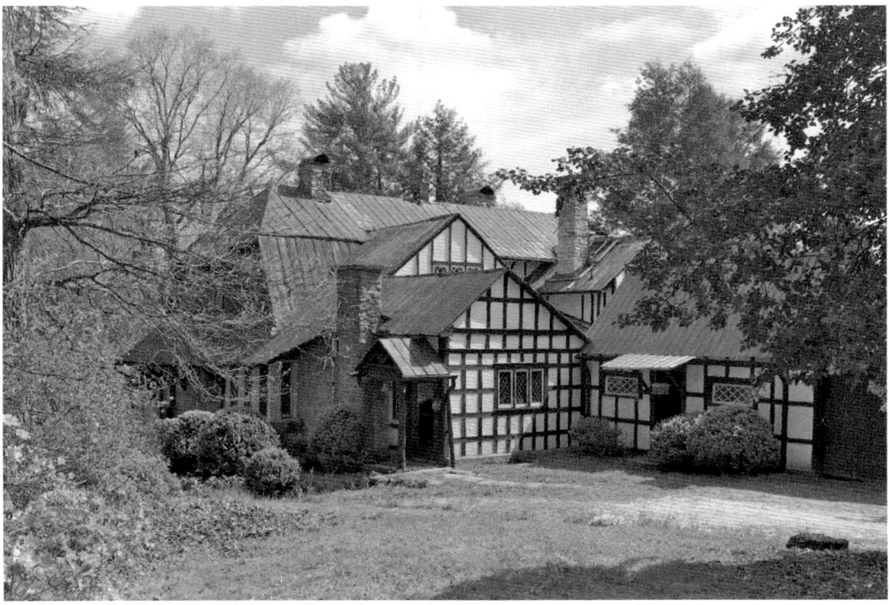

Bryn Avon.

Over the years, the colony at Bowman's Bluff diminished as residents moved on to Canada, returned to their native Wales or died in their homes on the bluff, leaving behind a fascinating microcosm of architecture. As time wore on, houses were razed and others burned, leaving only the heavily renovated Holmes home and the historically intact Bryn Avon, together with its associated buildings constructed in the twentieth century.

During the dismantling of the Gethsemane chapel after only two decades of use, parishioners once again salvaged the windows, bell, furniture and sacred vessels, conveying them to the now-defunct Episcopal St. John the Baptist Church of Upward. Before the latter church was lifted and moved from Jackson Loop Road to its present location—used now as the Community Bible Church in Upward—workers carefully removed the windows after David Saltonstall Mallett (1925–) secured permission from Bishop Matthew George Henry (1910–1974) of the Episcopal Diocese of Western North Carolina, Asheville, in the early 1970s. Mallett, current owner of the property Bryn Avon, had spoken with the Episcopal bishop in Asheville, requesting release of the stained-glass windows, "to bring them back home to Bowman's Bluff." The aged Bryn Avon already featured two of the Welsh church's windows within its front-door transom, and Mallett had decided to have a small family chapel erected on the grounds of the estate, in which he would install the émigré windows. Built by Jesse W. Bell (circa 1902–1991) and completed in 1976, the chapel stands in the midst of the Mallett family burial ground beyond a traditional Welsh lych-gate.

But the full story of the Welsh village and Bryn Avon begins in the late nineteenth century with the vision of two Welshmen: Morgan J. Evans (1847–?) and George H. Holmes (1833–1910). Together, Evans and Holmes established the Elizabethan colony at Bowman's Bluff. In 1882, the men bought in partnership from James Davis (1839–1920) 690 acres—originally the property of one of the area's earliest land grantees, Elijah Williamson (1755–1837), passed down to Williamson's daughter Malinda Williamson Henry (1824–1894). Evans at once set about building a house of stone for himself and his wife, Mary Emily, in 1884. Additional houses and cottages sprang up as a total of fourteen more families joined the settlement. Other family names in the colony included Jeudwine, Chenoweth and the Reverend Joseph Wainwright. John Simcox Holmes (1868–1958), son of George H. Holmes and for whom Holmes Educational State Forest is named, farmed much of the land surrounding the Elizabethan village.

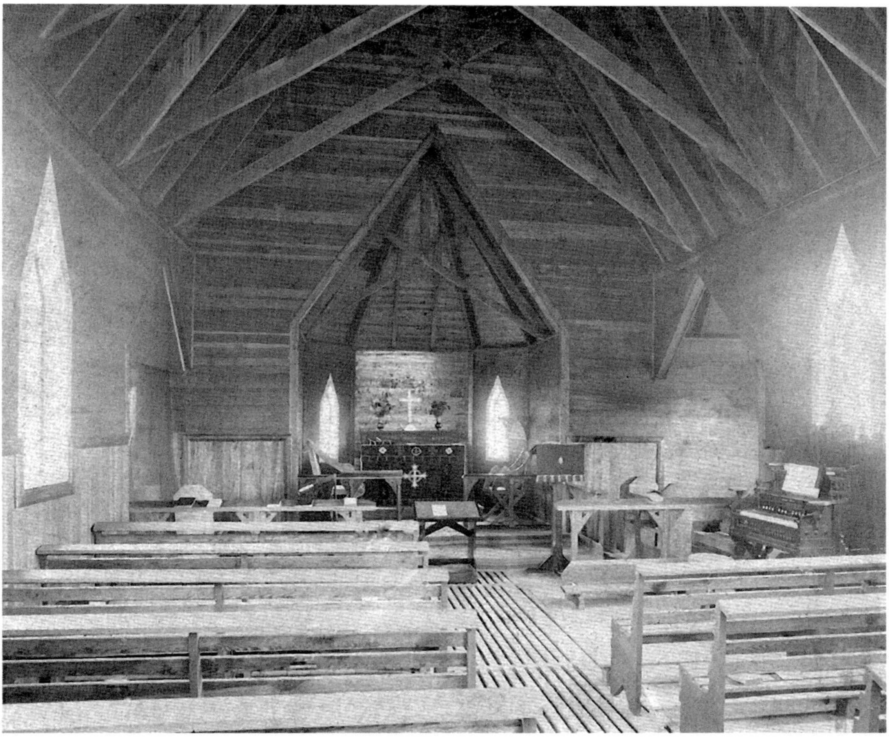

The Chapel of the Gethsemane at Bowman's Bluff. *Photo courtesy of David S. Mallett.*

The Reverend Theodore Benedict Lyman (1815–1893), Episcopal bishop of North Carolina, described the Gethsemane chapel as "a model of neatness and good taste" when he consecrated it on September 8, 1887.

John S. Holmes noted in this diary that Asheville architect Richard Sharp Smith (1852–1924) joined in the festivities at the Welsh colony in 1897 for a celebration of Queen Victoria's Diamond Jubilee. John S. Holmes was the first professionally trained forester hired, in 1909, by the State of North Carolina.

George H. Holmes sold to James Howard Cummings (1880–1959), the "Caroid" pharmaceutical magnate, and Cummings sold to J. Cason Ives (1904–1977), a dairyman from Miami who summered at Bowman's Bluff. In 1903, Morgan J. Evans had sold 130 acres of the Welsh colony and his home, Bryn Avon, for $1,750 to Ida Bellini Beach Mallett (1864–1950) and her husband, Charles Edward Mallett (1851–1924). The Malletts, of Huguenot heritage, had four children. Descendants including Ida, Charles's daughter

Anne Gibbs Mallett (1901–1995) and Lyra Beach Mallett (1870–1956) also lived on the property. Lyra Beach Mallett married renowned artist Wilford Seymour Conrow (1880–1957), and several of Conrow's portraits still hang in the halls and parlors of Bryn Avon.

David S. Mallett, grandson of Ida and nephew of Anne, acquired the property in 1997 and moved there from Asheville with his wife, Sarah Elizabeth Donaldson Mallett (1925–2005), after having summered and then lived full time at one of the Bryn Avon houses since 1965.

Morgan J. Evans built the core of Bryn Avon of stone, appended later with a framed upper story. The manor, stone and half-timbered in its exterior design, features multiple gables and jerkin-heads, double-hung sash casements, a double-leaf front door and pressed metal shingles. The manorial edifice incorporates exposed beams and other Old World appurtenances throughout its interior chambers, halls and cozy parlors. The dining hall feels not unlike an ancient one in Wales or in one of the wool barons' manors in England's Cotswold villages. Amidst its wainscoting of rich umber patination, a diamond-paned bay fitted with window seating graces one broad side of the room, and a fully paneled chimney breast at one of its short ends incorporates a niched mantel with cylindrical columns

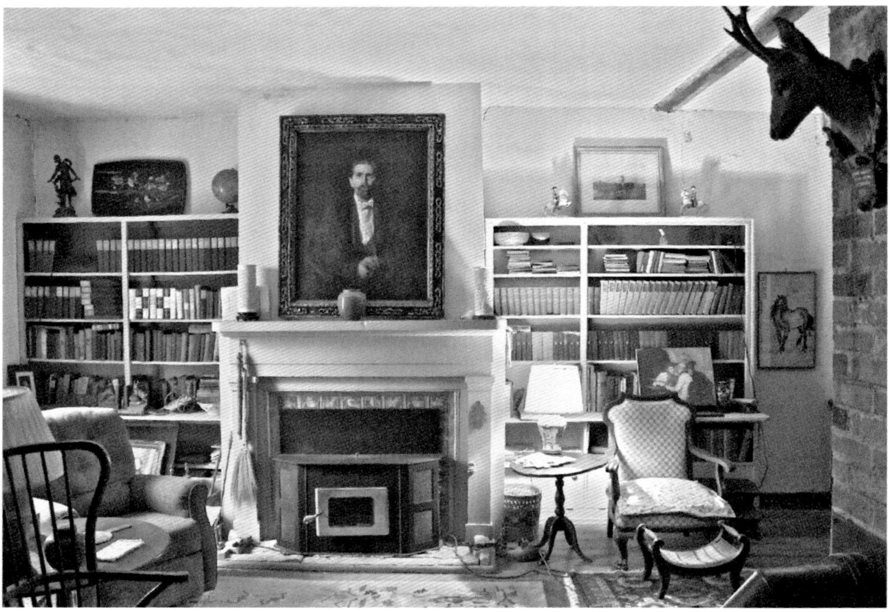

Library, Bryn Avon.

and projecting shelf with an arcaded tabernacle flanked by columns and a molded cornice. As do the many other fireboxes of Bryn Avon, the dining hall's is framed in decorative ceramic tiles collected by the Mallett family during their world travels. Other quirkily interesting features include an old-fashioned telephone alcove, a "drinks room" and a "winter kitchen."

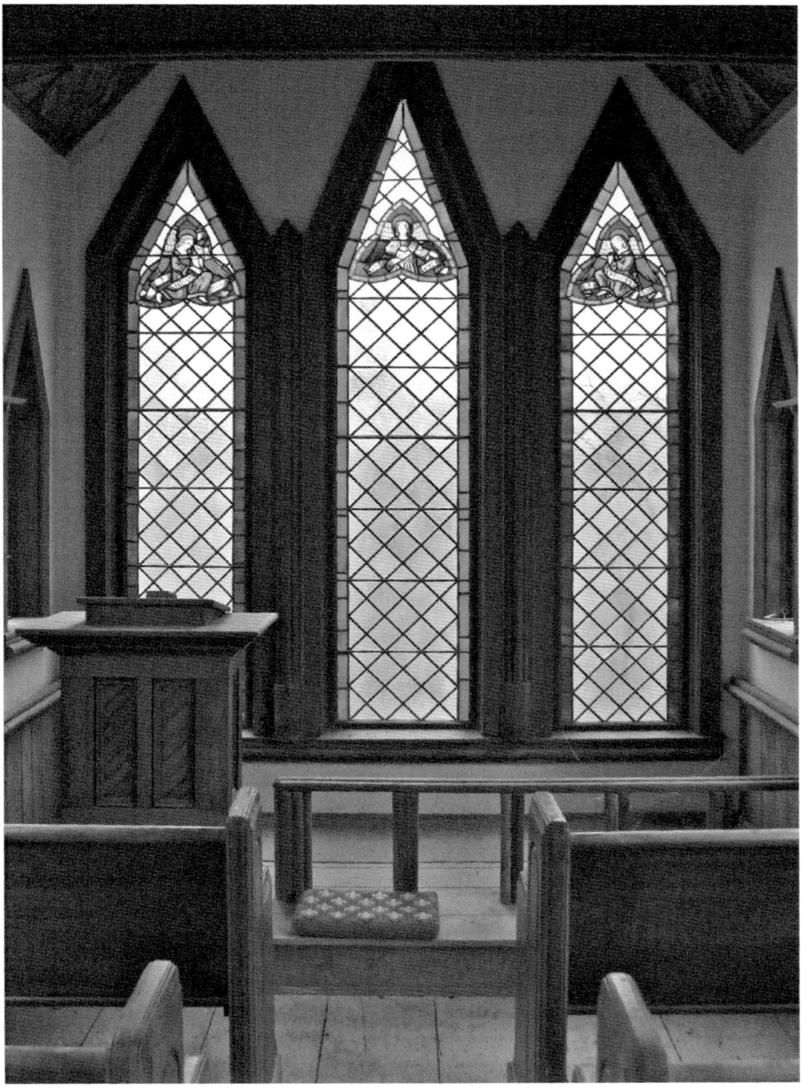

Mallet family chapel windows.

In its description of Bryn Avon, which means "hill above a river" in Welsh, the National Register of Historic Places mentions, "A country house with a bold, organic character, and an important example of the Tudor Revival style in North Carolina." The description continues, "[It] represents an organic strain of the style that might be described as 'vernacular' if the Tudor style was indigenous. The house is both a reflection of the Tudor-Revival style and the possibility within the English manorial tradition to create an unconventional 'period house' of unusual charm and personality."

Four cottages, named Mallett, Penne Bryn (Brown Cottage), Yon Way (constructed of saddle-notched logs) and Bellamy, occupy the land surrounding Bryn Avon. Other structures include a tea pavilion, Conrow Studio, Brown Playhouse, a stable and the Mallett family chapel, each of these structures having been added by Mallett family members since 1903. Lombardy poplars, ornamental trees and flowering shrubs, boxwood hedges and wild rhododendrons grace the gardens of Bryn Avon. Ida Mallett and her daughter Anne designed and maintained the English-style grounds. A pond, native stone terracing and a millstone outfitted with a sundial complement the casual ambience, and another millstone serves as a stoop.

The large family estate encompasses a horse pasture, croquet lawn and grass tennis court. In the 1930s, Caroline Mallett Bellamy (1891–1978) and Chesley Calhoun Bellamy (1887–1957) built the Bellamy Cottage within the estate, and Mrs. Bellamy operated Glen Carol, a small Girl Scout camp.

Mellowed by mosses and ivy, the Mallett Family Cemetery blends with the natural environment of Bryn Avon. In the midst of the burial ground stands the family chapel with the ancient Welsh windows illuminating its petite interior. Besides the graves of Mallett family members, the cemetery includes a white marble tablet inscribed with the name J. Thadeus [Thaddeus] Henry (1829–1857), a son of one of the nineteenth-century owners of the property. Reports of Henry's death include his having been murdered by slaves or freedmen.

DAWN HILL AND EDWIN DUBOSE HEYWARD

One of Henderson's cultural treasures lies in a sparsely populated sector of the southwestern county known as Valley Hill. A copse of laurels, rhododendrons and soaring white pines all but mask an expansive, albeit unassuming, property once called Dawn Hill.

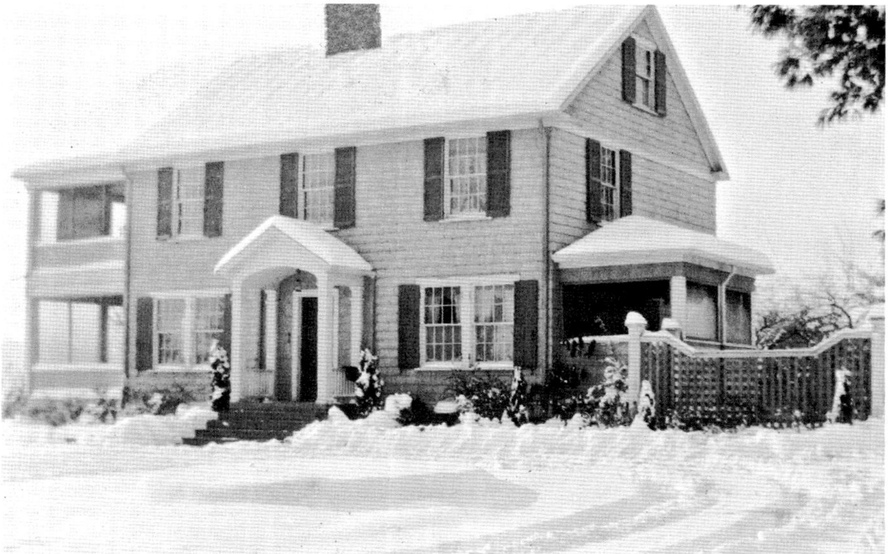

Historic shot of Dawn Hill used by the Heywards for a Christmas card. *Photo courtesy of Caroliniana Library, University of South Carolina, Columbia.*

Few who pass by the corner of Old Kanuga Road and Price Street realize the history concealed beyond the thickets. This was once home to DuBose Heyward, author of the bestselling novel *Porgy* and co-writer—with George Gershwin—of the American opera and Broadway and big-screen hit *Porgy and Bess*.

Born Edwin DuBose Heyward in Charleston, South Carolina, in 1885, the author, poet and playwright was a grandson of Thomas Heyward Jr. (1746–1809), a South Carolina signer of the United States Declaration of Independence and a colleague of George Washington.

With Hervey Allen (1889–1949), DuBose Heyward co-founded the Poetry Society of South Carolina. Heyward published his first poetry collection, *Jasbo Brown and Other Poems*, and wrote the novel *Mamba's Daughters*, the novella *Star-Spangled Virgin* and the children's book *The Country Bunny and the Little Gold Shoes*. With Allen, Heyward jointly published *Carolina Chansons: Legends of the Low Country*. Heyward's stage plays included *Brass Ankle* and *An Artistic Triumph* and a screenplay for the film adaptation of Eugene O'Neill's *The Emperor Jones*.

Before achieving literary success Heyward lived a less auspicious life, sometimes described as "genteel poverty." His parents' people, well-heeled plantation owners, were stripped of most of their wealth after the Civil

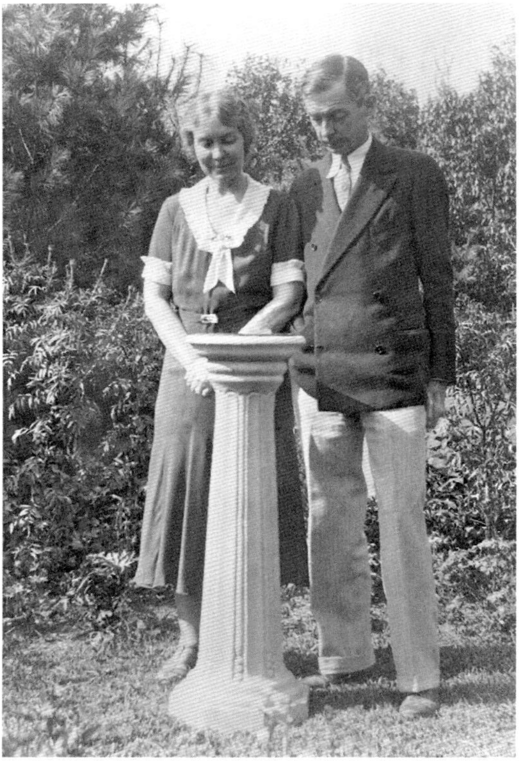

Edwin DuBose Heyward with his mother, Jane Heyward, at Dawn Hill. *Photo courtesy of Caroliniana Library, University of South Carolina, Columbia.*

War. A sickly child (polio, typhoid fever and pleurisy), Heyward struggled in school and dropped out at the age of fourteen. He worked in a hardware store as a means of helping to support his family. He later toiled as a customs worker on the cotton wharves of Charleston. Working with the black stevedores, Heyward became fascinated with the Gullah[3] culture and language. Heyward's mother, Jane Screven DuBose Heyward (1864–1939), a performer and interpreter of Gullah life in folktale and song, instilled a fascination that led to her son's novel *Porgy* and the ensuing stage plays and movie.

Literary critics hailed Heyward as an authority on southern black life, writing, "Heyward's attention to detail and reality of the Southern black's lifestyle was not only sympathetic but also something that no one had ever seen done before." African American poet and playwright Langston Hughes described Heyward as "one who saw with his white eyes, wonderful, poetic qualities in the inhabitants of [Charleston's] Catfish Row that makes them come alive." Heyward's biographer James M. Hutchisson described his subject as "a southerner who overcame social restrictions to perceive humanity beyond the class and color lines."

Earlier in his life, Heyward had sold insurance and real estate in partnership with his friend Henry John "Harry" O'Neill Jr. (1891–1952), the whole time

3. *Gullah*: A group of people of African ancestry (Angola and Congo) having been brought to America as slaves and inhabiting the Sea Islands and coastal areas of South Carolina, Georgia and northern Florida. "Gullah" is a corruption of the word Angola or Angolan.

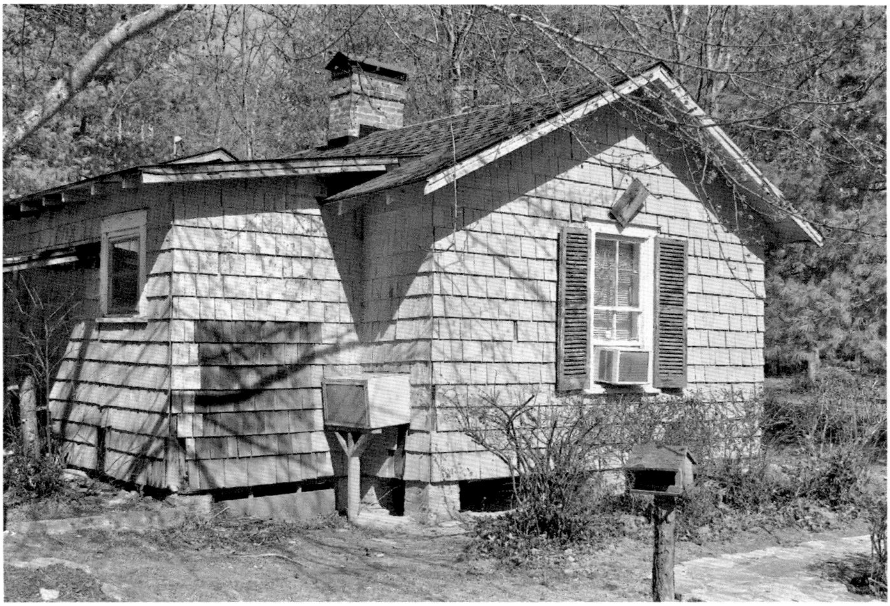

The Heyward studio at Dawn Hill.

penning poetry and book manuscripts. He also lectured at colleges and at Charleston's Porter Military Academy.

Heyward married playwright Dorothy Hartzell Kuhns (1890–1961) in 1923. In collaboration, Dorothy dramatized some of her husband's literary works for the stage and screen. The Heywards had a daughter, Jenifer (1930–1984).

In the early 1920s, the Heywards lived in a red cottage off Henderson County's Old Kanuga Road during the construction of their home, Dawn Hill, where they summered and then lived part and full time for nearly two decades. Adjacent to the house, one finds an unassuming cottage—the studio where composer George Gershwin (1898–1937), a guest in the Heyward home, spent months with Heyward as the two geniuses wrote such songs as the American classic "Summertime" while developing the opera *Porgy and Bess*. Ira Gershwin (1896–1983) composed some of the work's lyrics, but most of the lyrics—and all of the distinguished ones—are by Heyward.

Biographer James M. Hutchisson states in his book *DuBose Heyward: A Charleston Gentleman and the World of Porgy and Bess*:

> *Until now, Heyward's role in the writing of George Gershwin's acclaimed opera* Porgy and Bess *has remained almost unknown. He wrote the*

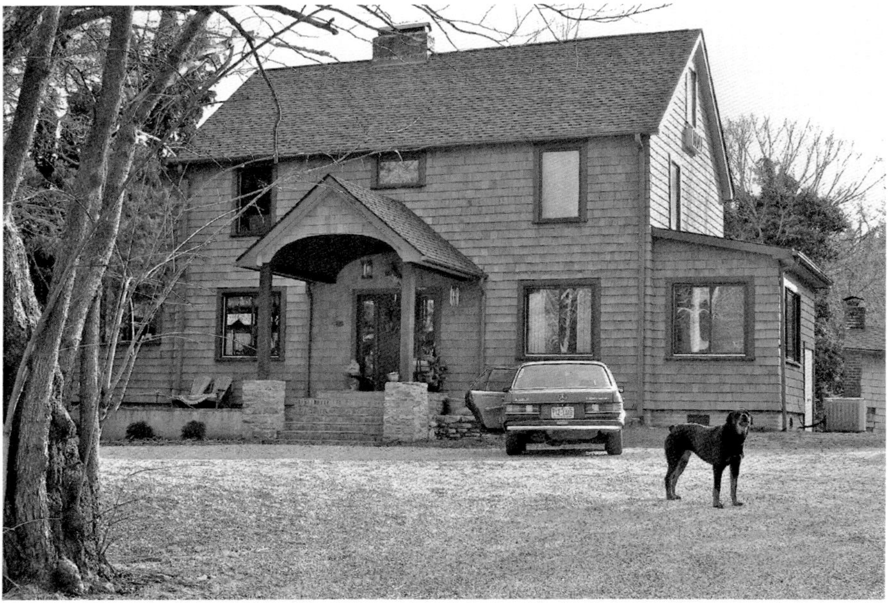

Contemporary view of the renovated Dawn Hill.

libretto singlehandedly, and nearly half the arias are by him. Long thought to have been merely an assistant to Gershwin, he actually was involved in most phases of the production. Although the opera eclipsed Heyward's book, it was Gershwin's foundation stone.

The Heywards sold Dawn Hill but continued to vacation in Henderson County. During a visit in 1940, DuBose Heyward experienced what he presumed to be a severe case of heartburn. His Henderson County hostess, Mrs. Margaret E. Matthew (1886–1963), drove him to Tryon, North Carolina, to be treated by Dr. Allen Jones Jervey (1881–1948), a friend and relative, but Heyward collapsed and died of a heart attack during the examination. The Heywards are buried at St. Philip's Episcopal Church Cemetery in Charleston, South Carolina.

Dawn Hill has changed, no longer sporting its mullioned windows and dark shutters. The current owners have expanded and modernized the house, and the swimming pool built by John Drake (a former Henderson County deputy sheriff) has been filled in. But one small structure looks much the same as it did in the time when Heyward and Gershwin spent months within its walls composing one of America's most time-honored musical masterpieces.

THE HOUSE OF SEVEN GABLES

Known also as "The Top," "High Gables," "The House of Gray Gables," "High Holde" and "COPISA Orchard," this English-style circa 1889 house on Macedonia Road in southeast Henderson County conveys a storied past. The acronym COPISA was derived from the first two letters of each of the names of an owner of the property, Cotesworth Pinckney Sanders (1845–1919), not an Indian name as most people had imagined. Orchards once covered the outlying acres of the House of Seven Gables. This property was, according to Frank L. FitzSimons, "one of the largest and finest apple orchards in Henderson County."

Leonard Hewett (1866–1912), an emigrant from the village of Binstead on the Isle of Wight, and his wife, Eliza Fry Maury Hewett (1856–1910) of Kentucky, bought the property from Sarah M. Blackwell (1847–circa 1880) and Andrew G. Blackwell (circa 1854/55–?) in 1888 for $125. The purchase included an existing cabin and springhouse. The Hewetts built the manor to resemble Leonard's home in Britain. When they purchased the property, it included 40 acres, and they added to it until they owned 187 acres. The Hewetts also bought an additional 127 acres in Macedonia. Frank L. FitzSimons described Leonard Hewett as an English "nobleman" in the second volume of his *Oklawaha* series, yet genealogical research brought up no references to nobility in Hewett's background, unless Episcopal priests, colonels, lieutenant colonels and consuls would be considered by some to signify noble bloodlines.

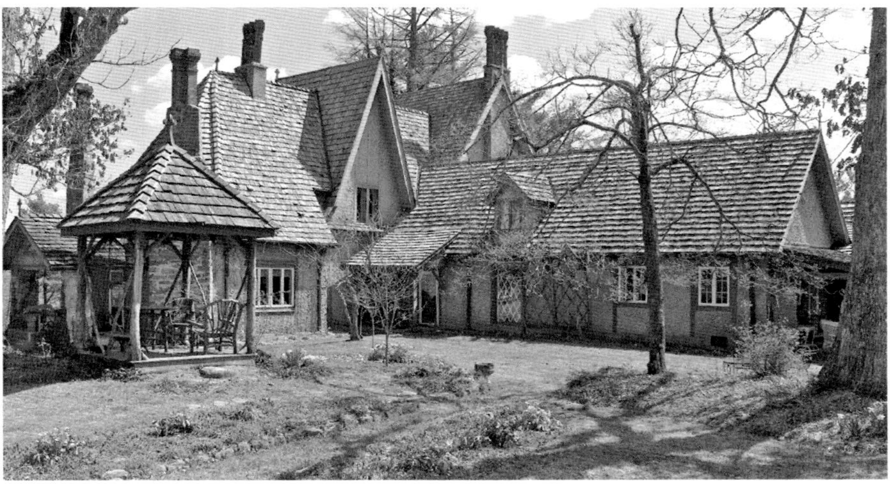

The House of Seven Gables.

After the Hewetts, Cotesworth Pinckney Sanders bought the property and house, for which he paid $3,500. Frederick and Elizabeth Yount owned it next, then Craig Kirkpatrick (1919–) and currently Oscar Wilson Harbin (1940–) and Cheryl Greene Harbin (1944–).

When Sanders held the property, his daughters discovered bundles of letters in the barn—correspondence between the Hewetts and between Mrs. Hewett and her brother, Austin Maury. After Mrs. Hewett died an untimely death, Mr. Hewett left from Charleston on an ocean liner, but when the ship arrived in New York Harbor, Hewett was nowhere to be found. The Hewetts had no children.

The rediscovered letters bring to life the Victorian spirit of The Top. In one of them, dated 1893, Lydie Healy wrote from New York to Austin Maury at The Top: "I have the photograph you sent me of the mountains around your home…I had so often photographed it in my head and so often thought about it, and although it does not look like my idea, it is very beautiful."

The compellingly handsome home sports a skin of pebbledash stucco, seven gables and five soaring "English-style" chimneys. Other features include a millstone set in the concrete front porch, original door hardware, bisque-in-relief tile details on an oversized mantel and a carved semicircular staircase. Gazing from the parlor proffers a vista of ancient trees framing an intoxicating view of Tryon Mountain. The old barn stands in good repair, and the Harbins have restored the house's pebbledash finish and the dry-stone terracing encompassing Mrs. Hewett's lavish gardens. Mrs. Harbin breathed new life into the semiformal landscaping, which sports a carpet of seasonal blooms and ivy purportedly brought by Mr. Hewett from Alfred Lord Tennyson's grave site on the Isle of Wight.

Brook Ledge (1900)

E. Hortence Potts (1926–) lives in her parents' 1900 home on the East Flat Rock property they named Brook Ledge. Hortence's parents were Ethel Kathleen Williams Potts (1896–1993) and Frederick Henderson Potts (1885–1975). Frederick was a son of freedman George L. Potts (1844–1926) and Lavinia F. Moultrie Potts (1846–1932). Lavinia was a daughter of Dr. Mitchell Campbell King (1815–1901) and granddaughter of Judge Mitchell King (1783–1862).

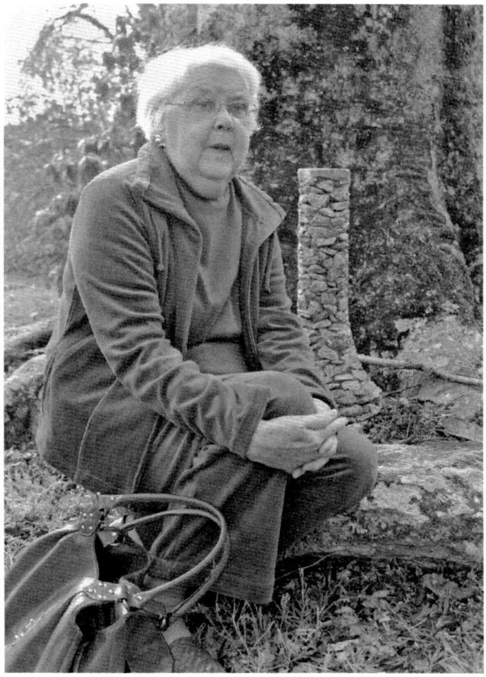

E. Hortence Potts seated on the hearthstone of her grandfather's log home.

The two-story frame house hugs a ledge above Bat Fork, surrounded by ancient hardwoods and lovingly maintained gardens that include colossal azalea bushes planted by Hortence's ancestors. One of the property's more interesting features would be a wide, thick slab of granite at the base of a majestic purple birch—the hearthstone from the two-story cabin built by Hortence's grandfather George Potts, who, with his wife, Lavinia, lived on Glassy Mountain on land they acquired from the King family after Emancipation. Lavinia was a well-respected yarb doctor and midwife in the East Flat Rock area.

The Reverend John Grimke Drayton (1816–1891), rector of St. John in the Wilderness, performed the wedding ceremony in 1871 for George and Lavinia in the parlor of Glenroy, home of Dr. Mitchell Campbell King. The Pottses raised their nine children in a log house George built on the side of the mountain. Hortence's father, Fred, began his life in the log house, from which, when later razed, Ms. Potts rescued its hearthstone and had it placed in her garden at Brook Ledge.

A flautist with an Asheville symphonic group and a chauffeur, landscaper and caretaker for Flat Rock estates, Fred Potts also looked after the mountaintop mausoleum of Roger Richardson Hill (1882–1927), which stands near the site of the former Potts cabin. Fred's father once owned the land on which the granite burial chamber stands atop Glassy Mountain. After vandals broke the mausoleum's stained-glass window, Fred gathered up the translucent green shards and set them in a shallow tray of concrete, which he fashioned into a table for his garden at Brook Ledge after filling in the window with granite blocks, not trusting that someone wouldn't repeat the same shenanigans.

E. Hortence Potts, a cousin of Louise Howe Bailey (1915–2009) and a retired schoolteacher, taught home economics for sixteen years in Rutherford

County and twelve years at West Henderson High School and special education in Henderson County schools. She earned a BS from Bennett Girl's College in Greensboro, North Carolina, and a master's degree from Western Carolina University in Cullowhee, North Carolina. A member of Alpha Kappa Alpha sorority and a former volunteer with the Henderson County Genealogical and Historical Society and the Henderson County Council on Aging, as well as a former board member of the Dispute Settlement Committee of Henderson County, she also involved herself in local civic organizations including the Society of Necessity, which her grandfather George helped found in 1889.

THE OLD BLUE HOUSE

Behind Dana United Methodist Church and Cemetery (known also by locals as "Blue House Cemetery") stands a moldering weatherboarded pile cosseted by chain-link fencing. If walls could talk, these would divulge the provenance of its core having been the "Old Blue House." This structure, now whitewashed, served a diverse purpose: schoolhouse, place of worship, post office, polling station and, before its abandonment, home of George W. Case (1902–1973) and his wife, Dollie Bell C. Case (1905–2005). The Blue House was built on the grounds of a Methodist camp—land owned by Leander Case (1830–1862), who erected a small schoolhouse on it about 1860 and served as its first schoolmaster.

Deed records from 1861 show indentures of Case having passed the land to trustees of the Blue Ridge Campground. Another indenture lists adjoining property as having been passed by James Jones (1826–1907) to the Blue Ridge Campground for the Methodist Denomination South. Case also served as the first postmaster, appointed in 1859, of Blue Ridge,[4] as the community was known at the time. The building hosted the post office and also church meetings where services were held for some forty years, during which time church members increased the size of the building.

Case enlisted as a private in 1861, Company G, Thirty-fifth Infantry Regiment, North Carolina, and was promoted to full commissary sergeant in 1862, the year he died of fever. As the student population of the little school grew, the Blue House Academy succeeded it, constructed farther

4. The post office name changed to Blueridge in 1894.

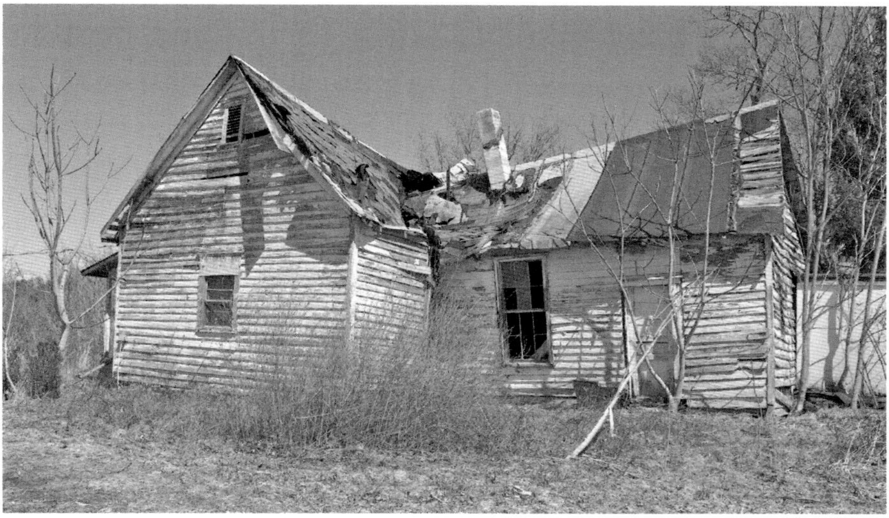

The heart of this building was once the Old Blue House at Blue Ridge, North Carolina. The original blue color shows behind the peeling white paint. *Photographed with permission of Archie Case.*

north between Academy and Owensby Roads, with Leander Case's brother Silas Case (1829–1877) as one of its teachers. Silas also served in the Confederate infantry.

In regions with no churches, the faithful organized camp meetings, and one such site included the Blue Ridge Campground, with its roots going back to the beginning of Methodism in the area. The faithful held camp meetings and revivals on the land where the Dana School now stands, north of the Old Blue House, as early as 1864. After the corn crop was laid by, religious camps generally ensued for two weeks. Circuit-riding preachers ministered to the camps at Blue Ridge until the Annual Methodist Conference gave money in 1897 to build a church. This conference, part of the Swannanoa Circuit, included North Carolina and eastern Tennessee and part of the Holston Conference (Buncombe County). A new sanctuary was completed and dedicated by 1910. Alfred J. Duncan/Dunkin (1839–1909) had donated the land.

Early pastors included Reverends R.J. Tuttle, J.D. Gibson (1848–1914) and David Riley Proffit (1870–1936). Early church records list a "Reverend Lanthan" as the first pastor, yet no first name or dates are mentioned. The earliest members included Thomas Jones Stepp (1825–1918) and wife, Nancy Elvira Taylor Stepp (1832–1917); Thomas Blackwell (1869–

1958) and wife, Mary (1871–1962); and Albert H. Blackwell (1876–1942) and wife, Alice B. (1875–1965). Thomas Jones Stepp (1825–1918), a Henderson County commissioner and deputy sheriff, gave land for the parsonage.

The cemetery predated the church, many of its original markers mere fieldstones with no inscriptions, with James E. Stepp (1754–1830)—grandfather of Thomas Jones Stepp—the first to be buried there. The present church was remodeled in 1976.

J.J. Blythe (1831–1912) taught at the Old Blue House and Blue House Academy. Captain William Gunaway Brownlow Morris (1840–1891), a Confederate veteran, was the first professor at this school. During Morris's nine years of service, Blue House Academy served as the educational hub of Dana, its influence extending beyond the county by attracting students from Rutherford, Transylvania, Polk and Buncombe Counties. Certain of these students became professional and civic leaders. Another of the teachers was Professor John H. Merchant (1845–1919) of Gloucestershire, England. Merchant is buried at Riverside Cemetery in Asheville, North Carolina.

In 1907, after construction of a larger building, Robert Gibson Anders (1882–1968), later a Henderson County superintendent known as "the superintendent on horseback," attained great strides for the improvement of education in the area, launching a countywide program for school consolidation and transportation of pupils to school by bus, as well as instigating improved professional training and standardized testing in the county. In 1928, the eight or more schools in the Dana area were combined, and a new modern school was built near its hub.

In 1960, when high schools in Henderson County consolidated, Dana contained grades one through eight. In 1974, a new facility was constructed after Dana School was destroyed by fire—by accused arsonist James Robert Arrowood (1946–1981). The present facility, named Dana Elementary School, serves grades kindergarten through five.

Refuge Baptist Church Steeples

Harry Z. Thompson rescued the old steeples from Refuge Baptist Church when the sanctuaries went through two restoration and enlargement phases. These historic features may be seen from Dana Road on the Thompsons'

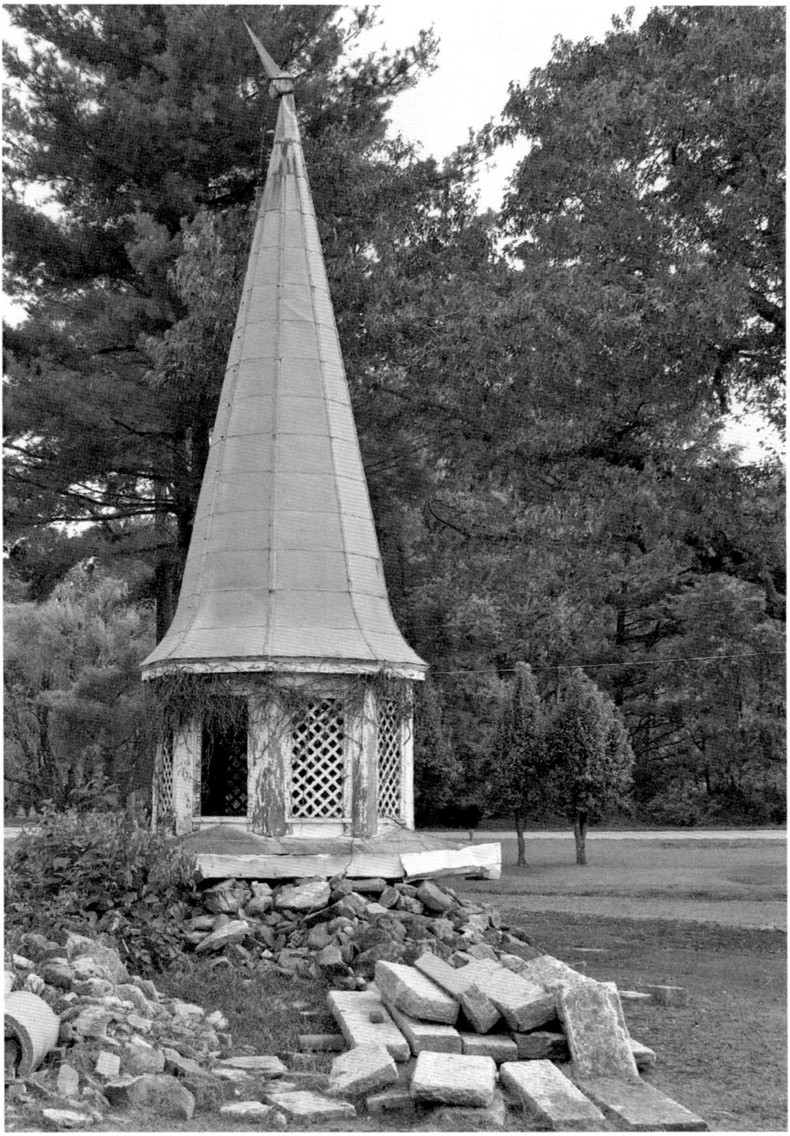

The 1958 steeple of Refuge Baptist Church. *Photographed with permission of Todd Thompson.*

property—one with an oxidized copper roof from 1958, upright on a rock foundation, and the all-wooden 1991 steeple lying prostrate.

Refuge Baptist Church began as the City of Refuge, an arm of Ebenezer Baptist Church organized on July 13, 1847. Members worshiped in homes and then at Ridge School until they completed their first sanctuary in 1856. A larger church was completed in 1898, and its tower in 1903, replaced with an even larger sanctuary of brick in 1951 and expanded in 1991. The church stands at the junction of Ridge, Upward and Dana Roads.

REESE HOUSE (1885)

One of the oldest houses in downtown Hendersonville stands at the southwest corner of South Washington and West Allen Streets. Queen Anne in style and on the National Register of Historic Places, this was once the home of William Patrick Reese (1842–1897) and his second wife, Harriet Louisa "Louise" Williams Reese (1851–1913). Mrs. Reese, who kept a vegetable garden on the property, had the reputation of being a marvelous cook.

Turner Williams (1809–1881) deeded the property to his daughter Harriet; she inherited it in 1881, and her husband hired local designer and carpenter James Brown (1850–1909)[5] to design a house for the site. The Reeses' son James Brown Reese (1885–1953), a mason and plasterer, lived in the home for sixty-eight years. Several other Reese descendants have also lived in the house.

Shannon Hudson acquired the property, which had become somewhat dilapidated, in 1996. Hudson worked with preservation specialist John Horton (at the time with the western office of the North Carolina Department of Cultural Resources, Archives and History, Asheville) to restore the historic house, repurposing it as Shannon's Restaurant. More recently, Kanaan and Sylvie Kassab operated their restaurant Sinbad in the Reese House.

GOSPEL TABERNACLE CHURCH

Reverend Miller, a Bible teacher, purportedly built the undenominational Gospel Tabernacle Church at a corner of South Washington and West Allen Streets in 1935, with members worshiping there until 1943, when the Fundamental Gospel Church moved in and used the sanctuary for its

5. The elusive Mr. Brown, born in Scotland, lived in many places in the United States, including Manhattan, New York; Greenville County, South Carolina; and Hendersonville, North Carolina. He was married to Mary Alice Henderson.

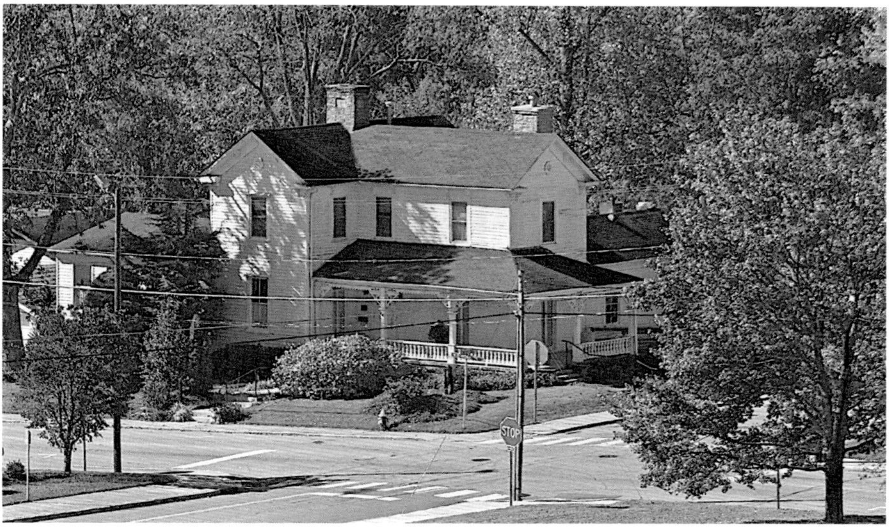

The historic Reese House as seen from the roof of Henderson County's historic courthouse.

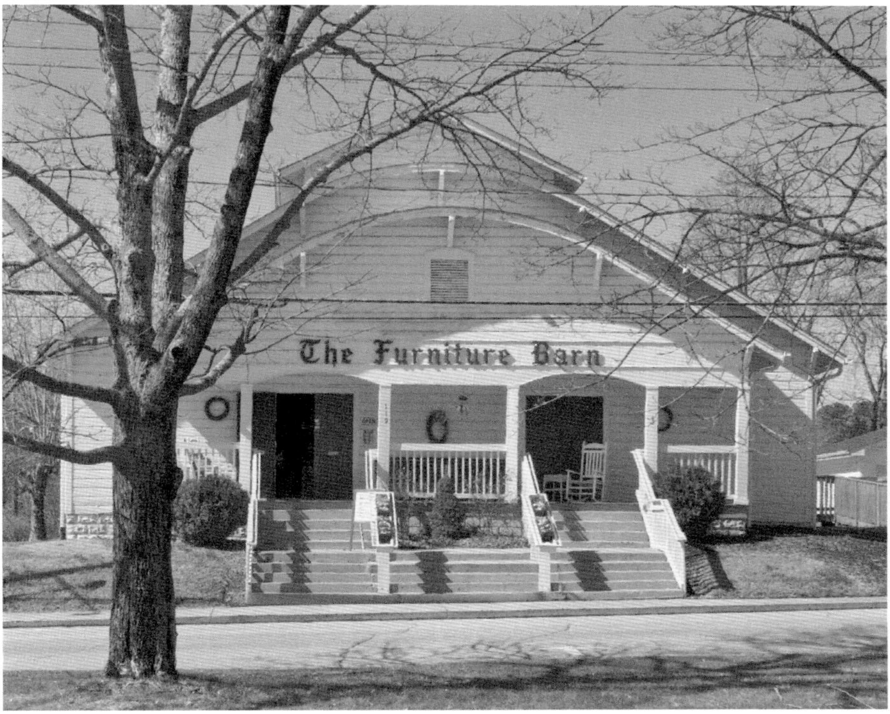

The former Gospel Tabernacle Church.

services until 1961. The First Alliance Church occupied the building between 1975 and 1980. Successive tenants included United Pentecostal Church and Grace Bible Church. A furniture consignment business currently occupies the building.

Brownlow Van Merrell (1912–1989) and Mary Jane Greene Merrell (1910–2011) lived in the house behind this property on West Allen Street. Mrs. Merrell ran a floral business for twenty-five years—Jane's Flower Shop—which she operated from the basement, and Brownlow worked as a ticket agent at Hendersonville's Southern Railway station. For Brownlow and Mary Jane's nuptials in 1934, Mary Jane invited guests to a piano recital and surprised them with a wedding event.

THE KING-WALDROP HOUSE/MAPLE GROVE (CIRCA 1881)

During summer and fall, mere peek-a-boo views of its façade may be glimpsed through the namesake of the property: enormous maple trees that put on a spectacular show each autumn.

Laura Virginia Ripley King (1851–1926), daughter of Colonel Valentine Ripley (1807–1879), one of Hendersonville's earliest businessmen and entrepreneurs, bought the title from her father in 1879 for the property on a corner of what are now South Washington and West First Streets. After Laura married Elias Pinckney Benjamin King (1858–1911), the couple built the large Queen Ann/Italianate–style house later named Maple Grove by the Waldrops. (The Kings later divorced.) No known records indicate the architect of this hefty white house, which sports first- and second-story porches with turned spindles, bracketed eaves and, perhaps the structure's most commanding feature, a square, three-stage cupola with concave pyramidal roof.

The Kings' neighbors, Dr. Joseph Grayson Waldrop (1847–1913) and his wife, Nancy Anna Carpenter Waldrop (1863–1941)—after having lived with Dr. T.A. Allen—moved to a small, modest house one block north of the Kings, on land now occupied by the State Employee Credit Union. As the Waldrop family grew (eleven children after the first one died in the womb), the Kings agreed to swap homes with the Waldrops in 1897.

The home's kitchen, as was typical of its era, was detached. The property sported a barn and three-stall garage built in the early 1920s, a well house

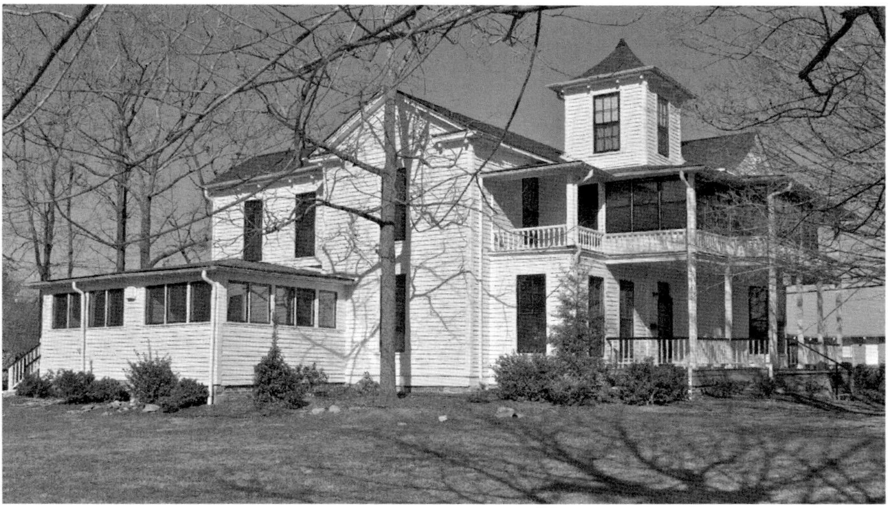

The historic King-Waldrop House.

and a three-hole privy. The Waldrops kept horses and chickens and grew apples and grapes on the property.

J.G. Waldrop, born in the Mill Spring area of what were Buncombe, then Henderson and now presently Polk Counties, moved as a youngster with his family to a farm on Howard Gap Road. His brothers operated a mercantile business in downtown Hendersonville, and J.G. kept a supply of drugs in his brothers' store. He studied medicine in Maryland, Charleston and New York and began practicing medicine in Henderson County about the same time he married. Hendersonville's leading physician from 1880 to 1910, Dr. Waldrop, chief surgeon of the Southern Railway, served as chairman of the Henderson County Medical Society and as superintendent of Sunday school at First United Methodist Church of Hendersonville for twenty-five years. He delivered all eleven of his children at home with the assistance of another doctor.

The Waldrop children were known to play with Captain M.C. Toms's children, who lived on the hill above Toms Pond. One of their playgrounds, Toms Park, featured three lily ponds, a stream and a swimming pool. The children also played pool in the Tomses' billiards room at their Victorian mansion on the hill.

The buggy being too small to accommodate their family of thirteen, the Waldrops oftentimes walked single-file when traveling as a group. Townsfolk often remarked on the large family strolling to the First United Methodist

Church on Sundays—"like a gaggle of ducks making their way northward along the sidewalk."

When Dr. Waldrop died, he left his wife and four children still living at home to fend for themselves. The enterprising Mrs. Waldrop converted her six-bedroom residence into a guesthouse, adapting upstairs porches into two more bedrooms and extending the front porch to increase the size of the dining room. Her advertisement read: "Mrs. J.G. Waldrop, owner & proprietor. Centrally located, two blocks from heart of city and city park. Modern conveniences. Large garage, shady lawn, excellent table fare." Known for her hospitality and delicious fare, Mrs. Waldrop also included special touches, such as fresh waterlilies from Toms Pond for table décor, and her daughter Ruth Gladys Waldrop Izlar (1901–2002) provided musical entertainment by playing piano for after-supper musicales. The tariff: a room and three meals a day for one dollar or twenty-five dollars per month.

One of only two surviving nineteenth-century dwellings in downtown Hendersonville, Maple Grove—listed with the National Register of Historic Places—retains much of its original essence both inside and outside. Waldrop descendants have restored and repaired their ancestral home in Hendersonville and formed an association to maintain it. A goodly number of them, South Carolina lowlanders, vacation at the estate in the summer and for reunions.

OTTARAY CANNING COMPANY AND JONATHAN CASE

Passing by it via Dana Road, how many have wondered about the provenance of the massive stone edifice standing alongside the connector between Four Seasons Boulevard and Ridge/Upward Roads? The "1850" posted on it would be an address, not its date of construction. Most recently, the building hosted Bill Holden's Used Cars and before that, the Dana Volunteer Fire Department. Long since deserted and eerily peaceful, this tract of land once knew a bustling enterprise. In the early 1900s, three structures stood on the site, just east of Refuge Baptist Church, owned and operated by Jonathan Case (1869–1942), in their heyday the Ottaray Canning Company—the largest cannery of its time in North Carolina and one of the largest in the Southeast. By 1912, Case was processing up to 50,000 cans per season—mostly tomatoes, green

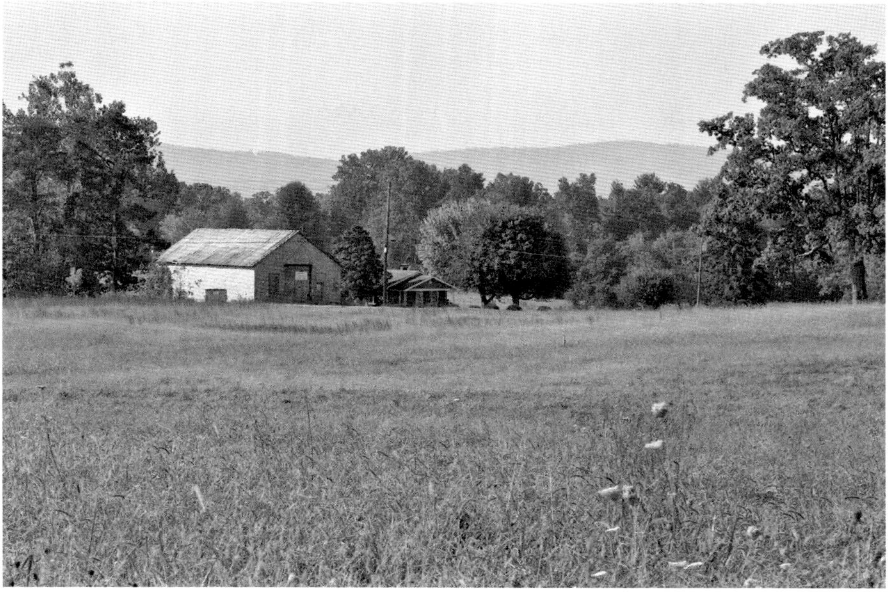

Distant perspective of the Ottaray Canning Company.

beans and corn. He also canned blackberries, potatoes, apples, peaches and pears. Eventually, the plant boasted a capacity of 500,000 cans, and Case also produced apple cider vinegar. His plant, named Ottaray, meaning "mountain" in an extinct Cherokee dialect, endured its shares of ups and downs.

According to the *French Broad Hustler* in March 1912:

> *Jonathan Case, of Dana, has returned from a trip to Baltimore and other eastern points where he went for the purpose of purchasing machinery for a new cannery and to make a study of canning methods in other sections. Mr. Case has been operating a vegetable cannery for about 15 years and after having become fully familiar with the possibilities offered such an industry in this section he has decided to install new and modern machinery, which will enable him to turn out nearly a million cans of vegetables each year. Mr. Case stated that he did not purchase machinery for the plant, but closed a contract for it and will endeavor, before purchasing, to ascertain what cooperation he will get from the farmers of this section...He says that he is thoroughly convinced that the soil of Henderson County for tomato cultivation is far superior to that of some of the best vegetable growing*

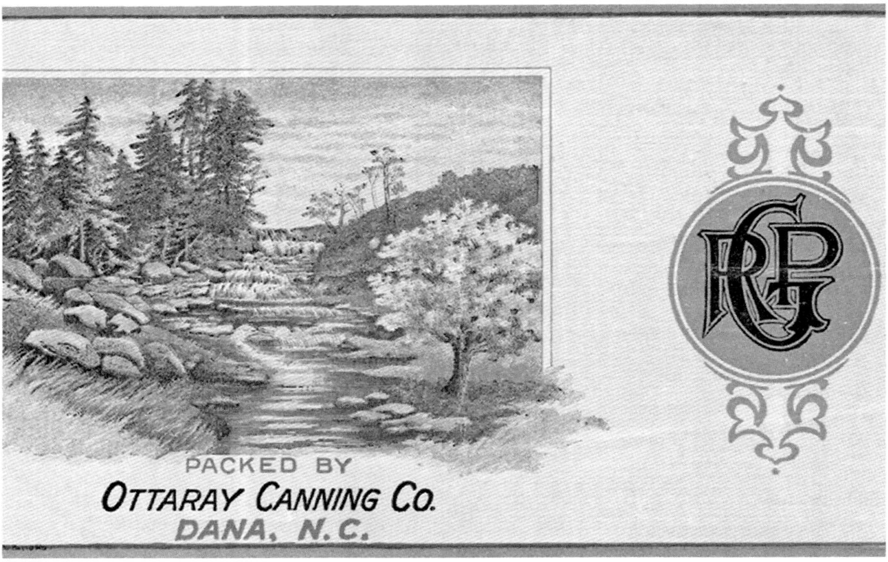

A vintage Ottaray can label. *Photo courtesy of Seth Swift and John Paul Jones.*

> *sections of Virginia...If the farmers will grow the vegetables, he says, his cannery will be prepared to handle unlimited quantities.*

Case owned four hundred acres in Dana and raised beef and dairy cattle. He was postmaster at Dana from 1894 to 1915, and he also owned a country store. His wife, Julia Waters Case (1872–1965), a musically gifted schoolteacher, ran a boardinghouse. The Cases had seven children.

Case enlarged his Dana store and took Emmett Bernard Freeman (1885–1963) of Calvert City, Kentucky, as a partner, calling the store Case & Freeman. Freeman was appointed postmaster in Dana in 1915.

Jonathan Case's father, William S. Case (1842–1904), a large landholder in Dana, was purportedly the first merchant in the Dana area in the mid-1800s. His industrious son Jonathan had the first telephone line from Dana to Hendersonville and also had the first Victrola in the community. Jonathan Case donated land for the Advent Christian Church of Dana.

When Jonathan Case expanded his business into the city of Hendersonville, the venture was less than the success he expected. He sold half interest in the cannery to Captain Marion Columbus Toms (1843–1917) and son, Charles French Toms (1872–1937). At the time, one hundred employees worked for Case and the Tomses, and operations included processing 120 bushels of peaches per day from Captain Toms's

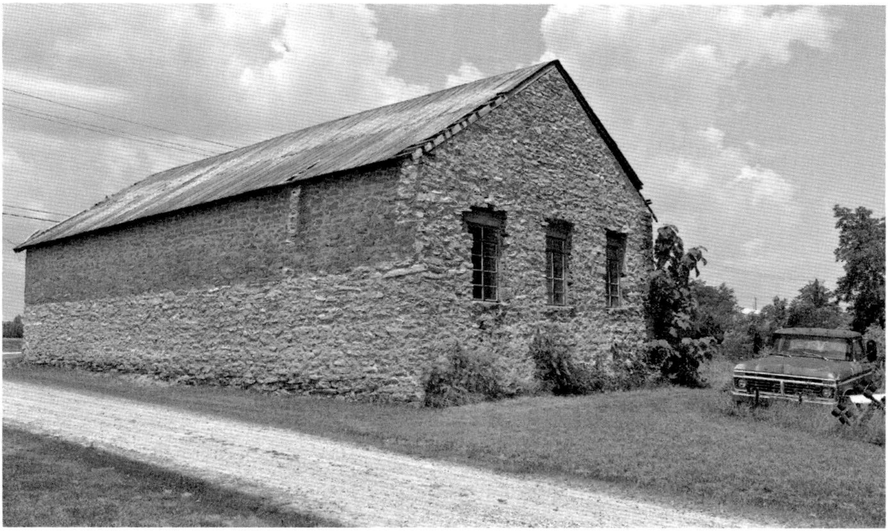

Jonathan Case's Ottaray Canning Company originally sported two such rock buildings, one of them with a wooden ell.

Essowah Orchards on Jump Off Mountain. By 1915, Case was out of his Hendersonville store and the Ottaray cannery and declared bankruptcy. According to the *French Broad Hustler* in February 1914:

> *By reason of excessive freight rates, which made it impossible for the Ottaray canning company of Dana, Henderson County, to compete with other canneries, this plant has been forced to reduce its operating capacity as a result of which the company, which was composed of Jonathan Case, Captain M.C. Toms and son, Charles French Toms, has dissolved. While the impression has gone out that the plant will discontinue, Mr. Case who owns half interest and who operated it several years before becoming associated with Captain Toms and son states that he will continue to run the cannery but on a reduced scale and gives the farmers and truckers of Henderson County assurance that he will handle all the products they will furnish him. It will continue to manufacture canned beans, sweet potatoes, tomatoes, apples, pumpkins, peaches, pears, fruit and vegetables, making jellies a specialty.*

By 1917, Case was back in business with T.L. Durham (1870–1940); soon after, Richard Parker Gregory (1868–1927) purchased the cannery and employed Case as manager, and operations flourished once again. Case and

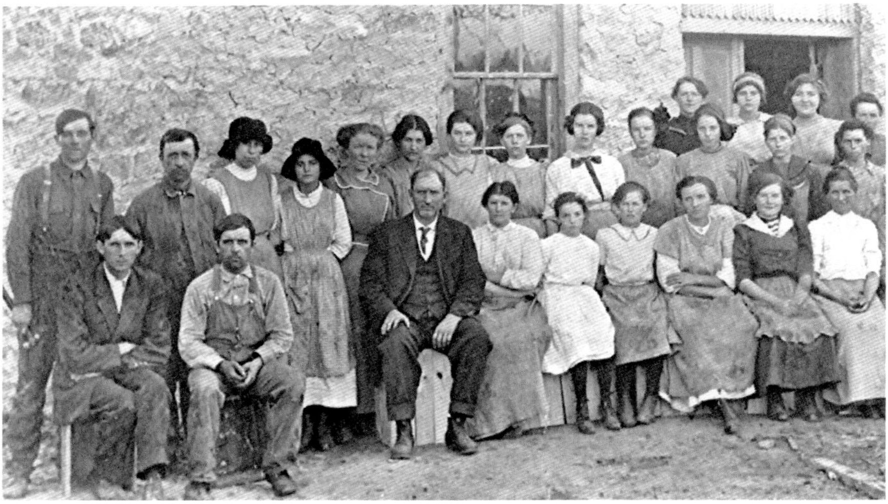

Jonathan Case surrounded by employees of his Ottaray Canning Company, at one time the largest canning company in North Carolina. *Photo courtesy of Chat Jones and John Paul Jones.*

his wife spent their last years in Asheville, where they died. They are buried at Refuge Baptist Church in Dana.

Note: The author worked through personal connections and local government agencies for special permissions to access and photograph historic sites and structures. The material within these pages is not intended for readers' use as a guide to the properties cited, nor does the author or his publisher condone trespassing on privately held land. Rather, enjoy an armchair tour through these passages and photographs, and please respect property owners' privacy.

Part III
Who Was That?

In Our Midst

Over the centuries, celebrated figures have lived and vacationed in the mountain retreat of Henderson County, North Carolina. There are people alive today who remember author F. Scott Fitzgerald having lodged at Hendersonville's Skyland Hotel—and all the big bands, including Cab Calloway's and Kay Kyser's, that performed in the Skyland's ballroom and the dance pavilion at Laurel Park. Few know of the more anonymous residents or vacationers, such as Hilda Marie Hult Brach (1892–1964) and her husband, the candy magnate Emil J. Brach (1859–1947) of Chicago, who summered at 407 West First Avenue. The more highly publicized visitors included the Gipper (Ronald Reagan), Captain Kangaroo (Bob Keeshan), GI Joe (Robert Mitchum), Gomer Pyle (Jim Nabors) and Minnie Pearl (Sarah Ophelia Colley Cannon). Some even claimed having made Elvis sightings when "the King" allegedly looked at the historic Beaumont estate when it was listed for sale in the mid-1900s.

In 1926, promoters of Laurel Park's Fleetwood Hotel brought in heavyweight boxing champion Jack Dempsey (1895–1983) to train at Laurel Lake Casino. Film actress Ann Jeffries summered in Hendersonville in the 1940s. Pat Hingle's family owned a house in Laurel Park, where the actor frequently visited. Hingle also acted at the Flat Rock Playhouse, as did Burt Reynolds, Dom DeLouise and Nelson Reilly. President Jimmy Carter's brother Billy participated in one of Hendersonville's Motorama events and, as Kermit Edney put it, "was a smashing hit."

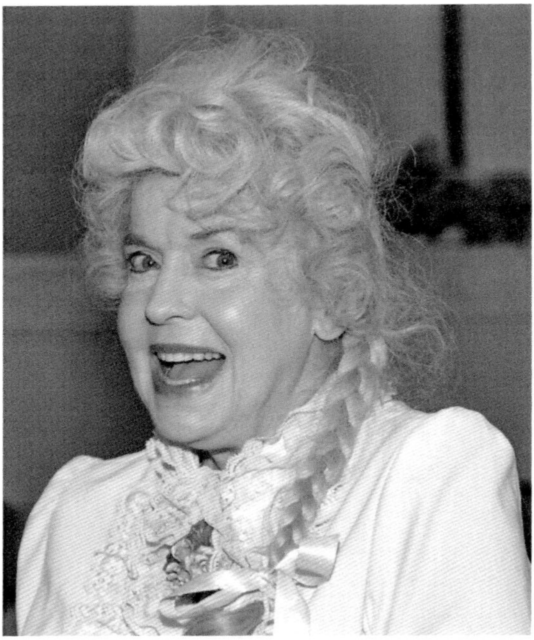
Donna Douglas at Etowah Baptist Church, 2004.

After a Hollywood career as a movie star, model, recording artist and actress in the popular sitcom *The Beverly Hillbillies*, Donna Douglas (1933–2015), who played Elly May Clampett, became a real estate agent, author of children's books and, more recently, a gospel singer and speaker at churches throughout the Southeast. On October 17, 2004, she graced Henderson County with an appearance at Etowah Baptist Church, where she preached a riveting forty-five-minute sermon comparing and contrasting her life of celebrity to various lines of Scripture. Douglas admitted to having been a tomboy in real life as she grew up in East Baton Rouge Parish near Zachary, Louisiana. She played softball and basketball at her Catholic high school and was later discovered in New York, "when I was one of those refrigerator ladies," she explained—a model in long gown and gloves gesturing at television game-show prizes. Soon after her discovery, the rest was history. "Hollywood is a sinful place," Douglas went on to say, "and havin' been brought up proper, I wouldn't play the game." The same day Douglas preached, renowned gospel tenor Rick Strickland (1977–) entertained at the church.

But what of our own unsung, homegrown heroes and celebrities?

A STEPP AT A TIME

Opinions shared through genealogical resources differ on the origin of the surname Stepp, many of them citing Holland and/or Germany or even Flemish Belgium (Flanders) as lands from whence the families migrated to England—more specifically to Devon and Cornwall. Spellings of the name over the centuries have varied, including Step, Steppe, Stapp and Stappe, derived, perhaps, from the Germanic Stapf or Von Stapf.

Henry Preston Scalf (1902–1979), a Stepp family historian, and the late Louise Howe Bailey believed the provenance of the Stepp name evolved from the Norse word *staup* or the Old English word *staepe*, meaning "a dwelling on a steep slope" or "a dwelling at the steppingstones." In time, this name took the Anglo-Saxon form of Steppan or Stapan, afterward shortened to Stepp or Stapp, indicating "a person living in a house by the stepping stones." Further origins include Stephan, Steventon, Steventone, Stephenton and the Latin *Stephanus*—each of them pertaining to "son of Stephan." Whatever the case, the name likely originated in Germany and evolved to its more popular, current spelling of "Stepp" in England and the United States. Scalf also believed there was likely a greater concentration of Stepps in Henderson County, North Carolina, than in any other county in the United States.

The 2013 Hendersonville telephone directory included nearly one hundred entries for the name Stepp. In my personal experience, the local Stepps have been and continue to be an upstanding and industrious lot.

Joseph Hamilton Stepp Sr.

Across from Refuge Baptist Church, at the crossroads of Ridge/Upward and Dana Roads, we find a grocery and sundries store—originally J.H. Stepp's general store, serving also as a post office, filling station, feed-and-seed outlet and café, with its second story a residence. The central building housed Stepp's packing plant. While serving as postmaster, first at Saconon and then Dana, for forty-one years, J.H. Stepp also operated his store, farmed and hauled truck crops to South Carolina markets.

In his early life, Joseph Hamilton Stepp (1886–1967) worked as a bookkeeper at Southern Railway's central repair shop in Spencer, North Carolina, and as an accountant for a cotton mill in Campobello, South Carolina. His experience at his uncle Jonathan Case's Ottaray Canning Company acquainted him with the packing business, and with his brother Thomas Dulus Stepp, he formed a canning operation known as Laureldale. Stepp had purchased the rock store previously owned by Emmett Bernard Freeman and twenty-two acres of farmland behind Refuge Baptist Church, the site of the Laureldale cannery. Freeman had been diagnosed with tuberculosis and, at the advice of his doctor, moved on to Arizona. Stepp

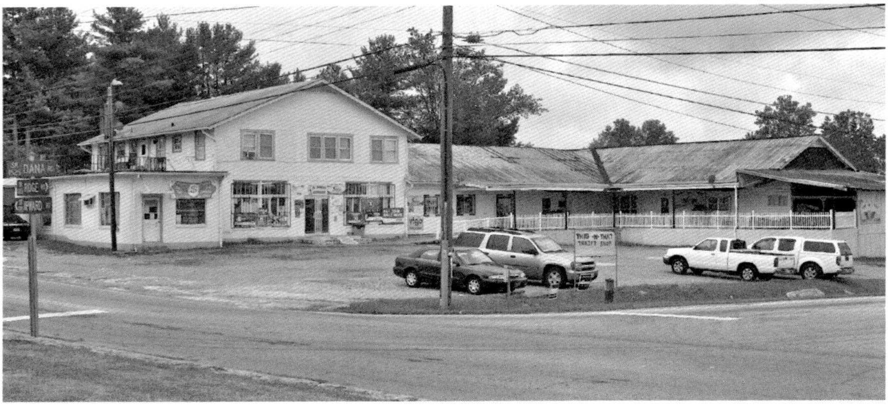

The former J.H. Stepp general store, café and packing plant complex.

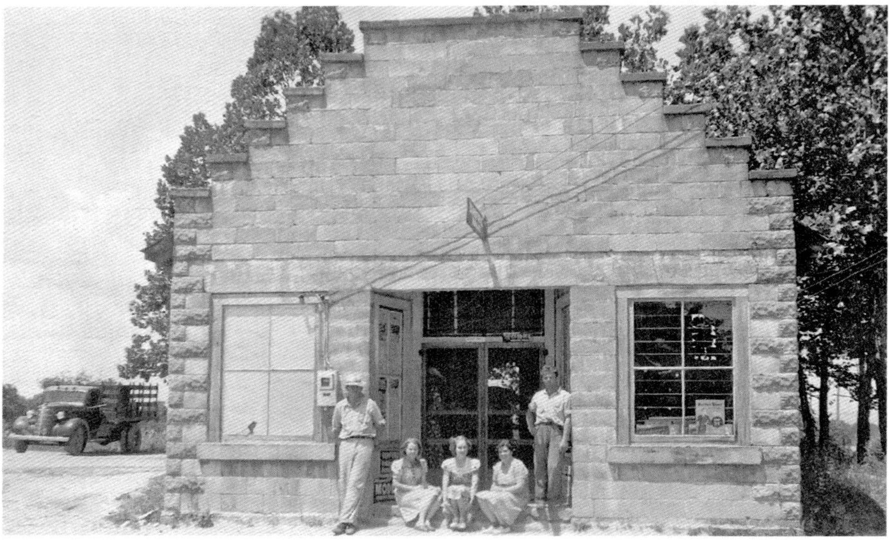

J.H. Stepp bought this rock store from Emmett B. Freeman. *Standing*: Leon Stepp (left) and J.H. Stepp Jr. (right). This structure was razed. *Photo courtesy of Sandra "Neicee" Stepp Johnson.*

later opened a store at East Flat Rock with Marion Lee Walker (1894–1964) but soon sold back to Walker and returned to Dana, where he bought out his brother Dulus's interests in the family enterprise.

Son of Arthur Fralo Stepp (1853–1913) and Martha Eloise Waters Stepp (1856–1951), J.H. Stepp worked to improve telephone service in Dana and to get electricity to the Dana area. He also worked diligently to promote the

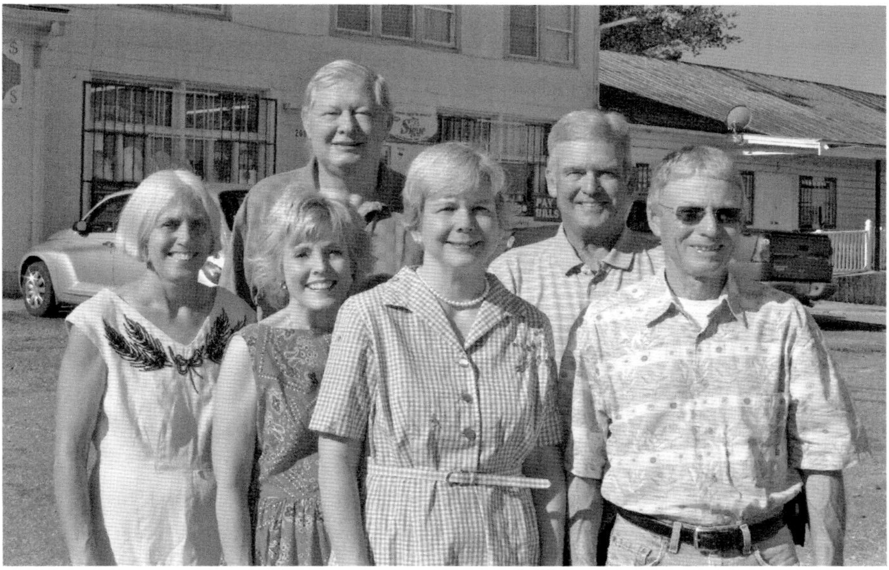

The grandchildren of Joseph Hamilton Stepp Sr. stand on the former site of the rock store. *From left to right*: Sonya Stepp Hollingsworth, Leon Stepp Jr., Colette Stepp Worley, Sandra "Neicee" Stepp Johnson, Joseph H. Stepp III and Mike Stepp.

consolidation of smaller schools in the region. He married Effie Arminta Pace (1890–1979) in 1908. The Stepps had nine children.

Stepp added a café to his one-stop shopping center at the junction of Upward/Ridge and Dana Roads to accommodate his packing plant workers. Word soon spread about the excellently prepared meals, seducing others, including General Electric Company employees, who drove out from East Flat Rock.

Those who knew J.H. Stepp considered him to be an industrious, practical and honest family man, and some went so far as to say, "Everything he touched was better for it."

Thomas Dulus Stepp

J.H. Stepp's brother Thomas Dulus Stepp (1878–1966) was also a Dana postal worker, but for only a few months. Dulus, who enjoyed playing the violin, attended Judson College and worked there as a custodian to pay his tuition. He married Anna Margaret Pace Pittillo (1884–1960) in 1910, and

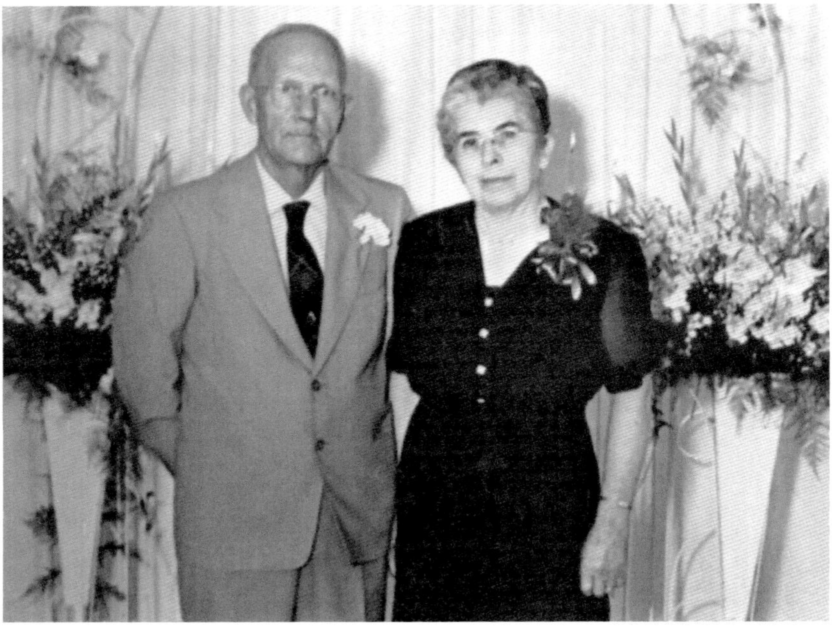

Joseph Hamilton Stepp Sr. and Effie Pace Stepp, 1953. *Photo courtesy of Sandra "Neicee" Stepp Johnson.*

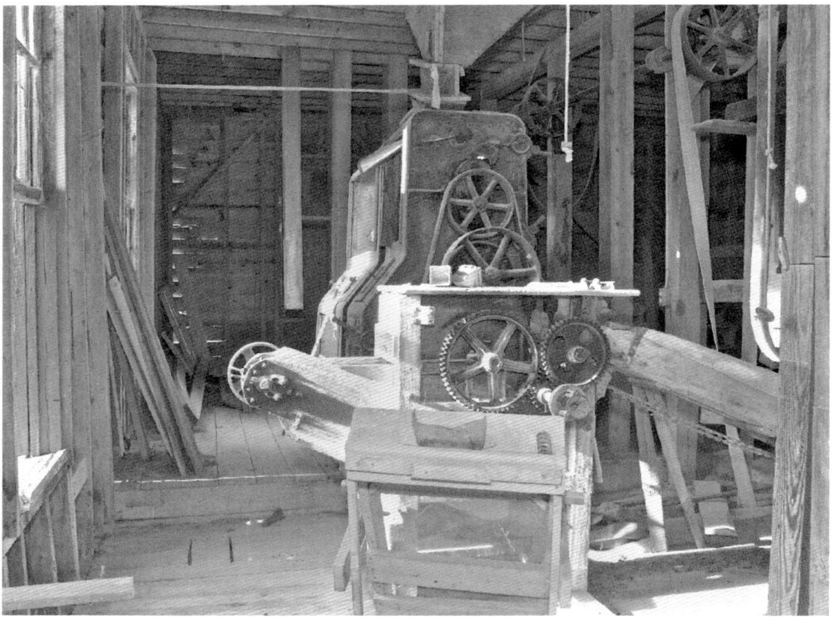

Inside the old Merrell/Stepp mill. *Photographed with permission of Carolyn Justus.*

with his brother J.H. formed a business partnership called Stepp Brothers Cannery and General Store. During the lean years, J.H. took a job in Whitney, South Carolina, while Dulus operated the business, and his wife, Anna, worked as supervisor of the Laureldale canning operation. Dulus bought out J.H. in 1925 and sold it back to him in 1927. Dulus and Anna had three children.

As a Henderson County commissioner from 1927 to 1930, Dulus proved influential in improving county roads and also in bringing electricity to Dana. He bought Ottaray Canning Company from his uncle Jonathan Case in 1924. An expert miller, considered an authority, he traded his Dana acreage for the gristmill property of Benjamin A. Merrell (1869–1935) on Tumblebug Creek at Saconon in 1933. Stepp learned the trade after having worked the Rhett Mill on Highland Lake in Flat Rock.

J.H. Stepp Jr.

One of J.H. Stepp's "quarter of a dozen sons," his namesake Joseph Hamilton Stepp Jr. (1920–2011), owned J.H. Stepp Farm's Hillcrest Orchard, a family tradition continued by two of his children, Mike Stepp (1950–) and Sonya Stepp Hollingsworth (1953–).

J.H. Stepp Jr. began his farming career as a child, working on his parents' farm. He married Yvonne Mann (1919–2008) in 1942 and joined the Army Air Corp the following week. After serving four years during World War II, he returned home at the age of twenty-six and worked at the family store

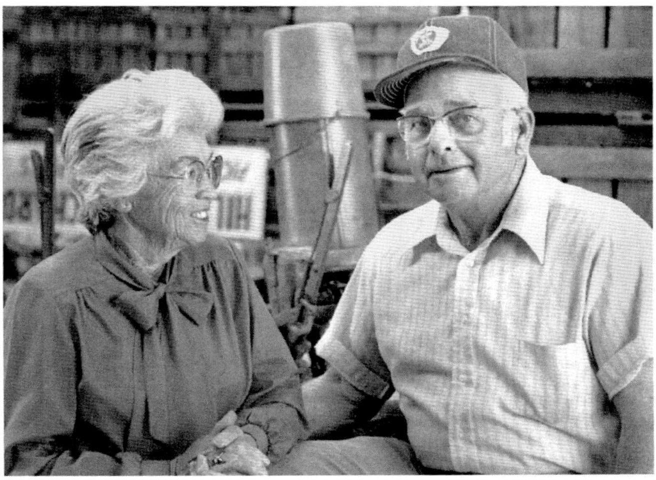

J.H. Stepp Jr. and his wife, Yvonne, 1986. *Photo courtesy of Sandra "Neicee" Stepp Johnson.*

and packinghouse in Dana. Apparently, the man had farming embedded in his DNA. Called "the grower" by family members, Stepp farmed in the Mills River valley for several years, cultivating beans, cucumbers, peppers, cabbage and apples. After laboring in the fields, he helped at the packinghouse and hauled and shipped truck crops to South Carolina markets.

In the 1960s, J.H. Stepp established a pick-your-own apples enterprise and moved to the Stepp farm at Stepp Orchard Drive, which he named Hillcrest in 1967. Stepp dedicated ten of the seventy-four acres to orchard with four varieties of apples, beginning with a wholesale business, which evolved into a retail operation. Today, the Stepps grow twenty-two varieties of apples on forty of the acres of their ancestral land, which has become a popular tourist destination.

Lucile Stepp Ray

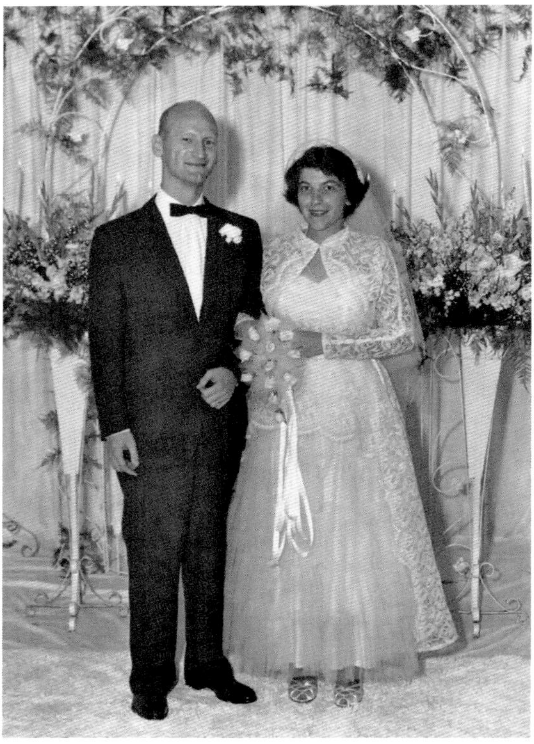

Charles Lenoir Ray and Lucile Stepp Ray, June 12, 1953. *Photo courtesy of Christopher L. Ray.*

One of the "half a dozen daughters" of J.H. Stepp Sr., Lucile (1924–2011) assisted in her family's business pursuits at Dana. At an early age, she worked at the *Western Carolina Tribune* as a photographer, reporter and advertising manager. She met her husband-to-be, Charles Lenoir Ray (1922–1971), at the newspaper office. Ray freelanced there and for other area newspapers.

Lenoir Ray, postmaster at Flat Rock for twenty-four years (1948–1971), wrote *Postmarks*, published in 1970—a book highly regarded by local and regional historians. Several of Lucile's photographs count among the book's illustrations.

The Rays married in 1953 and had four children. Lucile took a hiatus for motherhood and then returned to her newspaper career, working for the *Mother Earth News* and then the *Times-News* for fourteen years before she retired in 1989.

Born to X Ray (1897–1961) and Charlotte Berthel Blackwell Ray (1903–1991), Lenoir was a Renaissance man, having been an avid reader, researcher and writer, stamp collector, scoutmaster for the Boy Scout troop of East Flat Rock and member of numerous clubs and organizations. He involved himself also in drama, having acted—during his years of military service—in United States Army productions and later with the Hendersonville Little Theatre and Flat Rock Playhouse. He also wrote play reviews for the *Times-News*.

Lucile Stepp Ray left a legacy of rich photographic images. A browse through the collection bears out her innate talent for the art, with a keen sense of observation and composition and adeptness for capturing depth of field. Her subjects ranged from buildings that no longer stand to school, family and church activities to state fair livestock, including a three-legged chicken. The *Times-News* billed her as "a familiar Hendersonville personality offering up comments and curiosities concerning the people and places around her."

Charles Lenoir Ray and Lucile Stepp Ray are buried at Refuge Baptist Church Cemetery in Dana, North Carolina.

Gem Stepp Garren

Another of the "half a dozen daughters" of J.H. Stepp Sr., Edwin "Gem" Stepp Garren (1926–2014) went on to achieve regional and even national acclaim as a performing and recording artist. As a youngster, Gem helped with the family enterprise, working in the cafeteria and post office and later as bookkeeper for her father's business. She remembered having served the GE employees who frequented the café and doing "a lot of singing at home and in church"—and the shenanigans of "playing so hard" that she and a sister broke the family's sofa.

Gem's music teacher, Margaret Catherine "Kate" Dotson (1901–1971), introduced her and another pupil, Gerry Wilkie Shipman (1926–2010), to a talented musician who had moved to Hendersonville from New York, preferring the small-town atmosphere of his new digs in the mountains of western North Carolina. The musician, Raymond Thomas Taylor (1923–

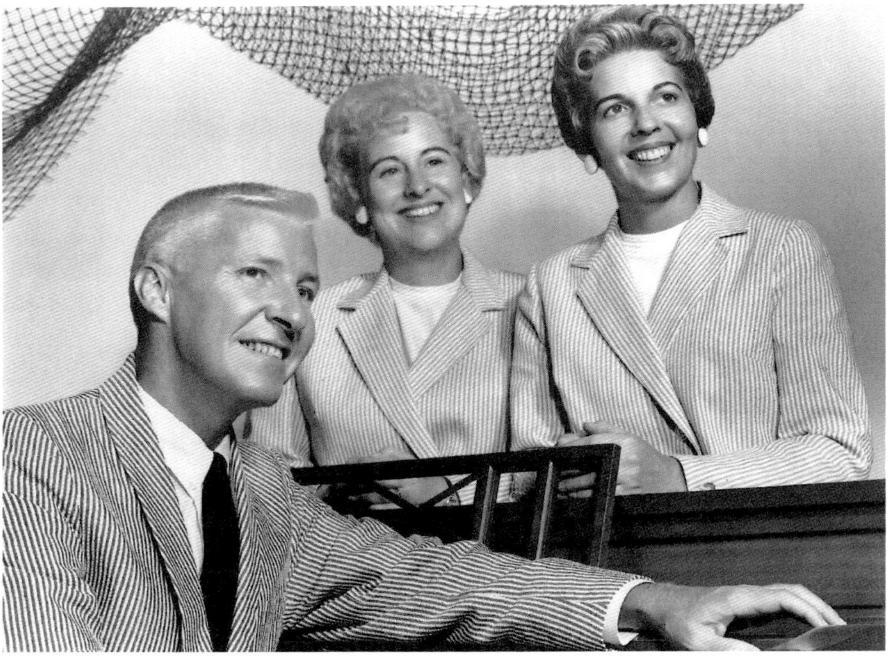

Ray Taylor and the Taylor Maids. *Photo courtesy of Linda Wilkie.*

1976), had written material for musical revues and for recording artists, including Jane Morgan (1924–) and Eartha Kitt (1927–2008), as well as Kitt's signature hit, "I Want to Be Evil." Ray discovered Hendersonville on a visit to his aunt Grace Etheridge and took up residence near the Shipman property on State Street.

Ray groomed Gem and Gerry, developing what would become the act known as Ray Taylor and the Taylor Maids. In the 1960s, the group entertained all over the Carolinas, including Asheville, Charlotte, Winston-Salem and Myrtle Beach; Sea Island, Georgia; Chicago; and New York. In Greenville, South Carolina, the group recorded "Blue Skies," "Any Time" and "Up a Lazy River" on the Dana Records label. Ray sang and played piano, and Gem and Gerry harmonized, with Gerry on drums and Gem on electronic bass keyboard. The group's floor shows also featured comedy skits.

Raymond Taylor studied music for twenty-three years at the Philadelphia Conservatory of Music, Oberlin College in Ohio and L'École Normale de la Musique de Paris in France. He wrote for musical reviews in New York, including six songs for Broadway shows. He organized the Show Barn, a musical theater held in the Shipman barn—later the home of Hendersonville Little Theatre—and also coached a number of Miss America entrants and piano students while living in Henderson County. After spending more than a decade in Hendersonville, he returned to his hometown, Batesburg, South Carolina, where he died from a self-inflicted gunshot wound.

In her eighties, Gem had her gowns that matched her partner Gerry's. She was married to Jack Ray Garren (1919–1989), a brick mason whose projects included Hendersonville's First Presbyterian Church.

Henderson County native and director of music and organist for First Presbyterian Church, Gayle Hamilton Stepp (1950–), well remembers Ray Taylor and the Taylor Maids and the impact they made on her life:

> *I learned professionalism by watching Ray and the Taylor Maids perform. Ray would introduce them: "The lovely platinum blonde is Gerry Shipman and the brunette is Gem Garren." Ray's piano arrangements required real skill, and Gem and Gerry sang in what seemed perfect harmony—harmony in voice and in their compatibility.*
>
> *Ray died young in his South Carolina hometown. Gem and Gerry retained a lifelong friendship. I'm grateful for their influence on my musical career.*

Reuben Miller Stepp and Oleeta

A monument inscribed "R.M. Stepp, Co. H 2nd N.C. Mtd. Inf. U.S. Army" marks a plot at the Stepp-Hyder Cemetery on Round Hill alongside Oleta Road at Dana. Not far from this small, rural cemetery, white water tumbles from Little Hungry River over a granite ledge within a wooded sanctuary and subdivision known now as Oleta Falls Retreat. In 1908, a post office was established at this site—a population center known as Oleeta. Sometime later, one *e* was dropped from the name.

While working the gristmill driven by the power of the falls, Reuben Miller Stepp (1839–1907) died suddenly, likely from a heart attack. Stepp married first to Mary Elizabeth Jones Stepp (1844–1894) and had thirteen children and second to Lucinda "Lou" Parris Stepp (1860–1941) and had six more children. R.M. and Mary's son Robert Coleman Stepp (1860–1942) resumed operation of the mill after his father's death.

But the history of the milling operation predates the Stepps' tenure. John Jones Sr., one of the first settlers in what is now the county of Henderson—Buncombe

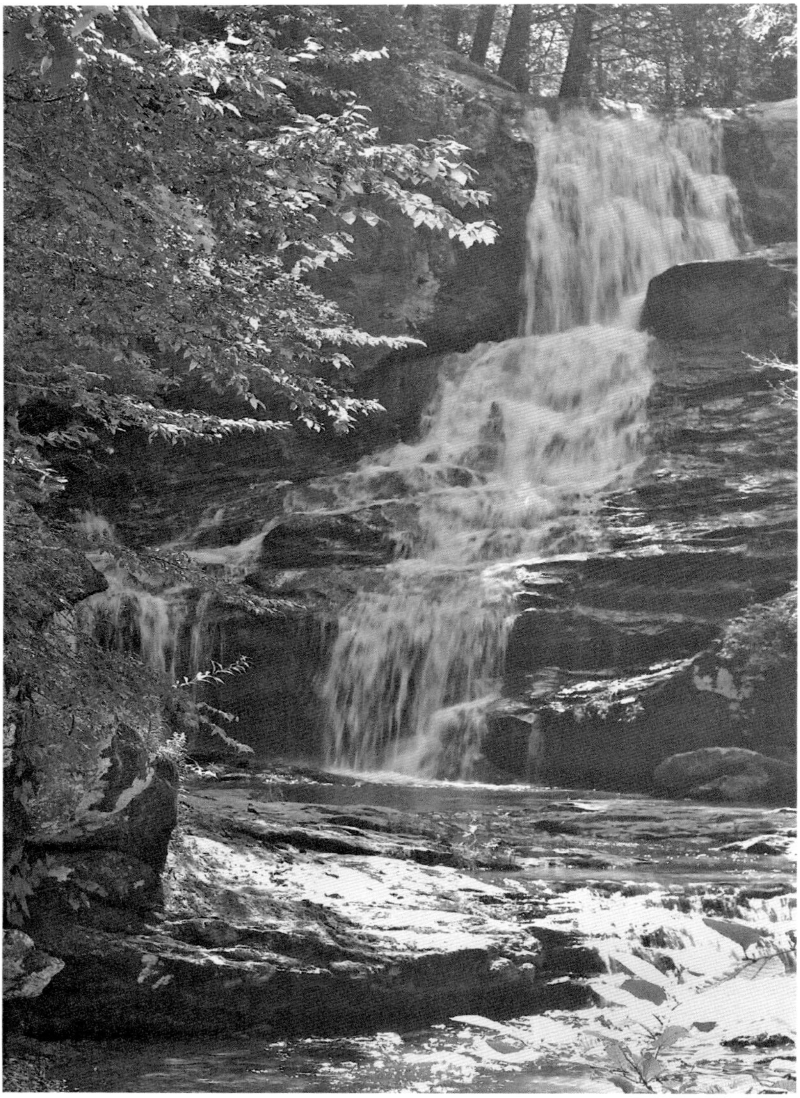

The visual and audio treat at the terminus of a half-mile-long trail: Oleeta Falls.

County at the time—held more than one thousand acres, including the site at Oleeta. Jones's log home, one of the first in the county, stood near this section of "The Ridge" between Dana and Upward.

Alongside the Oleeta waterfall, Jones constructed the county's first sawmill, essentially a "slash mill," operated with an up-and-down saw and

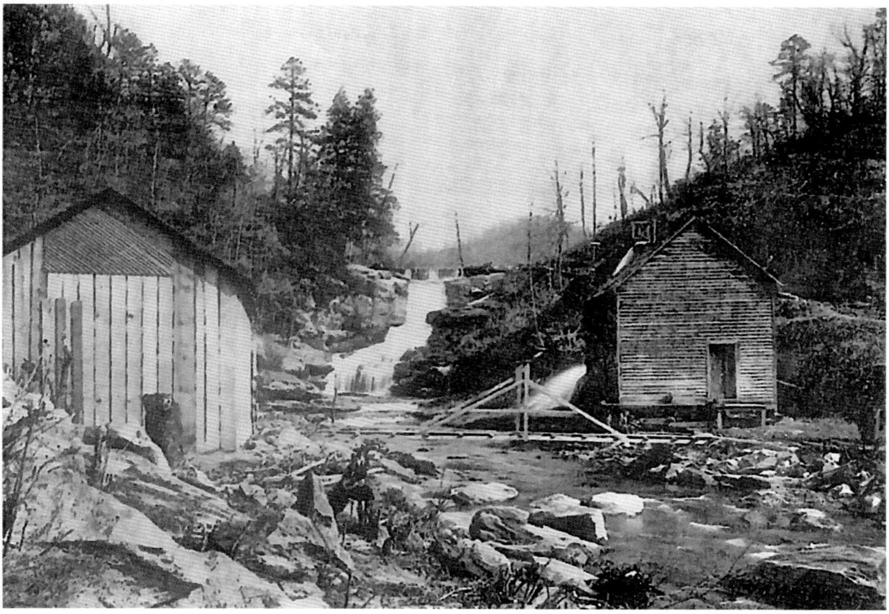

Historic view of the mills at Oleeta. *Photo courtesy of John Paul Jones.*

hydraulic system through a complex system of levers and gates to regulate the movement of water energy and the logs to be cut. Boards sawed at this mill furnished building materials for the early summer homes at Flat Rock, including Brookland, the mansion of Charles Edmondston (1782–1861). Jones also built one of the first gristmills on the site.

Alice E. Stepp Merrell (1880–1974), sister of J.H. Stepp Sr. and wife of Benjamin A. Merrell, worked as first postmistress at Oleeta until service was moved to Saconon in 1913. Besides the mills, structures on the site included the millers' house and post office—all washed away during the 1916 flood. After the devastating storms of 1916, the magnitude of floodwaters diverted the course of the river, forever changing the appearance of the falls.

Today, the site of Oleeta lies within a gated enclave proffering panoramas of Dana, Sugarloaf Mountain and beyond. Within it, one finds the preserved Revolutionary War–era Stepp Cemetery on "Red Hill." Homeowners association dues include pristine maintenance of trails, creek banks and bridges, enabling residents and their guests a much more leisurely course than that of the property's forebears and their oxcarts that moved tons of lumber and grain to and from the mill site.

DR. T.A. ALLEN

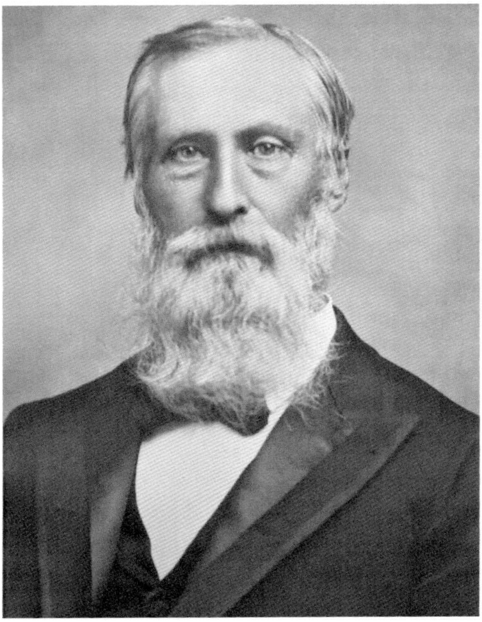

Dr. T.A. Allen, first mayor of Hendersonville, North Carolina. *Photo courtesy of Lu Ann Welter and Hendersonville City Hall.*

A lull exists in the recording of Hendersonville's seminal years because Dr. Thomas Alexander Allen (1824–1914), the city's first mayor, believed minutes to be unnecessary. Due to this gap in recorded history, some would argue whether Allen ever served as mayor, although his portrait hangs at city hall among the others of Hendersonville's mayors—his a most distinguished countenance with resolute eyes and long white beard.

In 1872, the North Carolina General Assembly granted all incorporated towns the right to elect a mayor and board of directors. Shortly thereafter, Hendersonville citizens voted Dr. Allen their town's first mayor, and he served between 1873 and 1878. Records were not kept until 1878 under Mayor Hamilton G. Ewart (1849–1918).

T.A. Allen was born to James B. Allen (1784–1853) and Kerron Happuch Braden Allen (1792–1849) of Rutherford County, whose family settled in Mill Spring in Rutherford County—now Polk County. He attended medical college in Charleston, South Carolina, and lived for a time in Alabama before settling in Hendersonville, North Carolina, around 1850. Allen practiced medicine in Hendersonville, owned a general store that included drugs, practiced dentistry as well as general medicine and dealt in land transactions. He served as secretary of the Western North Carolina Female College and was a member of the Henderson County Board of Health. According to an 1860 census, he owned four slaves.

In an article about Hendersonville and Dr. Allen in the 1870s that appeared in the *French Broad Hustler* on October 23, 1917, Thomas J. Rickman noted:

> *The number of inhabitants within the town limits was not over one dozen families and the highways consisted of one long main street and some roads leading into it, from the country, while about four storehouses graced the edges of this main street...On the east side he read a sign over the door, "T.A. Allen, General Merchandise, Produce taken in Exchange for Goods." He ventured inside and found the doctor and some of his clerks busy counting up eggs, weighing hams, measuring corn and some rye and a few bags of wool and some country knit-socks.*

Dr. Allen married Ruemma A. "Emma" Jones (1826–1913) in 1853 and served as a physician for the Confederate army during the Civil War. The Allens lived on Main Street—their private boardinghouse since 1865, at the time the oldest under continuous management—and were frequent over-winterers in Florida. They had four children and were among the early leaders of the Methodist congregation of Henderson County.

THE GODFATHER OF SOUL

Partway into a live performance of his hit recording "Please, Please, Please," James Brown—in a moment of rehearsed passion—would drop to a knee, at which point his emcee would drape a cape over his shoulders and assist him to his feet. Hendersonville sisters Bonnie Pilgrim and Melinda Pilgrim Lowrance vividly remember this moment from the late 1950s, when James Brown and the Famous Flames performed at the Carolina Theatre on Hendersonville's Main Street. The Pilgrim sisters recall, too, their mother having told them that, before achieving fame as a performer and recording artist, James Brown (1933–2006) toiled in the fields of Henderson County.

For decades, Henderson County farmers and orchardists have depended on the labor of migrant workers from South Carolina, Georgia and Florida. James Brown, who was born to unwed parents in rural Barnwell, South Carolina, knew his share of poverty and tribulations. Raised in a brothel and jailed as a teenager, he later tried his hand at semipro baseball pitching and wrestling and suffered from diabetes, drug addiction and prostate cancer. He traveled as a performer on the Chitlin' Circuit before his songs made the charts in the mid-1950s, skyrocketing the extravagant performer to fame and fortune. Brown, also an activist and staunch Republican, was inducted into the Rock-and-Roll

Hall of Fame in 1986, and the Songwriters Hall of Fame added him to its roster in 2000.

Hendersonville resident Robert H. Bittle (1956–) played with a band that opened for the James Brown Review during the last decade of Brown's life. "He would arrive in a stretch limousine," Bittle explained, "with bodyguards—some of the largest men I've ever seen. After each concert, the bodyguards would escort him back to the limo, and he was out of there. He didn't hang out much."

CHESTER ALLEN "CHAT" JONES

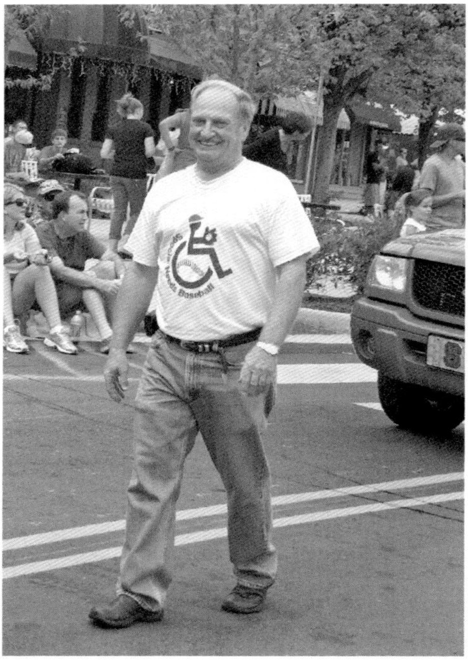

Chat Jones marching with special needs children in the 2012 King Apple Parade in Hendersonville, North Carolina.

Host to a bullpen for compatible fellows and history buffs, his office brimmed with files, folders and binders of historical data and old photographs and an eager willingness to discuss the past. Chat Jones not only loved history, but he also respected everyone who came his way.

Chester Allen "Chat" Jones (1949–2012), a friend to all who knew him—born to David Nathaniel Jones (1927–1982) and Marcene Corn Jones Alger (1930–2013)—graduated from Edneyville High School in 1969 and was a member of the First United Methodist Church of Hendersonville. He owned Jones Auto Sales on the Asheville Highway and was a member of the Hendersonville Kiwanis Club, serving as its president in 1987 and named Lay Person of the Year by the club in 2008.

Chat's head and heart were in the history and intricately woven heritage of his native Henderson County—and with all who were less fortunate.

As a civic leader and philanthropist, he launched programs including the Special Needs Baseball League with his brother Donnie Jones. He raised and donated funds for disposable diapers for his "Balfour babies" and spearheaded efforts to raise money for playground swings at Jackson and Etowah Parks, including a handicapped swing at Edneyville Community Park. In April 2013, officials named two ball fields at Hendersonville's Jackson Park "Chat Jones Memorial Fields."

Chat, married to Judith Lyda Jones (1952–), had two children, Michelle Mullinax and Lucy Brevard. He died unexpectedly one evening while working at his auto dealership—of accidental carbon monoxide poisoning.

A community treasure, Chat Jones is sorely missed.

GEORGE MULLINS

The mild clime of western North Carolina has long attracted summer visitors, but it was more than the coastal elite who found respite here from the exhaustive heat and humidity of their Lowcountry estates. A few old-timers still remember the many field hands who came up for the summers and others who took odd jobs and entertained on the streets.

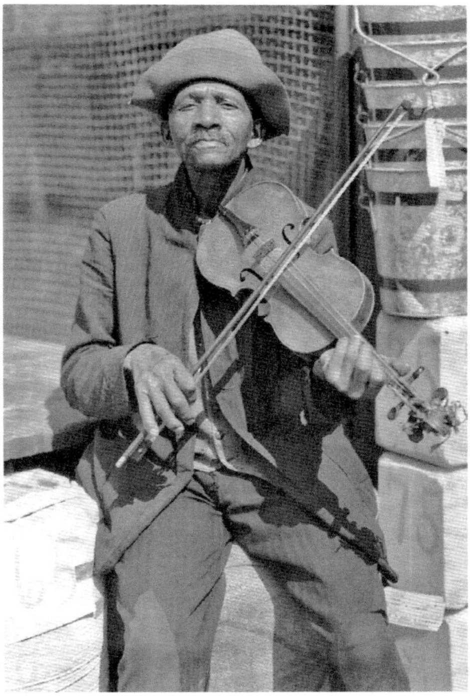

"Trottin' Sally." *Photo courtesy of the* Herald-Journal *Willis Collection, Spartanburg County, South Carolina Public Libraries.*

Eccentrics keep things interesting, and George Mullins (1855–1931) of Spartanburg County, South Carolina, counted among the more avant-garde of characters who passed through Hendersonville. Known more popularly as "Trottin' Sally," Mullins took odd jobs in Hendersonville and also performed as a street musician with his homemade violin, which he named Rosalie. Folks who remember him, including Samuel "Sammy" Williams (1919–2013), said Mullins could make his violin talk.

Mullins's most unusual characteristic, however, would have been his gait. He trotted and sometimes galloped, using the middle of the road in favor of more conventional footpaths. Sammy Williams could not forget the sight of Mullins trotting by his father's hardware store, Louis Williams & Sons on Seventh Avenue. Mullins, known to race trains—and win—pawed the ground, whinnied, nickered and snorted in the manner of a horse and barked like a dog if someone approached him too closely. Mullins was buried at Ridgeville Baptist Church Cemetery in Inman, South Carolina, in an unmarked grave.

DAVE GRAUE AND *ALLEY OOP*

Little River Road, the narrow and curvaceous connector between the Greenville Highway and Kanuga Road/Crab Creek Road, was widened somewhat and repaved only after tragedy struck near one of its bends on December 10, 2001. The victim: David Graue (1926–2001), a retired cartoonist of the *Alley Oop* comic strip.

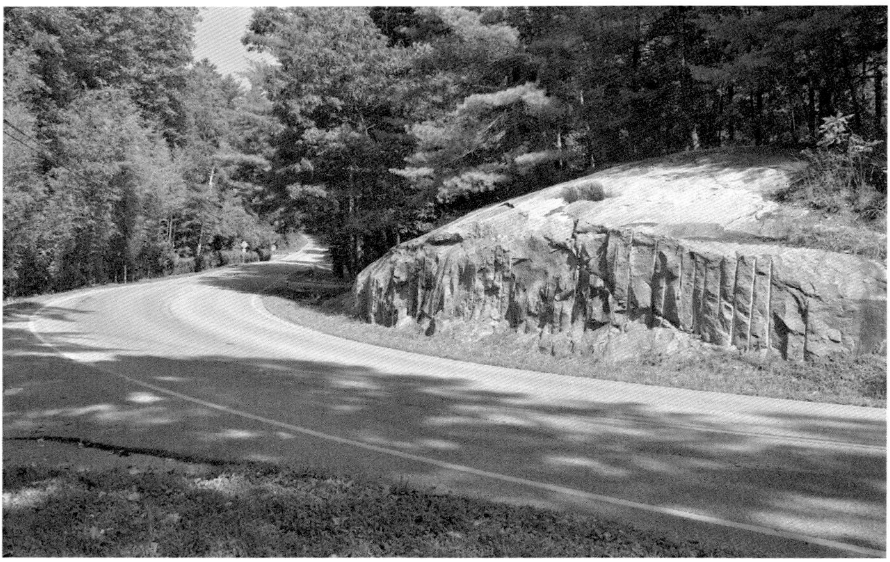

Site of the Graue fatality on Little River Road.

Alley Oop, the irrepressible, club-wielding Neanderthal, first appeared from the pen of Vincent Trout Hamlin (1900–1993) in 1932, and the comic strip went into syndication in 1933. At the peak of its popularity, eight hundred newspapers carried the strip. When Hamlin retired in 1971, his assistant Dave Graue took over, illustrating the cartoon through the 1980s, when Jack Bender took over the illustrative component. Graue, who enjoyed portraying North Carolina scenes in a pointillist motif, continued writing the *Alley Oop* strip from his studio in the Tranquility subdivision until he retired in 2001.

Dave Graue and Eliza B. Graue (1933–2012) lived in the Tranquility neighborhood off Little River Road. The Graues had complained about being run off the road, or nearly run off the road, by oversized trucks—a complaint not uncommon in the area. Then one day as Graue left his neighborhood, a dump truck struck him after the truck driver lost control of his vehicle, overcorrected and crossed the centerline, crashing into Graue's car. The truck driver was charged with death by a motor vehicle. Following the catastrophe, residents of Tranquility petitioned North Carolina's governor, Michael Easley, and the State Department of Transportation to restrict weight limits on Little River Road and also launched a movement to widen and improve the dangerous corridor.

KATHLEEN FEATHERSTONE WILLIAMS

Statuesque, handsome and determined, with eyes warm yet piercing, Kathleen Featherstone Williams (1920–2013) led a remarkable life. Reared in "the big city," she called Hendersonville "a cow town" when she moved there in her early twenties, but she nevertheless adapted to small-town ways, involving herself in business and civic affairs. "Hendersonville has come a long way since I arrived here," she said.

Kathleen, born to Forrest Featherstone (1878–1964) and Anna Featherstone (1898–1939) of Asheville, North Carolina, graduated with honors in 1938 from Stephens-Lee High School. She attended a beauty school run by Cordelia W. Stewart (1884–1967) in Asheville, where she "was the only student at the time." After apprenticing in Asheville for two years, Kathleen moved to Hendersonville to operate a beauty salon opened by Alberta Jowers Mooney (1907–1992) at 719 Maple Street—the first bona fide beauty shop, excluding those run from private homes, within the city limits. Jowers was the first African American registered

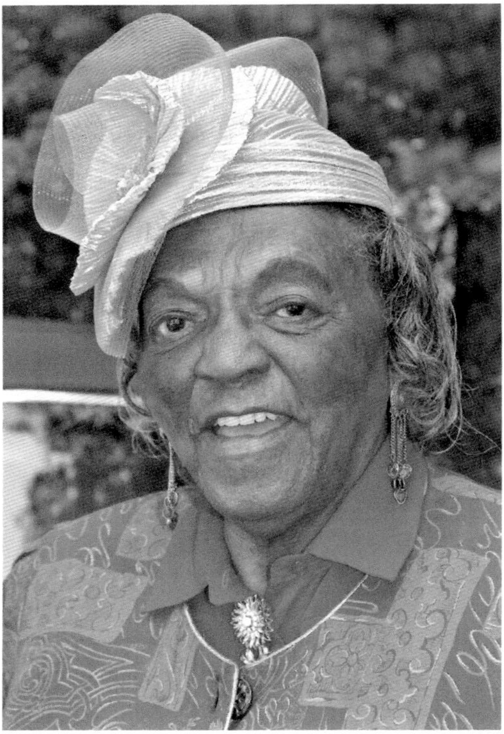

Kathleen Featherstone Williams at age ninety-two.

nurse at Hendersonville's Patton Memorial Hospital.

Kathleen took over the salon business, naming it Kathleen's Beauty Shoppe, and moved it to First Avenue in Peacock Town near her home, where she operated for forty years. She also kept a store and cafeteria in that building, where local youth would gather on Monday evenings. Customers came from beyond Hendersonville to Kathleen for hairstyling, including Phoebia Cheek Sullivan (1855–1956), the renowned faith healer from Saluda, North Carolina.

In 1943, Kathleen married Henry N. Williams (1904–1983) of Seneca, South Carolina. "We went down to Spartanburg to a justice of the peace to get married," she said, "because that's what people did then. I never asked why." Kathleen and Henry had four children. About racial discrimination, she remarked, "We had problems in those days, but they were minor." About the unspeakable subject of eugenics, she said, "I figured that one out myself, when someone would have a child and then could have no more."

A member of Star of Bethel Baptist Church, Kathleen served as chair of her church's Mission Circle, sang in the choir "and just about everything else," she said. She was president of the PTA at Ninth Avenue School, belonged to the North Carolina Beauticians Association and to the North Carolina Beautician and Cosmetologist Club, which she organized. Serving as secretary for the community council, she labored rigorously for desegregation. One such effort took her back to Asheville, to a superintendant of schools, who told her, "We are going to integrate in 1964 anyway." Meanwhile, she organized forty people to get the process established. "Everything went pretty smoothly," she said.

Involving herself further in civic activities, she was instructor of education of the Grand Chapter Order of the Eastern Star, DAR; member and co-chairperson of the Council of Women, Church Women United; secretary of the Henderson County branch of the NAACP; and served on the Council of Aging and the YMCA. She served on the board of Democratic Women, was a member of Diamond Circle Chapter #263 of Hendersonville and a den mother for Cub Scout Pack 611 and organized the Kids' Bible Club. As a member of the Black History Research Committee, Williams conducted interviews and research concerning African American residents of Flat Rock and its environs—work crucial to the publication of the book *A Brief History of the Black Presence in Henderson County*.

In 2011, Kathleen Featherstone Williams, a Henderson County resident for more than seventy years, was inducted into Henderson County's Martin Luther King Jr. Memorial Park, with her name engraved into the park's brick pathway. Inductees include county residents who significantly impacted the community by "promoting racial harmony, enhancing cultural diversity, and advancing opportunities for achievement." Kathleen Williams not only witnessed the scores of changes in the county but also contributed to the positive outcomes.

RABBI CHARLES MANTINBAND AND AGUDAS ISRAEL

A 1950s poster in the archives of Henderson County's Agudas Israel Synagogue reads: "Jewish Religious Services: Traditional • Modern • 4th and King St., next door to the Public Library. Charles Mantinband of Hattiesburg, Miss., Summer Rabbi. Jews and Non-Jews Welcome!"

Born in 1895 to Samuel and Delia Gottlieb Mantinband of New York, New York, Charles Mantinband spent his formative years in Norfolk, Virginia. As rabbi, he served the congregation B'nai Israel in Hattiesburg, Mississippi, during much of the civil rights era, when most southerners did not support such notions. Mantinband, considered the moral compass of Hattiesburg and an outspoken proponent of racial equality and civil rights, argued that because of their own experience with discrimination, Jews should empathize with the plight of blacks. He crossed racial lines in association with out-of-state civil rights activists to the point where members of B'nai Israel futilely attempted to quiet Mantinband on these issues after the local white citizens' council made threats to members of the synagogue in Hattiesburg, insisting on dismissal of their rabbi. In 1963,

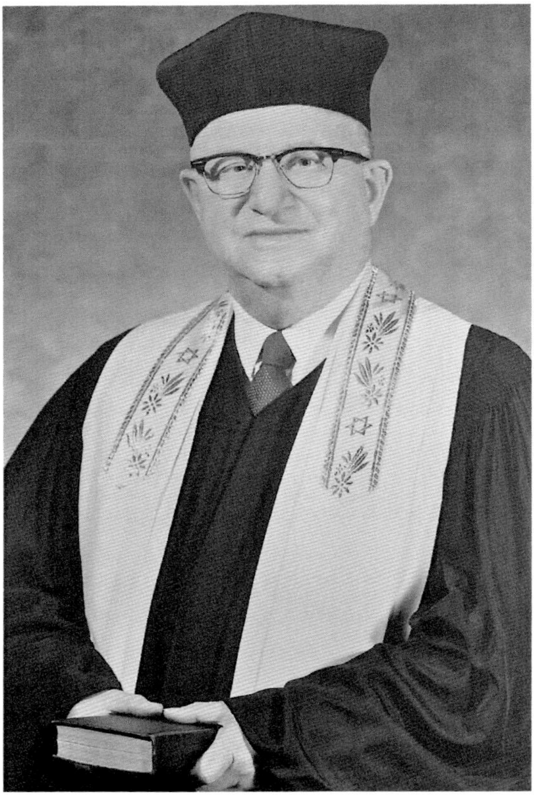

Rabbi Charles Mantinband. *Photo courtesy of Carol Mantinband Ginsburg.*

Mantinband left Hattiesburg for the Temple Emanu-El congregation in Longview, Texas. In June of that year, Mantinband was one of more than two hundred clergymen and religious leaders of all faiths invited by President John F. Kennedy to attend a White House conference on the "present aspects of the nation's civil rights problems."

Mantinband, who married Anna Kest (1891–1981), spent much of his life in the South, accepting his first job as director of the Young Men's Hebrew Academy in Memphis, Tennessee. He received his religious training at Rabbi Stephen S. Wise's Jewish Institute of Religion in New York City and earned his bachelor of science degree from City College in New York City in 1916; a master of arts from Columbia University in 1918; his doctorate from Barton College and Seminary at Wilson, North Carolina, in 1958; and an honorary doctor of humane letters from Lincoln University, Pennsylvania. He served as a chaplain at Camp Forrest in Chickamauga, Georgia, and in the tri-cities area of Florence, Sheffield and Tuscumbia, Alabama. He died in 1974, having spent the last years of his life blind. The Mantinbands had two children, Carol and Bill, and adopted Dan and Frank Aaron, who were orphans of the Holocaust.

Mantinband's daughter Carol Ginsburg (1922–) remembers the letters her father wrote to her mother, Anna, "one each morning, waiting for her on the breakfast table. Love letters. I saved all of them."

Agudas Israel member and Hendersonville native Rebecca "Becky" Sherman Banadyga (1948–) of Sherman's Sports and Navy Store shared memories of Rabbi Mantinband, who asked for a lock of her blond hair in the 1950s, when she

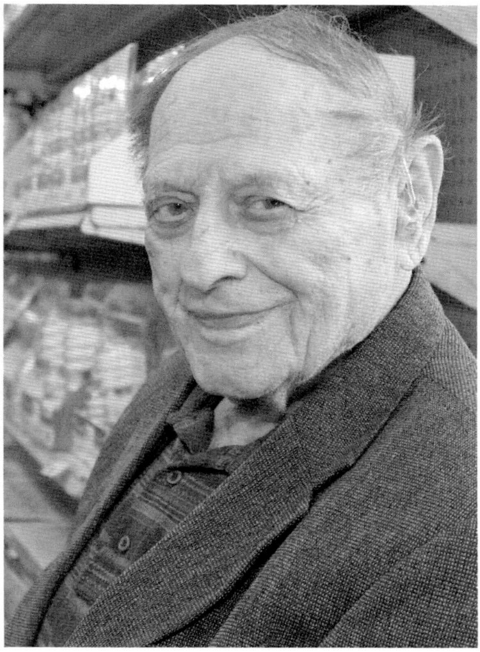

Samuel Williams at age ninety-two.

was a toddler. "I was so young then, but I do remember him as a good man," Becky said. Years later, the Mantinband family returned the lock of hair to the Shermans. Another Agudas Israel member, Dr. Michael Beckerman (1945–), remembers Mantinband as "a wonderful man, stout and plump with cherubic red cheeks." As a child, Beckerman enjoyed Mantinband's classes, adding, "He didn't get on the particular subject of civil rights here in Hendersonville." Beckerman also recalls the congregation's excitement in having a rabbi to officiate instead of having only lay readers for religious services. Sammy Williams agreed with Beckerman's statement. "Quite personal," Williams said. "Everyone liked him. He gave us genuine leadership after having been led by lay members for so many years."

The building first occupied by the Agudas Israel congregation was built in the early 1900s for Home Electric Company on Hendersonville's King Street near Fourth Avenue. Deed records show E.W. Ewbank as grantor to Robert Marcus Oates (1869–1922) of Home Electric Co. in 1918 and the Oates estate as grantor to Agudas Israel trustees A. Lewis, H. Patterson and L. Sherman in 1925. After Agudas Israel moved to its new location in Laurel Park, other occupants of the building on King Street included the Community Club and the Salvation Army.

The original Agudath Israel movement was established in Europe in 1912 by some of the most famous Orthodox rabbis of the time, including the Chofetz Chaim (Yisrael Meir Kagan Poupko, 1838–1933). The movement grew during the 1920s and 1930s to be the political, communal and cultural voice of those Orthodox Jews who were not part of Zionism's Orthodox Jewish Mizrachi party. An Ashkenazic phrase, *agudat achim* in Sephardic Hebrew, means "society of brothers." According to the *French Broad Hustler* of October 1, 1913:

> *The people of Jewish faith are celebrating today the feast of Rosh Hashanah, which corresponds to the Christian New Year. All orthodox Jews observe the feast and in consequence the business house of H. Patterson in this city will be closed today and tomorrow until 6 p.m.*

Hendersonville's Agudas Israel Congregation, affiliated with the Union of American Hebrew Congregations, took root in Henderson County when twenty-seven men and women attended the founding meeting held at the home of Abe Kantrowitz (1891–1969) in 1922. Before that time, Hendersonville Jews had been meeting together informally to worship in people's homes on a rotation basis. The group continued congregating in private residences until later, when they used the local Masonic Temple for worship services. Henry Patterson (1874–1953) was president of the seminal congregation. Additional founding members included Morris and Leah Kalin, Sam and Ray Kalin, Dan and Sophia Michalove, Harry and Pearl Mottsman, Harry and Minnie Patterson, Jacob and Jennie Rosenberg, Louis and Rosena Sherman and Louis and Minnie Williams. In its seminal years, traveling qualified persons and senior student rabbis conducted Rosh Hashanah and Yom Kippur services for the congregation.

According to the Goldring/Woldenberg Institute of Southern Jewish Life:

> *The desire to fit into the heavily religious culture of the town motivated Hendersonville Jews to push quickly for a permanent synagogue. The members of Agudas Israel soon began to raise money for a Jewish house of worship, yet since the congregation consisted of only a handful of extended families, the cost of a building seemed beyond their means. In response the members who owned businesses sent a fundraising appeal to their business associates asking for donations. They wrote that "the majority of the non-Jews in this community are under the impression that we have no religion of any kind owing to the fact that we have no permanent place to worship...this situation is very embarrassing to us, and in order to hold the esteem of the non-Jews of the community, we must have a suitable edifice for religious worship.*

Trustees for the congregation purchased the Home Electric Company building in 1925 and made it their synagogue. Member Louis Williams (1899–1971) brought his brother Chaim Williamowsky (1896–1971) to Hendersonville to serve as rabbi. Williamowsky, who served from

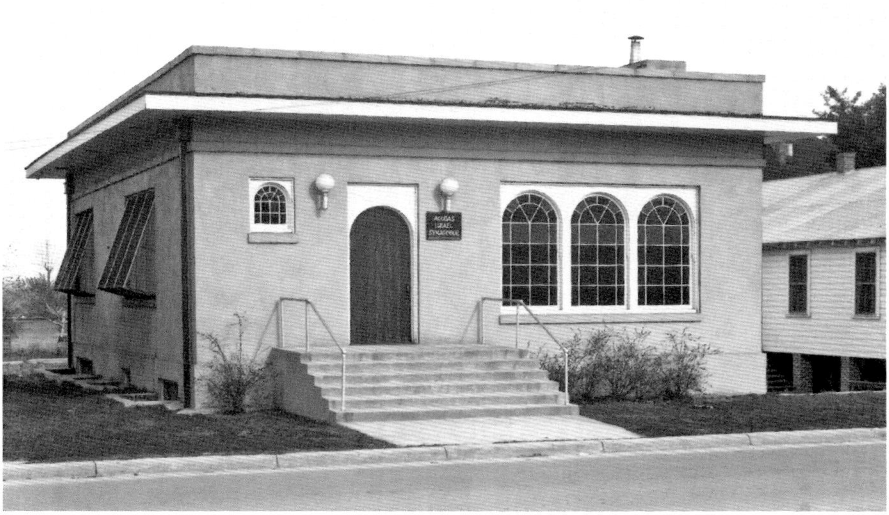

View of the Agudas Israel Synagogue's location on King Street. *Photo courtesy of the library of Agudas Israel.*

1927 to 1929, also taught Hebrew to the Sunday school children of the congregation and slaughtered kosher meat for Orthodox members. When, due to lack of funds, the congregation found difficulty in paying the salary of a full-time rabbi, the Jewish Ladies Auxiliary hosted a series of fundraising events to finance the rabbi's salary. Rabbi Williamowsky remained with Agudas Israel until 1929, when he moved to Durham, North Carolina, and Rabbi Beryl Cohen succeeded him, but only on a part-time basis until 1964, when he died—the same year the King Street synagogue was remodeled.

By the 1950s, the congregation had moved away from Orthodoxy, embracing Conservative Judaism. In 1958, the congregation bought land for a new synagogue but postponed construction and sold the lot to the YMCA after the number of congregants had fallen away or had moved.

An influx of retired Jews to Hendersonville in more recent years led to a resurgence in membership of Agudas Israel. In 1996, new members pushed to officially join the Judaism Reform Movement. By 1997, approximately 250 Jews counted among Henderson County's population, and Agudas Israel had a full-time membership of 86, plus 64 additional members during the summer months. The congregation launched a building campaign in 2000, and by 2002, the new synagogue had been completed in Laurel Park. Philip J. Bentley became the first full-time rabbi employed by Agudas Israel in seventy-five years. Rabbi Phil Cohen succeeded Bentley in 2011.

Part IV

The Road Less Written

Tour of Crab Creek Road

Much has been written of the "great flat rock," the granite outcropping from which the western North Carolina village takes its name, yet little exists in print with regard to the vast lands just west and south of the storied village of Flat Rock. And few alive today recall when the artery now called Kanuga Road (County Road 1127), Kanuga Street and Crab Creek Road (County Road 1127) was called Crab Creek Road all the way from the wee villages of what is now eastern Transylvania County to downtown Hendersonville.

Under orders in 1792, Sergeant Lambert Clayton (1755–1828) and his militia built a road from the Catawba Trail, near what is now Flat Rock, through the Little River and Crab Creek settlements to the Estatoe Path—a primary Cherokee hunting and trading corridor—to the Davidson River. This conduit, known as the Crab Creek Path, coursed through the Blue Ridge Mountains to the Cherokee village of Estatoe in South Carolina—one of the first routes to navigate and open up the rugged, densely forested terrain. Clayton, born in Kent County, Delaware, relocated to Rowan County, North Carolina, before acquiring large tracts of land in what became Transylvania County. Clayton served as this area's first postmaster and justice of the peace.

Not so long ago in this sublimely mysterious valley, sawmills buzzed and gristmills clunked, and the fragrance of freshly mown hay permeated the atmosphere. These pastoral lands that juxtapose the heritage of Henderson and Transylvania Counties still reflect a sense of what was—rolling with grain fields, dotted with iconic scenes and vacant structures that served as homes and post offices and country stores. Mundane, perhaps, yet the passage of time has conferred a special romance on these workaday buildings where farmers and others toiled at their trades, and here, in some respects, rural life proceeds as it has for generations.

Here grain fields and pastureland unfurl for miles to a horizon serrated with blue ridges—a panoply of geography: forested mountains, sprawling valleys and tributaries of one of the planet's most ancient of rivers. A popularly held notion alleges that the French Broad River is the third oldest in the world behind the Nile and the ironically named New River, part of which flows through North Carolina. The Cherokee named the French Broad River *Agiqua*, meaning "long man." Historians attribute its current name to French explorers.

Let's take a road trip from points where Transylvania was Henderson, through population centers known as Penrose and Little River, to the Crab Creek Valley, up Kanuga Road and into Hendersonville. Along the way, we'll pause at structures, taking a peek into state forests, camps, cemeteries and the farms, homes and stores now mostly lost to nature and time.

PENROSE

The tiny population and agricultural center known as Penrose stretches from the southern foot of Fodderstack Mountain, bounded by the French Broad flood plain. Within the midst of these rural reaches, the Calhoun Post Office was established in 1856 and the Penrose Post Office in 1889.

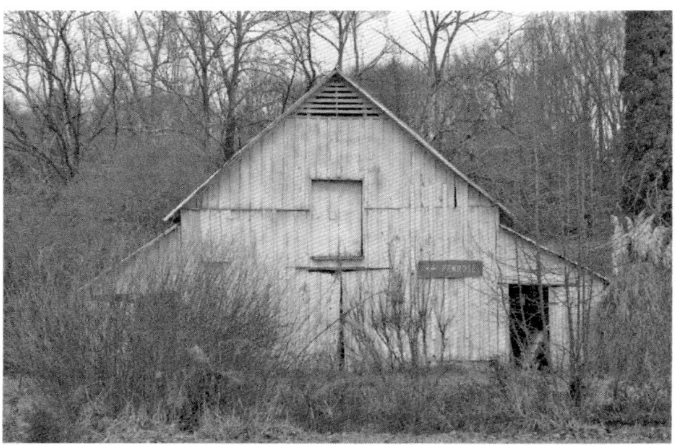

The W.L. Talley barn.

THOMAS GLADIOLUS FARM

Thomas's Gladiolus Farm once counted among the thriving agricultural enterprises in this sector, where, in 1950, Alexander P. Thomas (1910–1971) began propagating gladioli in the fertile flood plain and sold and shipped corms and flowers to markets all over the country. A founding member of Sacred Heart Catholic Church in Brevard, North Carolina, Thomas raised a considerable amount of money to construct the first Sacred Heart Church by selling his flowers. He and his wife, Edith Lowe Thomas (1909–1999), also lived in Florida and owned gladioli farms there as well, in Cocoa and Fort Myers, cultivating the plants in North Carolina during the summer and in Florida during the winter.

The Thomases, who purchased the property from the Everetts of Cleveland, Ohio, sold to the Ecusta Mill (1939–2002) in 1971. Ecusta, which produced flax pulp and cigarette paper, added the Thomas land to its holdings for warehousing purposes, using part of the property for an employee shooting range. The Lenz family currently holds the property.

Distracted by traffic signals, cellphones, iPhones and offensive driving, it's easy for commuters to miss the historic aspects surrounding them. History keeps reminding us that nothing stays the same, yet a few tangible traces of

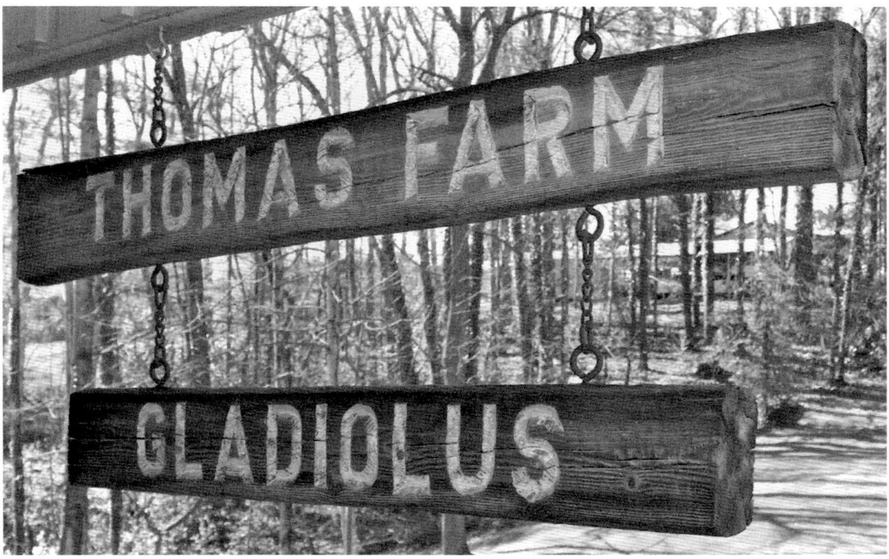

The Thomas Gladiolus Farm sign now hangs at the home of Andrew P. and Jackie Thomas in Brevard, North Carolina.

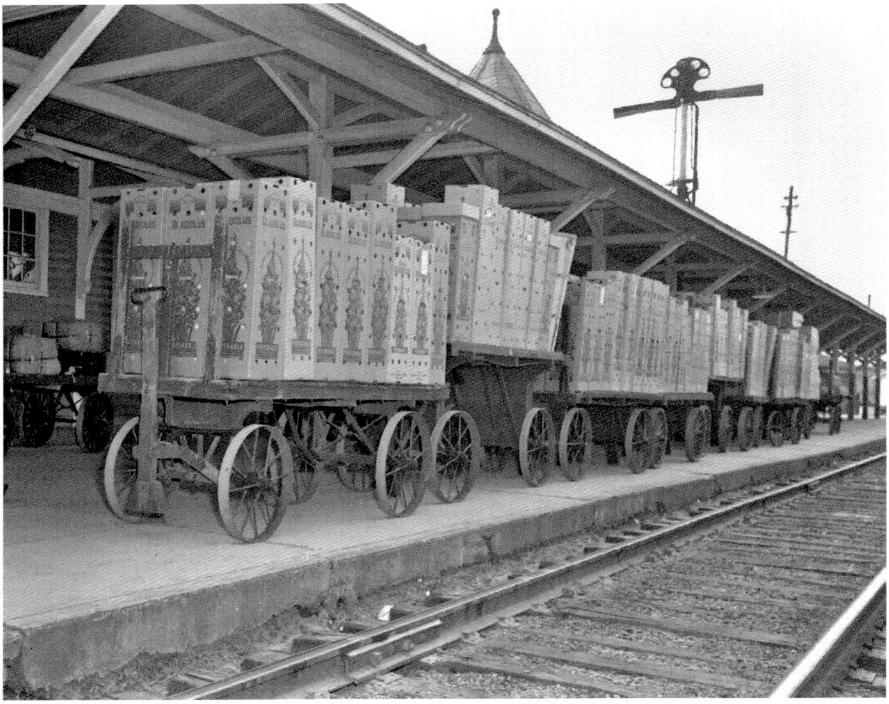

Gladioli awaiting shipment via train cars. *Photo by Lucile Stepp Ray, courtesy of Henderson County Genealogical and Historical Society, Inc.*

earlier life along the periphery of Henderson and Transylvania Counties remain as cues of a vast rural culture. Landmarks in this sector include an excavated granite massif known as Vulcan Penrose Quarry, the Triangle Stop (formerly the Penrose Grocery), the Transylvania County Airport and a span of railroad tracks—all within a stone's throw of sweeping farmland. East of Highway 64, we find the Old Hendersonville Highway and branching from it a little-used section of the old Crab Creek Road, which crews realigned and paved in 1947–48. The Old Hendersonville Highway was rerouted in 1956, and the segment of Crab Creek Road known by locals as "Little River Highway" was re-looped to meet U.S. 64 at a more westerly position, with a bridge added. Horace Clayton Lyday (1895–1969) owned the land under the quarry at Penrose, just west of the moldering vestiges of Evan Talley's farmstead.

EVAN AND CATHERINE TALLEY HOUSE AND FARM

Classic examples of demolition by neglect may be glimpsed alongside U.S. 64. The clutch of sagging farm buildings and derelict I-house belonged to Evan O. Talley (1838–1916). His wife, Ellen Catherine Talley (1843–1916), was daughter of Wilson Picklesimer (1816–1897). The Talleys' circa 1880 weatherboarded house, swathed in white and trimmed with green, stands on native stone foundations and sports an asymmetrical façade; two cut-stone, gable-end chimneys; a hip-roofed front porch; and a painted, standing-seam metal roof. Three bays wide and one room deep, the house incorporates a hall-and-parlor plan, its rear ell at one time connecting a separate kitchen to the main house. A smokehouse and springhouse join the rear ell by a breezeway, and originally there may have been a spring trough on the back porch. The approach to the property—in the Talleys' time encompassing approximately one hundred acres—rambled much longer before the rerouting of U.S. 64 in the 1950s, and a snapshot of the farm would have proffered a view of hayfields flanking the scene. The Talleys' son Carl Wilson Talley (1885–1959) and his wife, Bonnie Aiken Talley (1890–1952), were next to occupy this farm.

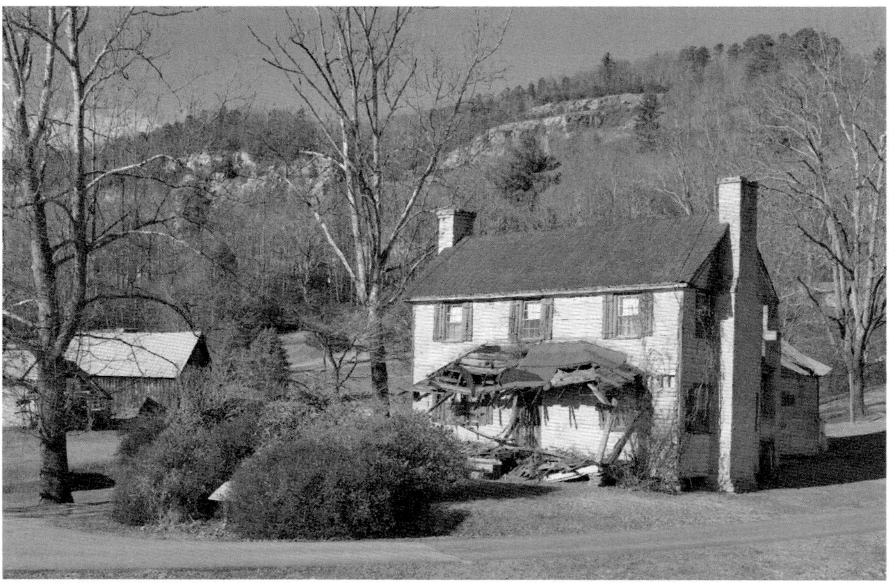

The Evan Talley home with Fodderstack Mountain in the background.

One of the oldest standing buildings on the Talley tract would be the corncrib of mortise-and-tenon timber frame, slatted siding and gabled roof. The gable-roofed frame barn features handmade, metal-strip hinges and has been evaluated by National Register scholars to be the same era as the house. Other structures include a concrete silo built in the 1920s, a poured concrete bank house/root cellar "built like a bomb shelter" and a hog pen.

Today, a pair of Hydro stone tablets inscribed with the Ten Commandments remains planted in front of the sagging Talley house—a silent vestige of faith-based, diligent farmers.

TALLEY HO

William Luther Talley (1868–1945) and his wife, Louetta Talley (1870–1920), built Penrose Cottage, their characteristically Victorian-style home—later renamed Talley Ho—on the Old Hendersonville Highway (SR 1504). Traveling salesmen and vacationers passing through the area lodged at this boardinghouse until the late 1930s.

Reports vary on the completion date of Talley Ho, some suggesting circa 1890 and others, circa 1902. The Talleys added a wing to the dwelling in

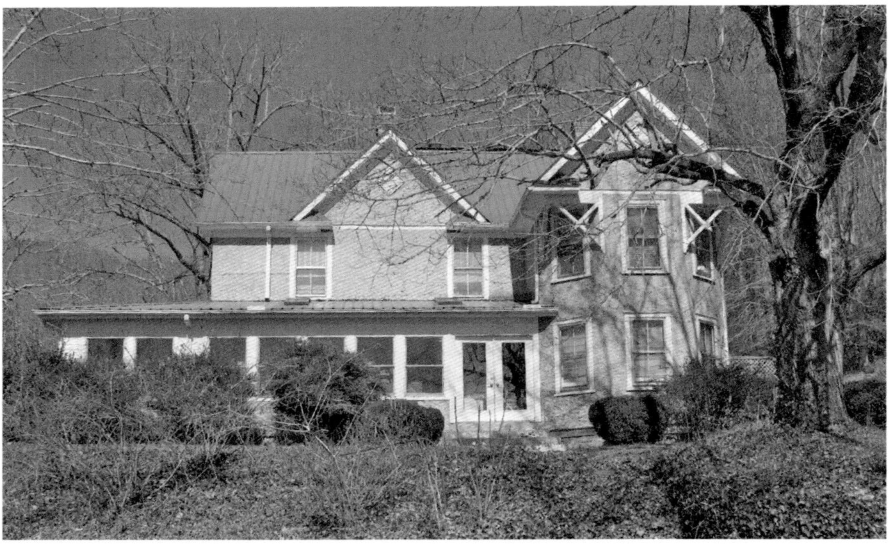

Talley Ho.

1904. The well-preserved and maintained frame house sports a pebbledash[6] exterior, a polygonal front gable ell and Victorian and stick-work details. The interior features what have been described as a notable Colonial Revival mantel with ionic colonettes, door and window surrounds with bull's-eye corner blocks and turned newels and balusters adorning the staircase.

A white, gable-fronted stock barn with vertical plank siding and enclosed side sheds occupies a space between the old boardinghouse and Crab Creek Road, as do a milk shed and stuccoed springhouse.

Across the road from the barn, William Luther Talley kept a general store known as the Penrose Store. His son William Everett "Scad" Talley (1898–1960) took over operations after his father's tenure. Exemplary of earlier country emporiums, this one featured a potbellied stove, wooden chairs for gossipers, a candy counter and displays of dry goods, meats, cheeses, canned goods and household products. A small loading dock out back served farmers who bought feed and seed from the Talleys. Mrs. Ina Rustin (1896–1977), William's sister, served as postmistress in a corner of the store. When the county moved the road, channeling most traffic away from the store, William built a store of brick at the intersection of Crab Creek Road and the new Highway 64 and repurposed the old building, using it for storage until it was razed.

Clyde Nicholson (1916–1999) and Nell McCrary Nicholson (1911–1997) later owned and operated a store called Nick's Grocery, constructed of cinderblocks and still standing on Crab Creek Road across from Everett Road. According to Lenoir Ray, this site hosted the Calhoun Post Office, established in 1856, where David Shuford (1788–1862), Jane P. Shuford (1830–1898) and Alexander Gray (1824–1895) served as postmasters.

Talley also operated the county's only cooperative cheese factory on the family farmstead in the 1910s. Between the old and new stores, a sawmill counted among the business concerns of this now hauntingly hushed nook off Crab Creek Road.

Everett Road was named for Sylvester Thomas Everett (1838–1922), a financier, industrialist, politician and philanthropist from Cleveland, Ohio, and the man indirectly responsible for Hendersonville's first library. Everett's family kept a summer home at Engadine Farms in Transylvania County, North Carolina.

---

6. *Pebbledash*: an external finish popularized in the region by Asheville architect Richard Sharp Smith, consisting of small stones or pebbles embedded in plaster.

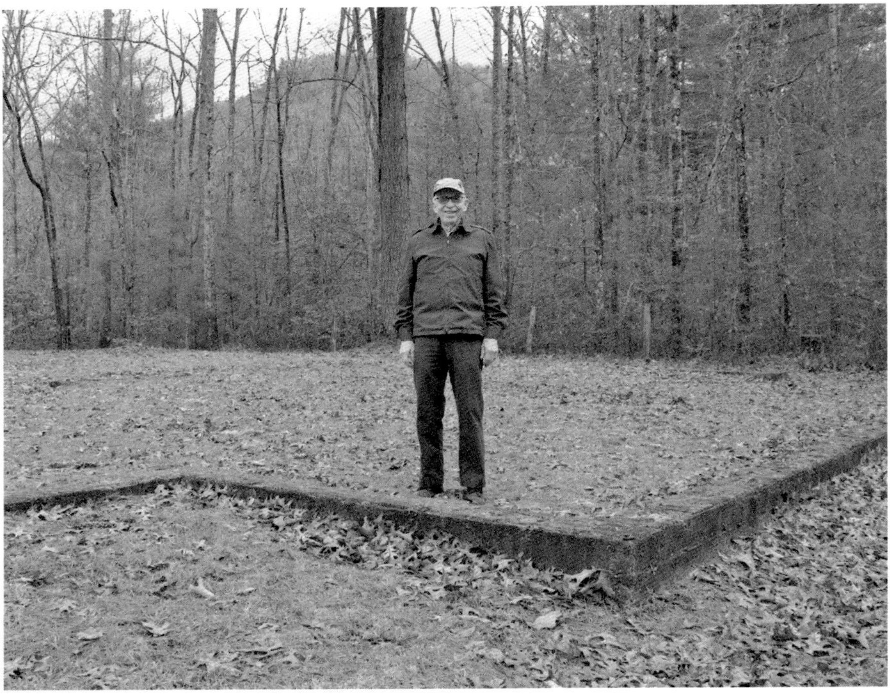

V. Leon Pace stands within the foundations of the former Piney Grove Methodist Church.

PEACE IN THE VALLEY

Sundry stone tablets fleck the periphery of a slope rising from the right side of Talley Road where it veers sharply northeast from Crab Creek Road. This is Piney Grove Methodist Cemetery, where, under a canopy of hoary pines and oaks, foundation stones trace the footprint of Piney Grove Methodist Church betwixt a medley of monuments bearing the names of Gray, Galloway, Allison and more.

JETER MOUNTAIN

Meandering south on Crab Creek, we come to Jeter Mountain Road, which scales a peak straddling Transylvania and Henderson Counties. Around 1800, when the geological prominence fell within Buncombe County, Revolutionary War veteran William Sentell (1756–1837) of Virginia was one of the first pioneers to settle there. Sentell and his wife, Elizabeth Stevens Sentell (1760–1847), raised their eight children on the mountainside. They were buried in the now nearly obscured family cemetery on a knoll above Big Willow Creek. The elements have mostly erased the tombstones' inscriptions, but the more legible ones show variations in the spelling of the surname. Like spokes of a wheel, several Sentell family members lie buried around the hub of a now-dead cedar tree in this partially cleared recess sometimes referred to as "the Yankee burial ground" because its interments included Sentells who fought on the Union side during the Civil War.

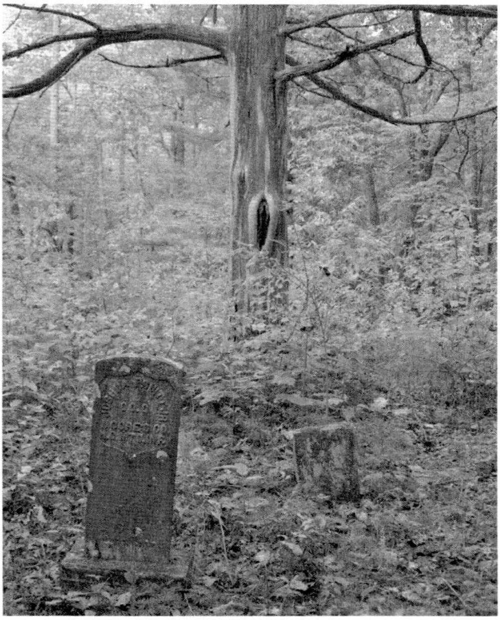

Like spokes of a wheel, graves of Sentell family members radiate from the base of a now-dead cedar tree. To access this burial ground, the visitor must ford a creek, scale a steep bank and negotiate a laurel hell.

Near the apex of Jeter, Richard Fitz Randolph Sewell (1907–1987) raised white-faced Herefords on pastureland on both sides of Jeter Mountain Road—a farm he named Fairfolly. Sewell's wife, Blanche Todd Sewell (1893–1970), worked at nearby Eagle Nest Camp. The Sewells' barn now sags from age, as does the two-story frame house, which at one time headquartered the Tuckasegee Beagle Club.

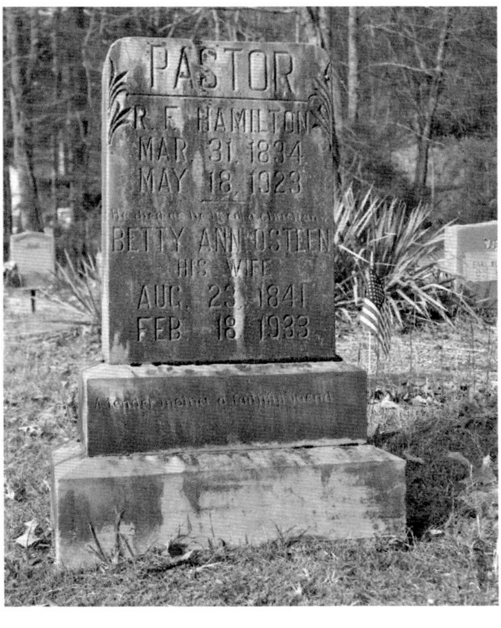

Reverend Robert F. Hamilton's plot at Holly Springs Baptist Church Cemetery.

Named for the Tuckasegee River, the club moved in the 1980s from Bryson City to Jeter Mountain and has since moved to Ellenboro, South Carolina.

Reverend Robert F. Hamilton (1834–1923) had a mill, and he and his wife, Elizabeth "Betty" Ann Osteen Hamilton (1841–1933), farmed 640 acres on Jeter. The Hamiltons are buried at Holly Springs Baptist Church Cemetery. The Osteen/Patterson Cemetery also occupies a slope of Jeter. Today, Carl Sandburg's granddaughter Paula Steichen Polega (1943–) and her husband, Stanley, live on the mountain.

LITTLE RIVER VALLEY

Populated by white settlers when it was part of Buncombe County, the community of Little River, bounded by the French Broad River, belonged to Henderson County from 1838 until 1861, when the county of Transylvania was formed from segments of Jackson and Henderson Counties. At that time, one of the largest population centers in the area, Little River evolved between what are now Shuford's Bridge (Penrose) and the Crab Creek community and maintains to this day much of its bucolic character.

Long before the arrival of Anglo-Saxon pioneers, the feet of aboriginal people and buffalo herds beat the trading path known as Estatoe from South Carolina to what is now Transylvania County. Some of the first white settlers who populated the banks of the Davidson River and a township known still as Little River included Benjamin Davidson (1742–1825) and his wife, Ann Patton Davidson (1748–1833); David Barnett (1798–1864); Robert Franklin Hamilton (1770–1822); and William Merrill (1781–1858).

The Merrills of Little River maintained what was likely the first mill in the area—a primitive mechanism known as a tub mill or horizontal mill with its water wheel inside a building, the wheel mounted on the same shaft as the turning runner millstone. The miller set the wheel parallel to the ground in a tub to cut down on the waste of water, which funneled through a flume to the blades on the wheel, with the sheer force of moving water turning the helm. The main shaft and its runner millstone turned at the same speed as the wheel—a contrivance easily transported to a more suitable locale if waterpower proved inadequate. A standard tub mill structure measured about twelve by fourteen feet.

William Merrill operated his gristmill on Bullen's Creek, which empties into Crab Creek. Merrill, also a blacksmith, amassed one thousand acres in the area, including the land received from his father, Benjamin Merrill (1752–1836). The milling operation persevered for nearly one hundred years. Merrill married Elizabeth Ashworth (1785–1853), and the couple had fourteen children.

Merrill and Ashworth family histories suggest that Elizabeth's mother, Nancy "Ann" Wood Ashworth (1745–1833), a self-trained yarb doctor and even a witch, put spells on anyone who crossed her. The wife of John Ashworth (1733/34–1805), she became known as Fairview's first doctor. The Ashworths lived on the Hickory Nut Gap above Fairview, North Carolina, in what was Rutherford County at the time. Henderson County author Sadie Smathers Patton (1886–1975) was a great-great-great-granddaughter of Ann Ashworth.

One of Ann Ashworth's treatments read:

> *To cure cancer: Go to a Savannah bush and say what did you come here for, to cure a cancer and brake* [sic] *off a twigg* [sic], *then say who it is on, brake another twigg then say where the cancer is, brake another twigg down and go away. This must be done before sunrise three mornings in succession before speaking to any person.*

Though the newly settled region did not encompass a plantation economy, the mountain elite indeed owned slaves. When William Merrill purchased a slave from his mother-in-law, the bill of sale read:

> *Know all men by these presents that I, Ann Ashworth of the County of Buncombe and the State of North Carolina, have bargained and sold unto William Merrill one Negro boy, about 16 years of age named Edmund for the sum of five hundred dollars to me in hand and paid by William Merrill. Which said Negro boy I do warrant to be sound in body and mind…Witness whereof I have here unto set my hand and seal this the 27th day of December 1832.*
>
> *Signed: Ann Ashworth*

Ann Ashworth bequeathed some of her slaves to her heirs and also left a gallon of whiskey for the men who would dig her grave. She handed down her medical skills to her granddaughter Margaret Williams Casey (1797–1887). Margaret passed her grandmother's cures and spells on to her daughter, Rachel Casey Sumner (1817–1913), who in turn passed them to her daughter, Nancy Albertine Sumner Wright (1838–1917).

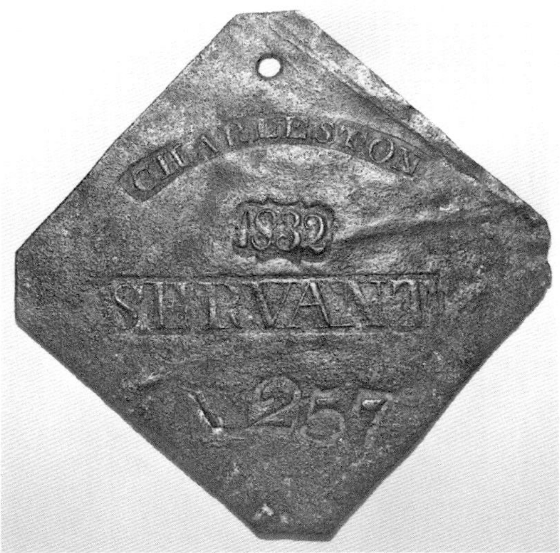

Copper slave-hire badge unearthed in Henderson County. A manner of annual licensing—inscribed with trade specialties such as "stonemason" or "carpenter" and, in this case, "servant"—permitted slaves to hire out for money, which they shared with their owners. These artifacts, produced from 1783 to 1865, originated in Charleston. *Photographed with permission of C.E. Staton, Hendersonville, North Carolina.*

Transylvania County's first census (1870) tabulated for the Little River community a total of 403 residents—"388 white and 15 colored." In those days, Little River was also called "Hogtown" because of its importance as a stopover point for drovers and their livestock from other parts of the county along the "Hogtown Turnpike" to the Buncombe Turnpike and on to points north and south. Historical texts mention an Ashworth Tannery in the vicinity, yet further research has revealed no details on this enterprise.

SHUFORD HOUSE

The circa 1825 home of David Shuford (1788–1862) and his wife, Sarah Orr Shuford (1793–1883), stands forsaken on Everett Road within view of Crab Creek Road—disturbingly renovated rather than historically restored. Architects would refer to its overall styling as an "I-house," a design trend emblematic of houses constructed in the I states (Iowa, Illinois and Indiana)—an architectural technique rooted in English folk culture. This style typically incorporated a tall, narrow profile two stories in height, with a center hall plan of single-room depth to two to three rooms wide and the main entrance on the house's long side; it frequently included a service wing or an ell attached to the back. This design presented the largest façade possible for a house featuring only four rooms with a center hall on each level. We find prolific use of the I-house throughout the southern United States, its popularity attributed to its effective ventilation qualities and a look of "grandness" in spite of its size.

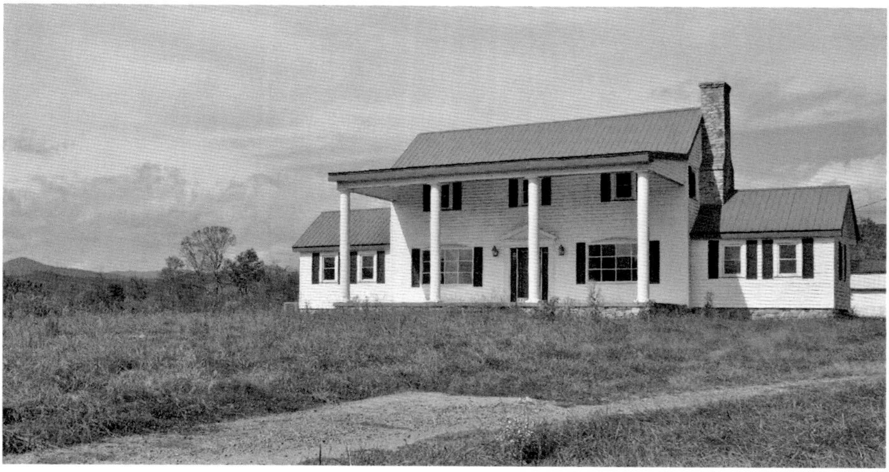

The David Shuford house on Everett Road.

According to Michael Ann Williams in *The Architecture of Henderson County, North Carolina* (1980), "The I-house became popular in the rural areas of Henderson County during the mid-19th century, mostly built on large tracts of farmland owned by well-to-do South Carolina families."

The Shufords' son, Jason Israel Shuford (1822–1895), and daughter, Jane, never married, continuing to live in the family home with their mother. David Shuford, one of Transylvania County's founding fathers, was the first postmaster at Calhoun. Genealogical blogs state that with only few exceptions, these Shufords never partook of whiskey or tobacco.

PISGAH VIEW FARM

Commanding attention from the midst of cornfields and dwarfed by a backdrop of hazy blue ridges, a massive gray barn nevertheless perseveres as a sentinel of Americana, albeit silvered and tattered by time and the elements. A rock house stands closer to Crab Creek Road, on a rise south of the circa 1940 barn. This land was part of the original Shuford holdings in the area and the house and farm of Merrimon Hamilton Shuford (1916–1994) and Gladys Elizabeth Blythe Shuford (1912–2007). The M.H. Shufords were members of Little River Baptist Church. Gladys, born to Arthur Blythe (1884–1966) and Emma Blythe (1891–

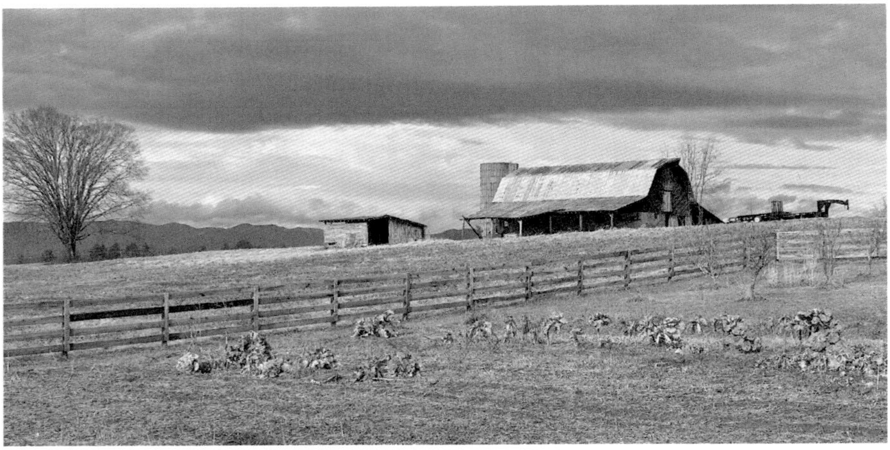

The M.H. Shuford barn against a background of Blue Ridge Mountains.

1984) of Henderson County, taught first and fifth grades for thirty-one years in Transylvania and Henderson County schools. Known as a superb cook, she also involved herself in the Little River Community Club and the Extension Homemakers Club of Little River and was a member of the North Carolina Retired School Personnel and Alpha Delta Kappa Teacher's Education Sorority. The Shufords had two daughters, Jane Francis and Julia Elizabeth.

The rock house, also built in 1940, features poured concrete sills and a brick-sheathed interior. Erected before power and water came to the valley, the house sports what the current owners described as "the most unusual of plumbing."

Clay Sykes, an environmental engineer, and his wife, Lisa Sykes of Brevard, who recently bought Pisgah View Farm, replaced old fences and added a mile of new fencing with the intention of operating a sustainable farm with red Angus cattle, free-range poultry and possibly an equestrian facility for special-needs children. The Sykes plan to rename the property the Shuford Farm.

Bumble Bee Trail, bordering the southern perimeter of this farm, winds west to another massive barn, this one featuring two brick silos of behemoth proportions. This was part of the homestead of Wilson Pickelsimer (1816–1897) and his family, who moved to the Little River community in the mid-1860s from Macon County, North Carolina. Nothing remains of their home, and piles of lumber demarcate where outbuildings once stood. Bub Hyder currently owns the property that surrounds Pisgah View Farm.

THOMAS LAGRANT PICKELSIMER HOUSE

An uncoated track named Cliff Road joins Crab Creek Road just southeast of Hamilton Road, and a short distance up the potholed track loom the relics of the farm of Thomas LaGrant Pickelsimer (1857–1948) and his wife, Nancy Elmina McCall Pickelsimer (1861–1947). Set on granite foundations with matching front steps, the circa 1875 house, in its state of decay, evokes sympathy. Its white, symmetrical façade features three evenly spaced windows on the second story, with a pediment eyebrow above the central aperture, and under a shed porch, the front of the ground story reveals a central door flanked by two windows all set in line with the upper windows. One stone chimney bookends the left of the façade; another chimney of stone stands perpendicular to it, located on the ell; and a brick chimney stands free in the midst of a caved-in kitchen. Brick-red tin shingles sheathe the roof, and four square pillars support the porch roof.

The Pickelsimers' granddaughter Elmina Eileen "Enie" McCrary Pace (1927–), born here, said, "I grew up in that house." Enie's grandmother Nancy taught her to sew, and Enie also recalls pulling green onions from her granny's kitchen garden and eating them on the spot. Her grandfather Thomas was baptized in the Little River, and the couple attended Little River

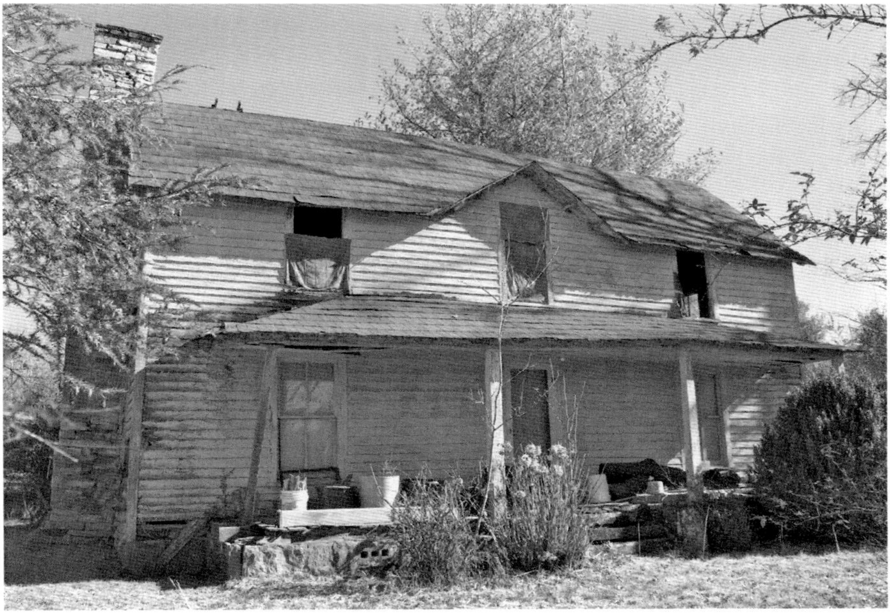

Thomas LaGrant Pickelsimer house.

Baptist Church. Enie's parents, Frank Benjamin (1893–1980) and Mary Pickelsimer McCrary (1899–2001), lived in the house during their first years of marriage. Mary's sister Nancy Myra Pickelsimer Merrill (1896–1999) and husband, Robert Leroy Merrill (1893–1970), occupied the homestead after Enie's grandparents' tenure. About twelve years ago, a couple from Florida bought the property with the intention of refurbishing the house, but according to Enie, "a family emergency kept them in Florida and the old home place deteriorated, especially after a large tree fell and cut the back of it in half."

Cascade Grocery/Hamilton Meat Market

Martin Luther Hamilton (1853–1937), who built the original Cascade power plant, also built the fine rock store at the edge of Cascade Lake Road in 1908 for W. Sylvester "Vess" Ashworth (1856–1930). Vess's son Charles Delis Ashworth (1894–1964) operated the grocery until Volney C. McCrary (1869–1941) bought it in the 1930s. Fred and Christine Hamilton took over operations in 1940. Older photos of the store show two gas pumps standing in front of it.

Volney C. McCrary erected the now-neglected one-story, German-sided cottage that stands to the right of the rock store, replacing an earlier two-story dwelling owned by the Ashworth family. Between the store and the house stands a stone well house with a gable roof, converted into a privy.

Old-timers in the area say Laurel Creek Church sits at the bottom of nearby Cascade Lake, now part of a 160-acre campsite recreation center with private beach, fishing and boating amenities.

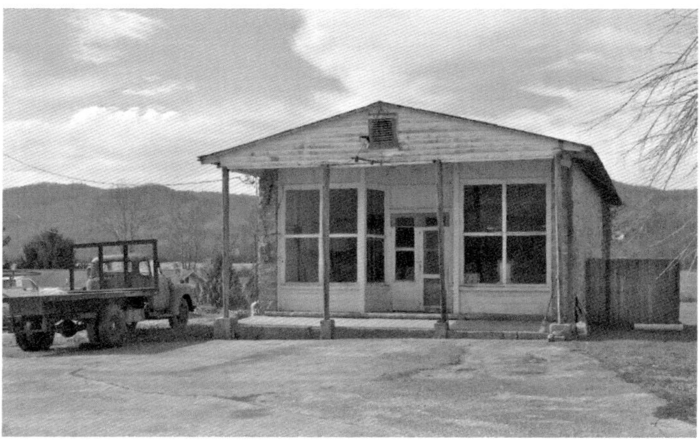

The abandoned Cascade Grocery.

LITTLE RIVER BAPTIST CHURCH, CEMETERY AND SCHOOL

In 1838, members of Beulah Baptist Church constituted a church at Little River, a shed-style meetinghouse where a small group of Baptists, Methodists and Presbyterians worshiped. The growing membership built a sanctuary in 1851, replacing it with a larger one in 1877 and again in 1905–06. The first pastors were James Blythe (1808–1897) and Robert F. Hamilton. The present church of brick was built in 1962.

Little River Baptist Cemetery spans a hillside behind the church, once home to a school. Here, alongside cattle pastures, lie some of Little River Valley's earliest residents, including Allison, Ball, Blythe, Cantrell, Capps, Hamilton, Heath, Kilpatrick, McCall, McCrary, Merell, Merrell, Merrill, Orr, Pickelsimer, Pridmore, Sentell, Sentelle, Shipman, Shuford and Talley—family names that spill over into Crab Creek Valley and beyond.

When Little River School, a one-room structure built in 1908, filled beyond capacity by 1910, a second room was added to accommodate an enrollment of sixty-eight, and eventually a third room followed. The Penrose School was established when, with consolidation, Little River School merged with Enon School in 1951. Such early institutions were known as "Old Fields" schools, which implied that until all the crops were in and the roads passable, only then would school sessions commence. Sallie S. Merrill (1889–1972) was one of the teachers at Little River School, and Seva McCall Mackey (1894–1986) taught there for many years.

An 1872 census of schoolchildren in Little River counted "90 white males and 80 white females, and two colored males and two colored females."

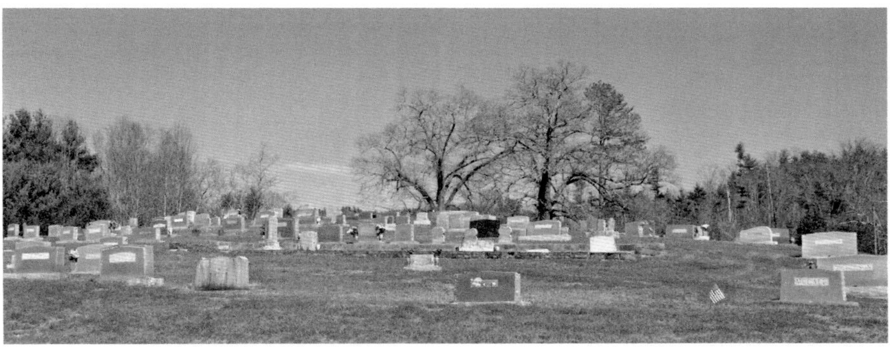

Little River Baptist Church Cemetery.

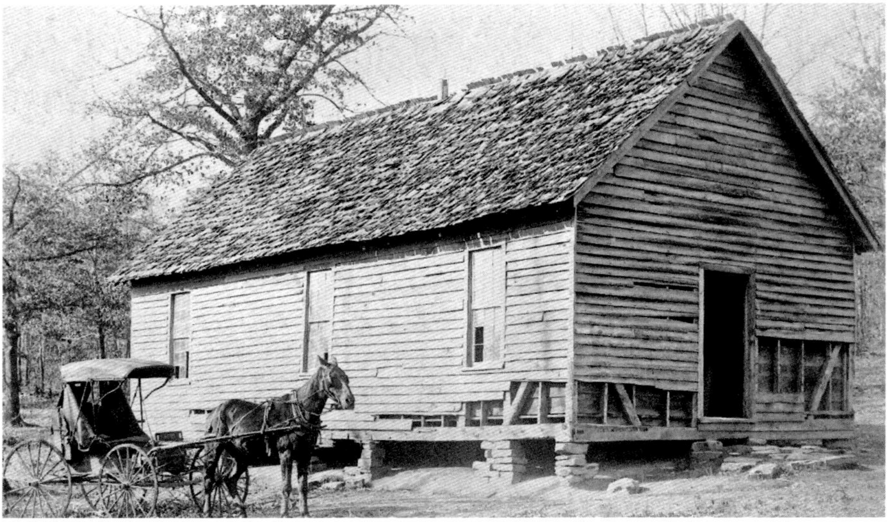

Little River School. *Photo courtesy of Rowell Bosse North Carolina Room, Transylvania County Library.*

A bit farther up Little River Church Road, one finds a farm known as Edgewood since 1901, currently owned and operated by brothers David and Taylor Mackey, grandsons of Edgar H. Mackey (1889–1973), who farmed this land after the tenure of John Merrill (1818–1880), their great-grandfather Taylor McCall (1855–1920) and their father, Edward Henry Mackey (1918–2009). The elder Taylor McCall moved to this site a circa 1849 log house—now weatherboarded—still standing amidst the farm buildings.

Another of John Merrill's farms sits on either side of Maple Hill Road, just east of Little River Baptist Church. Directly across Crab Creek Road from the church, Thomas Roscoe McCall (1927–), son of Taylor Roscoe McCall (1899–1987), operates a produce stand fronting the farm that belonged to his father and his grandfather Joseph Taylor McCall (1855–1920). The elder McCall also farmed the Edgewood acres.

MERRILL STORE

With a number of small convenience stores situated alongside the route through Little River and Crab Creek Valleys, local farmers and campers hadn't the need to travel all the way over and up to Hendersonville for groceries and camping provisions. One such store stands across Crab Creek Road from the home of Perry Merrill (1842–1931) at Maple Hill Road. The abandoned white building with rusted metal roof was the Jot 'Em Down Store, built in 1943 and owned by Wade R. Merrill (1877–1964) and his wife, Katherine "Kate" Shipman Merrill (1880–1964). Through the early 1950s, the couple lived in the back of the building and operated a store from the front, having moved to this location from another building near the Cascade Grocery Store.

Son of Wade and Kate, Donald E. Merrill and his wife, Alma Moss Merrill, took over operations, rebuilding the store in 1966. The business, featuring a sandwich shop, groceries and camping supplies, as well as a grease rack and gasoline pumps, closed in 1981.

PICKELSIMER-ORR HOUSE

Continuing eastward on Crab Creek Road, one cannot help but notice an exemplary model of an I-house on the south side of the road. Even in its ghostly state, the abandoned dwelling stands stately on its foundations of fieldstones, its weatherboarding warped and gray, its windowpanes shattered

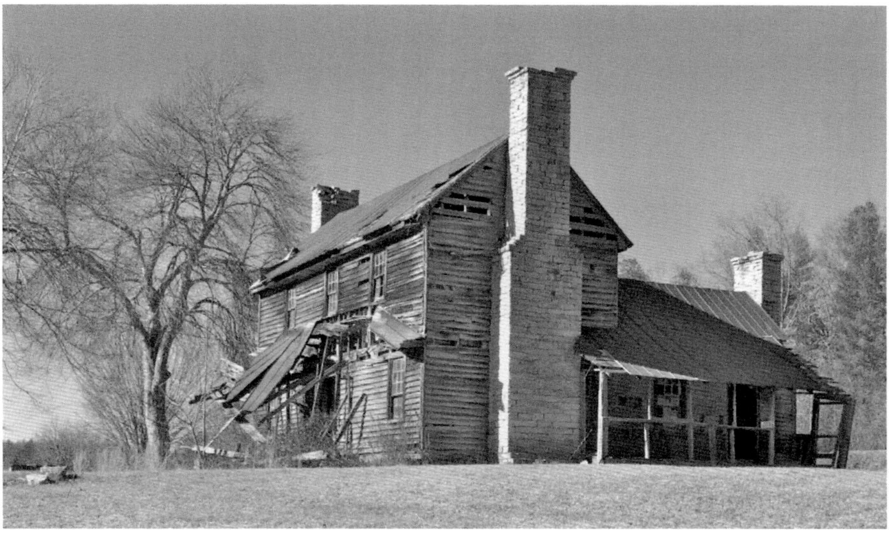

The Pickelsimer-Orr house, oddly elegant even in its state of ruin.

and its shed porch roof caved in. One of its three cut-stone chimneys bears the inscription "1868," tempting the inquisitor with this as a possible date of its erection. Whatever the case, John Merrill built the house for his wife, Mary "Mollie" Cantrell Merrill (1817–1874), and their family. Their daughter Margaret Malena "Lena" Merrill (1861–1925) married John Luther Pickelsimer (1855–1902) and occupied this homestead, acquired later by Vonley C. Orr (1884–1955) and Ellen Allison Orr (1897–1981). Ellen was the last to live in the house before its abandonment.

Records of the property list several outbuildings—now gone—including a barn, smokehouse, woodshed and chicken house.

The clean, simple lines and proportions of the house rival the work of renowned architects, and its chimneys stand nothing short of exquisite. Considering its status as possibly the second-oldest extant structure in the Little River Valley, it strikes one as tragic that someone hasn't shored up and saved this fine structure from the cruelties of time and neglect.

HOLLY SPRINGS

Between Allman Cove Lane and an abandoned blue building that last served as a florist at Coral Cove Lane stands the small brick church of Holly Springs Baptist, built in 1996. The congregation's wooden church, built around 1860, once stood above the other side of Crab Creek Road, at the crest of Holly Springs Church Road and East Lester and Kinard Lanes, near the Holly Springs Cemetery. That church was razed, and a concrete block structure replaced it, on the same site, in 1959. Voltaire Condorsed Volney Hamilton (1822–1908), who served as the church's first deacon, gave the land for the cemetery and church, which was constituted from Crab Creek Baptist Church and organized in 1860 with thirty-four charter members.

Continuing eastward, we find E.M. and A.S. Cartwright's farm on Ponderosa Farms Drive, and east of it, before Bulling Creek Road at the dividing line between Transylvania and Henderson Counties, stands a lean-to-style building—another of the convenience retailers in the area—this one the Orr Store, owned by Homer A. Orr (1902–1968) and Grace Owen Orr (1904–1985).

DUPONT STATE FOREST

A branch snaps under a hiker's foot, startling from its sun-drenched perch a terrapin that instinctively slips into the safer haven of the Little River as a sugar-maple leaf swirls randomly on the chaste currents of mountain flow. Alongside dewy banks, random shafts of daylight pierce the forested canopy, dappling a klatch of polypore fungi in color combinations rarely before glimpsed, and rock ledges flaunt verdant beards of peculiar mosses, liverworts and lichens. The adventurer may find all of this and more—a mere sampling of blessedly unspoiled vignettes flourishing today within a state forest—accessible to the public due to the benevolent efforts of late twentieth-century environmentalists who rescued these precious resources from the threats of development.

Branching northward and then westerly from Crab Creek Road, DuPont/Staton Roads convey the traveler up a serpentine mountain swath to the natural wonderland known as DuPont State Forest. These lands, through which the Little River courses, were once home to some of the region's earliest settlers, evidenced by traces of stone foundations and three identified cemeteries within its boundaries and historical accounts of gristmills at Hooker Falls. Tombstones within the protected Hooker-Moore Cemetery disclose the surnames Anders, Ashworth, Heath, Moore and Sentelle, with approximately sixty-five burials between 1859 and 1905, including Union veteran James Lewis Sentelle, who died in 1864. From Clinton Moore, three Hooker brothers—Edmund, John and Spencer from South Carolina—purchased land with a gristmill near the falls later named for them and built there a second mill in 1882. Other landholders included Micajah S. Thomas (1808–1883), who lies buried in Buck Forest's Thomas Cemetery, another of DuPont's preserved burial grounds. Thomas family deeds to this land date back to 1799.

Late nineteenth- and early twentieth-century loggers and industrialists voraciously harvested much of western North Carolina's old-growth forests, clear-cutting mountainsides, obliterating natural habitats and creating massive runoff crises. By the early 1930s, much of the region's forests had been stripped due to wholesale logging. Moreover, the contagion of greed induced others to lay to waste woodlands for the sake of superfluous subdivisions. Owing to the valiant efforts of environmental groups and the enactments of state and national governmental agencies, much of the clear-felled areas continue to reclaim their natural milieus, and the 10,268-acre DuPont State Forest exemplifies such reclamation.

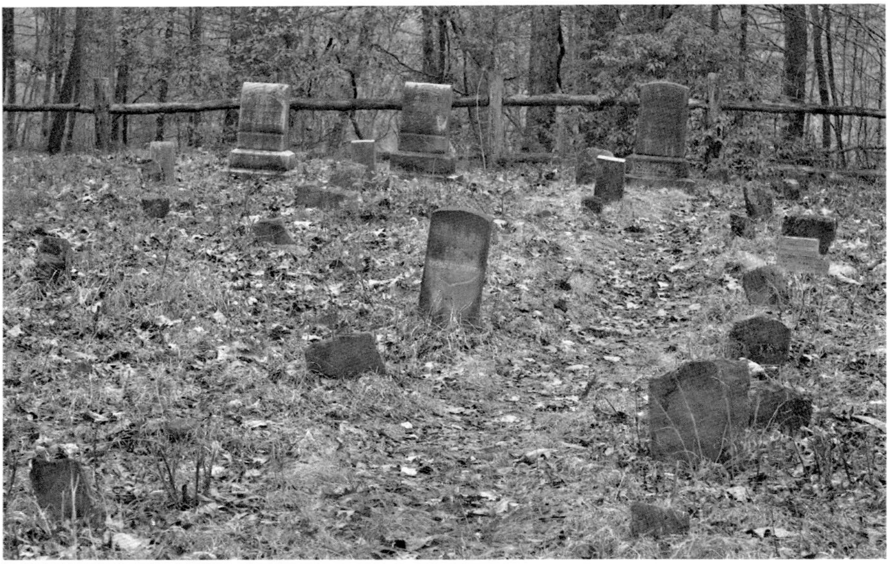

Hooker-Moore Cemetery.

In the mid-1950s, the American chemical enterprise E.I. DuPont de Nemours and Company, Inc., of Wilmington, Delaware, began acquiring large parcels of property spanning Henderson and Transylvania Counties—in what is now the DuPont State Forest—with the intention of utilizing more than 7,600 acres for the recreational pleasures of its company officials, employees and clients. DuPont opened an industrial plant east of Cedar Mountain—"in John Paul Staton's old wildcat hunting grounds," according to Lenoir Ray—in 1958 for the purpose of manufacturing silicon for computer chips, which changed later to an X-ray film plant.

John Paul Staton (1917–1992), a highly regarded trapper and backwoodsman, held deep-seated interests in managing bobcat predation and watershed and general woods problems, according to Mead Parce (1901–1997), who penned an article about Staton in the *Hendersonville Times-News* on July 2, 1958. Parce wrote, "I'd like to think maybe Staton inherited a drop or two of blood from two men who knew this country, Davy Crockett and Dan'l Boone."

In the 1970s, DuPont acquired Camp Summit, a popular boys' and girls' camp. Timber harvesting occurred on several tracts of the property during the forty-year period following the company's acquisition. Alternatively,

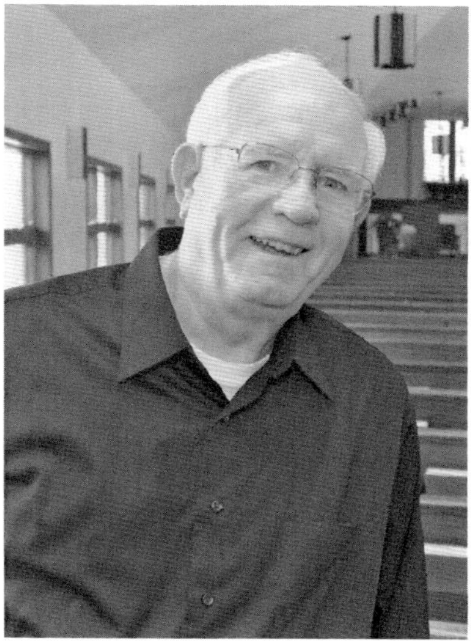
Reverend D. Lewis Staton.

IN 1962, REVEREND DAVID LEWIS STATON (1936–), son of John Paul Staton, wrote his first letter to Merrill Evans, chairman of the North Carolina State Highway Commission, appealing to the department to improve road conditions for the four hundred Henderson County employees of DuPont Company. An accountant for DuPont for twenty-five years, Staton was also minister of Green River Baptist Church and has been minister of East Flat Rock's Maranatha Baptist Church since 1983.

FOTOFAX, a Dupont Company newsletter, in March 1970 noted, "He wrote, called, reminded, visited, attended meetings, formed a road committee, and spent a period of five years and nine months before achieving success."

When Staton began his appeals, most employees of DuPont traveled to and from work via Cascade Lake Road between Little River and Cedar Mountain, which could be muddy and rutty or dusty depending on seasonal conditions. Staton and others deemed the state of affairs inconvenient and even dangerous, and Staton acted on his wish for improvements by working through various channels of state government, writing copious letters, gathering signatures on petitions and even meeting with governors and other statesmen during the tenures of three North Carolina governors: Terry Sanford, 1961–65; Dan K. Moore, 1965–69; and Robert W. Scott, 1969–73.

Staton appealed to the Highway Committee of the Upper French Broad Development Commission and met with Governor Dan K. Moore in Raleigh, accompanied by Hendersonville attorney Francis M. Coiner (1923–2004). He also captured the attention of DuPont plant manager Jack Dense, who endorsed the road project. When, during the course of seven years, Staton met with what he prefers to call "roadblocks," including landowner disputes, he continued writing letters. He saved copies of his correspondence and all return letters, telegrams and press coverage, assembling the paperwork in a comprehensive scrapbook.

In the interim, North Carolina governor Terry Sanford ordered improvements to Cascade Lake Road, including stonework, retention, guardrails and the softening of sharp curves. "This helped," Staton said, "but it did not solve the problems and certainly did not satisfy all the commuters."

At last, in 1971—nearly a decade after Staton wrote his first letter—Raleigh approved the project of putting in a new road, which opened in 1972. President John F. Kennedy's Appalachian Access Road Fund, through the Appalachian Regional Commission, financed the lion's share of the $1.2 million cost, and Raleigh picked up the balance.

In honor of Staton's diligence and years of work to see his vision through to completion, officials voted to name the new road for him, and the road from Crab Creek Road was indeed named Staton. This, however, presented another roadblock when Henderson County officials pointed out some years later that the county's township of Dana already had a Staton Road. Simply renaming the brief segment through Henderson County "DuPont Road" and the much longer portion through Transylvania County "Staton Road" solved the dilemma.

Two handwritten words—printed large and bold—close Staton's road-project scrapbook: "THE END!"

DuPont employees and subcontractors reforested much of the area and also carved miles of trails through the site.

During 1996 and 1997, the North Carolina Division of Forest Resources purchased the property from the DuPont Corporation. Meanwhile, Sterling Diagnostic Imaging had taken over the industrial plant on the remaining 2,700 acres. Agfa, a Belgian concern, currently owns the 450-acre industrial tract adjoining the forest.

In October 2000, through the actions of the North Carolina Council of State, the state acquired 2,223 adjoining acres by eminent domain from developer Jim Anthony of the Cliffs Communities of South Carolina. This portion of the property included three waterfalls (Bridal Veil, High and Triple), Lake Julia and several buildings and lodges. The actions transpired because the denial of access to the property by the public would have created dead ends on trails leading from the state forest toward the proposed residential property. There also existed a good deal of local concern and public pressure to protect sensitive environmental resources. Additionally, had the land fallen into the hands of a developer, the public might have been permanently denied access to it.

Beginning in 1999, Chuck McGrady—at the time a Flat Rock commissioner, chairman of the Henderson County Planning Board, former president of the Sierra Club and executive director of ECO and currently a North Carolina representative—lobbied for the salvation of the waterfall sector, raising awareness in Raleigh concerning the impending real estate development and its impact on the natural resources. North Carolina attorney general Michael Easley suggested that the state should use its power of eminent domain to acquire the waterfalls, and consequently the state condemned the waterfall tract. Additional efforts by grass-roots environmentalists furthered awareness of the situation, and at the request of Governor Jim Hunt, the board of directors of the Clean Water Management Trust Fund authorized subsidies for state acquisition of the site. In October 2000, Governor Hunt and the Council of State voted unanimously to invoke eminent domain on the tract, and following intense legal battles, the state paid the Cliffs Communities for the property, thus adding the valuable natural resources to the state forest's domain.

Today, the hiker may savor the forest's natural offerings, pausing to take in the shimmery music of falling water, feasting on unexpected patches of Oconee bells and trilliums in season or briefly locking eyes with a timid white-tailed deer before the lithe creature bolts for deeper cover. Indeed a nature lover's sanctuary, 1,750 acres of this forest's acres—due to their distinctive ecological significance—fall under the management and protection of the North Carolina Natural Heritage Program.

Hollywood crews filmed the movies *Last of the Mohicans* (1992) and *The Hunger Games* (2012) at various locations throughout DuPont State Forest, focusing on its waterfalls. The park's cascades include High Falls at 150 feet, Triple Falls with a total of approximately 120 feet, Hooker Falls at 15 feet, Bridal Veil Falls at 100 feet in a series of steps including a 10-foot freefall, Wintergreen Falls at 25 feet and Grassy Creek Falls at 30 feet. A major eco-tourist and recreational locale, the park also features stretches of Little River; Fawn Lake, Lake Imaging and the one-hundred-acre Lake Julia; Corn Mill Shoals; picnic facilities; and miles of hiking, bicycle and equestrian trails. Managed by the North Carolina Division of Forest Resources in cooperation with other agencies and volunteer groups, the property is registered as North Carolina Game Lands, with special hunting permits available from the North Carolina Wildlife Resources Commission.

CRAB CREEK VALLEY

Crab Creek Road bisects a fertile valley crisscrossed with creeks named Dismal, Dry Branch, Mud and Crab—the latter once known as Crab Tree Creek. Crabs have never populated the tributary flowing alongside Crab Creek Road; rather, old-timers have written and said that crabapple trees once grew prolifically alongside the banks, hence the road's name up to the confluence at Little River Road, where the name changes to Kanuga. Derived from a Cherokee term, the name Kanuga was selected by wheeler-dealer George Erwin Cullet Stephens (1873–1946) for his private Kanuga Club—now the Episcopal Kanuga Conferences—above Arrowhead Hill, which has hosted camps and conferences for several decades. But when was the span of Crab Creek Road from Little River Road renamed Kanuga Road and Kanuga Street?

Maps as early as 1913 show Crab Creek Road connecting from what is now U.S. 64 the entire way north to what became known as "the Busy Bend" and into Caswell Street on the southern boundary of downtown Hendersonville, yet a 1904 county map shows the northernmost span labeled as Kanuga Road. North Carolina State Highway and Public Works Commission maps from 1926, 1944, 1953 and 1957 label the section of what is now posted as Kanuga Street just south of downtown Hendersonville as Mangum Road, likely named for Dr. Charles Staples Mangum Jr. (1902–1980) who worked at the Kanuga Club in the early 1900s. Since roadmaps do not exist for each year of the county's existence, it may only be speculated that part of the road was renamed in the early 1900s as a measure of directing potential members to Stephens's private club. And old-timers claim that Little River Road was so named because it conveyed a route to the Little River community from the Greenville Highway.

Earlier in its history, the community of Crab Creek boasted its own post office, run by Loveda Hamilton Johnson (1850–1878) from 1875 to 1878, when Sabrina Hamilton Blythe (1816–1888) took over for a few months until the office closed in the same year. Lenoir Ray speculated its location to be near the Crab Creek Baptist Church. Loveda married John V. Johnson (1851–1880) in 1877 and moved a year later to Pliny, South Carolina, where she died at the tender age of twenty-eight.

SHOAL FALLS FARM (CIRCA 1887)

An eye-catching house swathed in crimson stands atop a wooded knoll at the western periphery of Shoal Falls Road. Known as the "Old Henry Place" and built by James Monroe Henry (1853–1900), it would predate the suggested date on tax records. The property has remained in the Henry family, belonging also to James's son Talmage McNeil Henry (1890–1989) and currently to Talmage's granddaughter Melissa Matthews (1952–).

The meticulously kept home features original stone piers, hand-hewn floor joists and rafters, a rock chimney and rock-lined well. The wooded setting and wildflowers proffer to its landscape an unspoiled glimpse of yesteryear.

From this corner of the county, Shoal Falls Farm tantalizes passersby, proffering an absurdly picturesque setting against tree-studded hills. Joseph Hamilton (1811–1887) once owned the two hundred acres of land composing this farm until he sold it to his son-in-law Martin Luther "Calvin" Patterson

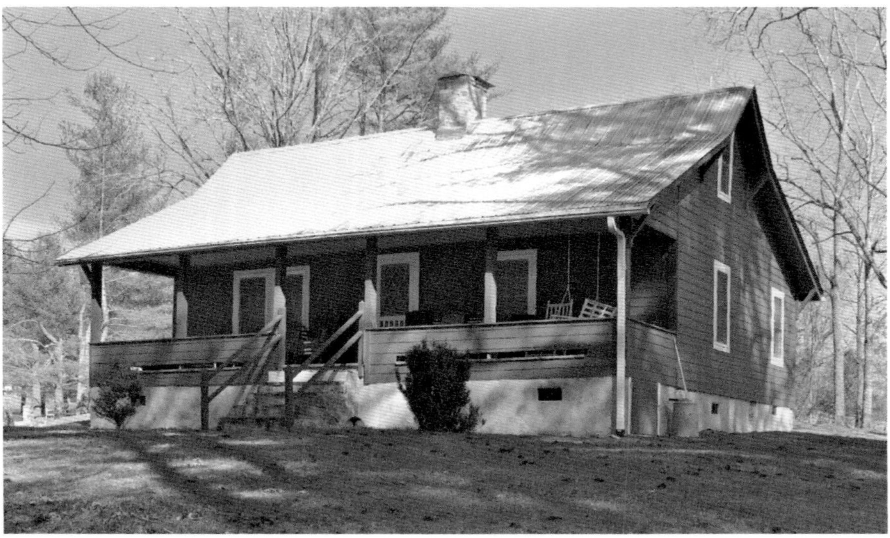

The "Old Henry Place."

(1844/45–1932) in 1885. Prominent building contractor King Gallileo "K.G." Justus (1877–1941) and William Henry Pridmore (1855–1935) next owned parts of the property, and Pridmore built a house for his wife, Wilmouth Shipman Pridmore (1860–1940), and their family on the spot where David Kemp built the present farmhouse in 1945. Justus's widow, Ella Florence Hollingsworth Justus (1878–1971), sold to David Kemp (1898–1966), founder of Diamond Brand Canvas Products Company of Naples, Henderson County. Asheville entrepreneur and philanthropist Harry D. Blomberg (1904–1991) bought the land from the Kemp estate in 1966, and Bearpen LLC has owned it since 2006.

During the World War II years, with the labor of German prisoners, David Kemp founded the quintessential farm—named Shoal Creek Farm and then Shoal Falls Farm, Inc.—so admired today. Adding to several buildings that already stood there, Kemp had more structures built, including a three-story, forty-stall barn and lodgings for his employees and guests. The barn features a milking parlor on its ground level, a ramped lounging area for cattle in its second story and a haymow in its third story.

Kemp housed his herd of champion Guernsey cattle in the behemoth concrete-block barn whitewashed and trimmed in crimson and added an adjoining structure with an office and creamery and an apartment for his personal quarters. Kemp's herd earned blue ribbons for setting

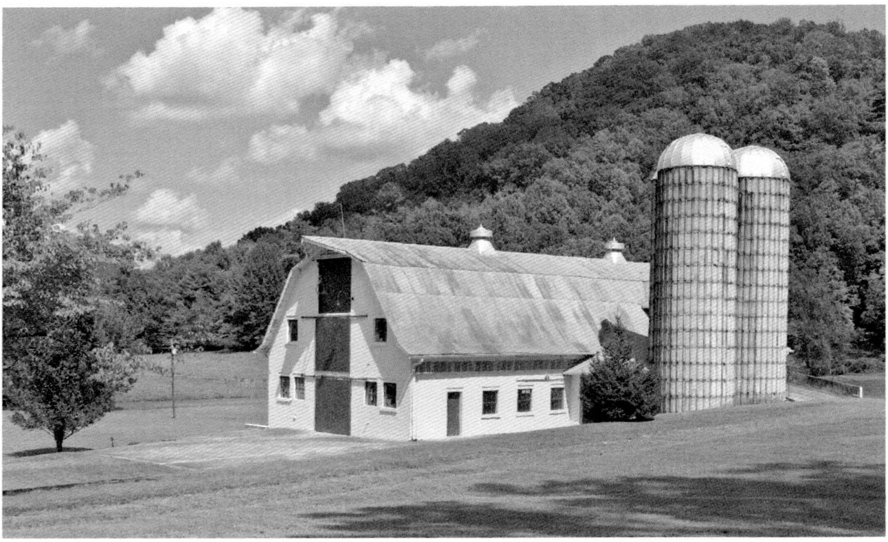

Shoal Falls Farm.

records in milk production and butter fat percentages. John S. Hollamon (1911–1980) served as the farm's secretary-treasurer and manager, and Ivan Wilbur Byers (1918–1992) was herdsman. Kemp's prize herd lived the life of Riley, feasting on a diet supplemented with molasses and beer. Farmhands clipped the Guernsey cows' fur in summertime to keep them cool, bathed them regularly and changed their sawdust bedding on a daily basis.

A surprise lies beyond, deep in the woods, the namesake of the farm: Shoal Falls, a forty-five-foot drop rarely seen by the public. Within viewing distance of the falling water, alongside Shoal Creek, stands a log house built by King Gallileo Justus and later expanded by David Kemp.

Successive owner Harry D. Blomberg achieved local and regional fame in western North Carolina, having taken over the failing Biltmore Industries (Biltmore Homespun Shops), making it a huge success. Blomberg also owned the Harry's Motor Inn chain and Harry's Cadillac-Pontiac—originally Harry's Cadillac-LaSalle, founded in 1923, and currently known as "Harry's on the Hill"—Asheville's first new-car dealership and western North Carolina's first Cadillac dealership. Civic-minded Blomberg was noted as having been particularly generous to the cause of healthcare.

V. Leon Pace well remembers life alongside the halcyon cove and falls from his childhood when his parents farmed part of the land composing Shoal Falls Farm. His father, Claudie Pace (1912–2004), milked Kemp's test cows.

Pace recalls:

> *I lived with my family at Shoal Falls Farm from 1945 to 1949 and again from 1952 to 1958. These were happy and exciting times. When we first moved to the farm, everything was new and pristine, with some buildings still under construction. My earliest memory there was seeing German POWs working on the roof of the big barn. This was my first experience with a language other than English.*
>
> *There were a lot of places for my brother and me to play. With other families with children living on the farm, we played from house to house and barn to barn. The maternity barn and the calf barn were interesting places to visit. There would be at least one newborn calf each week, and when we were in the calf barn at feeding time the herdsman would let us bottle-feed the calves.*
>
> *When we were younger, Mr. Kemp would sometimes drive my brother and me to the Jot 'Em Down Store in the Little River community for ice*

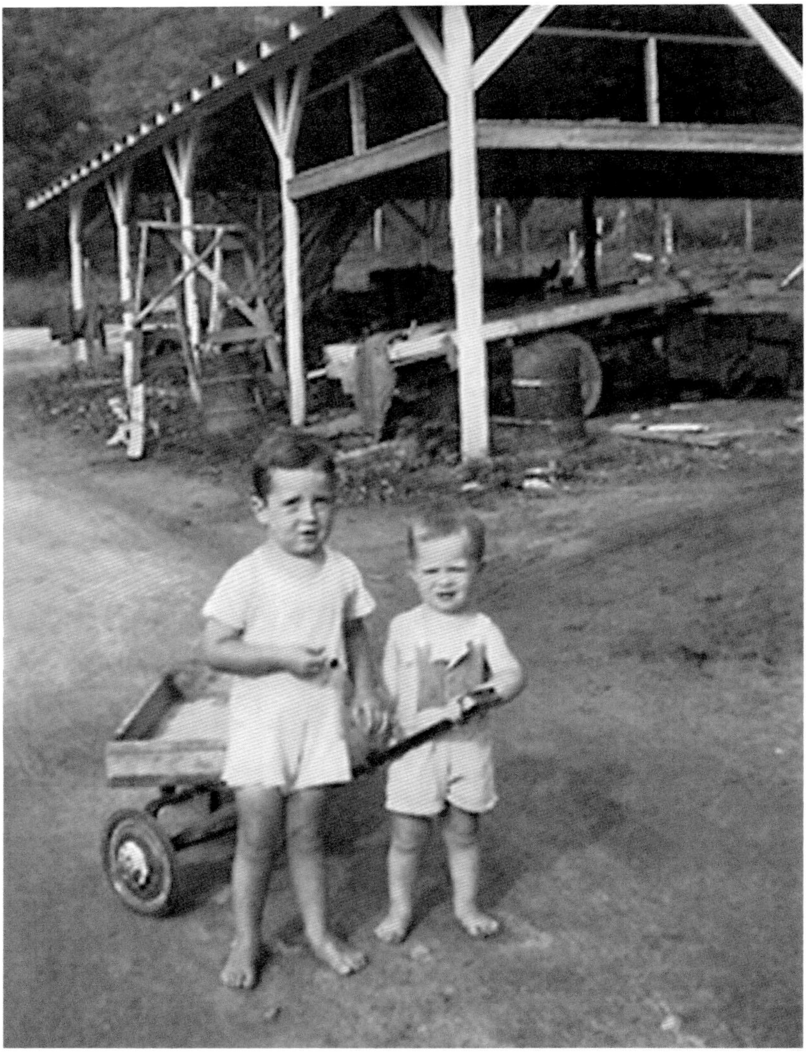

Brothers V. Leon (1942–) and Joe Pace (1944–) at Shoals Falls Farm. *Photo courtesy of V. Leon and Jean Pace.*

cream—a rare treat since ice cream wasn't readily available out in the country at that time.

Mr. Kemp occasionally hosted barbecues for his employees and their families at the log structure that stands near the falls on Shoal Creek. After eating and while the adults socialized, we children would walk the swinging bridges up to the base of the falls and enjoy the coolness of the spray.

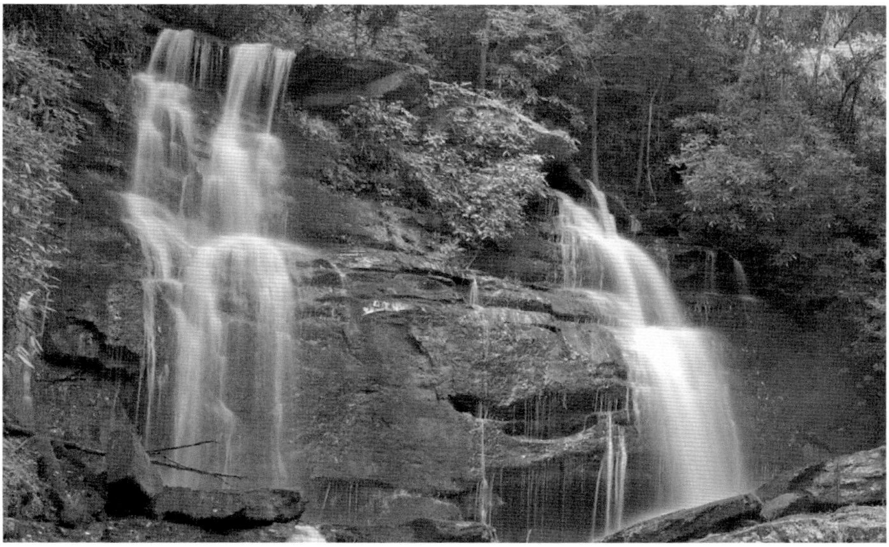

Shoal Falls.

Other enjoyable events were the square dances held in the big hay shed during summertime, with live bands and refreshments. The neighbors were invited, as well as the farm families, bringing together a large number of people.

We would sometimes walk with another family up the mountain to the springhouse above Shoal Falls—a shady, cool spot in the summertime and a most pleasant setting for picnics. There were always baskets filled with good food. Those really were the good old days.

Pace remembers the days when several dairy farms occupied the idyllic scenery flanking Crab Creek Road, ranging in size from two head to six or twelve cows. Shoal Falls Farm was the granddaddy of them all.

On the market again in the twenty-first century, a real estate firm markets the farm with its herd of Black Angus cattle as a potential family compound. The owners work with a nature conservancy group to ensure the protection of the property's natural resources.

Tracing the loopy conduit of Crab Creek Road by way of its myriad sharp curves, narrow shoulders, blind driveways and the occasional impasse of farming vehicles, the posted limits of forty-five to fifty miles per hour may seem dangerously excessive on this two-lane country thoroughfare. Roadside memorials attest to its hazards. Furthermore, why should anyone wish to travel at breakneck speeds through scenery so blissful?

For the cautious observer, glancing between pastures, wooded breakfronts and the occasional modern subdivision, certain aspects stand out, begging the questions: What was that old store, and who lived in that sagging, long-abandoned ruin?

Ruins no longer extant include the Holly Springs School, which sat on a knoll above Pridmore Hollow Road. A two-room clapboard schoolhouse replaced one constructed of logs. Not a trace of the school remains.

ZANDER MCCRARY FARM

Directly across from Pridmore Hollow Road, a silvery gray edifice stands remarkably close to the north edge of Crab Creek Road. This barn was once a house (circa 1850), which was converted in 1945, with its former windows boarded over and a broad shed attached to its west-facing side. Charles Alexander "Zander" McCrary (1891–1980), a farrier in the United States Army during World War I, and his wife, Clara Geneva Shipman McCrary (1899–1986), owned this farmland and had their home across the road from it. Zander passed the smithy trade along to

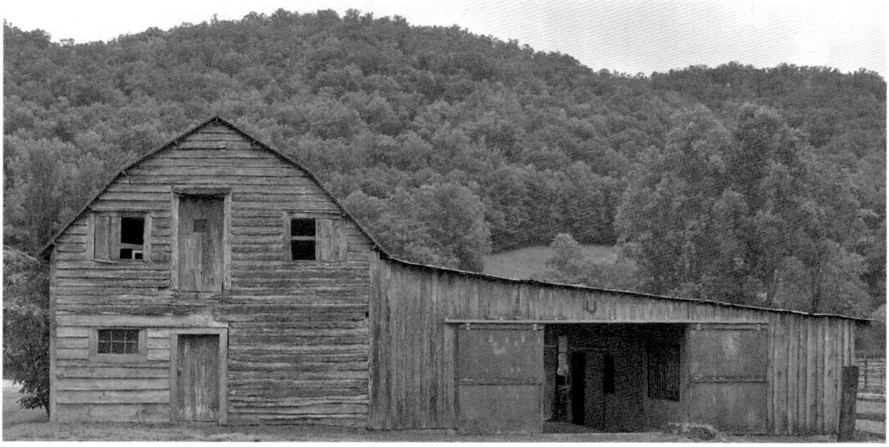

The McCrary barn was a house in the 1800s.

his son, Daniel Sherman Shipman McCrary (1941–), who now owns the farm. Dan McCrary, a lifelong farrier and one of the top rodeo riders in the United States, specialized in steer wrestling and worked the rodeo's team roping with his son Greg McCrary (1963–). Dan's wife, Patricia Lewis McCrary (1944–), also participated in rodeo goat-tying events.

Just east of the McCrary farm, a wooded cove nearly masks a mustard-colored house. This was once Pruitt's Crab Creek Grocery and is now a private residence.

An Outdoor Classroom

While reforesting in the 1930s, the Civilian Conservation Corps (CCC) camped at the 231-acre plot known now as Holmes Educational State Forest, and in 1972, the site became a recognized state forest named after North Carolina's first state forester, John Simcox Holmes (1868–1958). During the Great Depression, corpsmen operated a tree seedling nursery within this rugged terrain alongside Crab Creek Road.

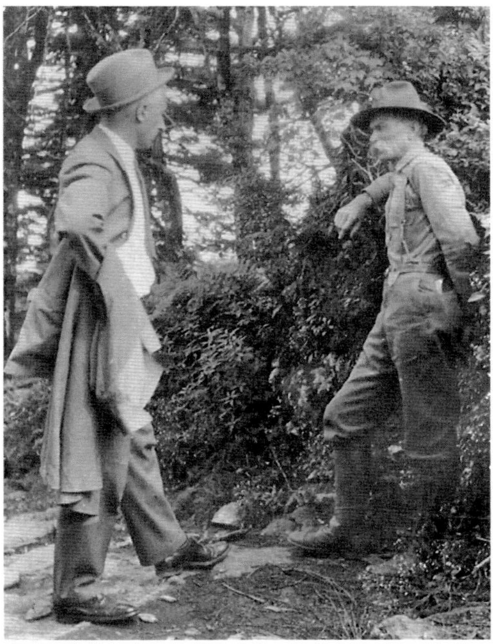

John Simcox Holmes (left). *Photo courtesy of the Forest History Society, Durham, North Carolina (CD9).*

Formed in 1933 as one of the most popular New Deal programs to provide vocational training and to relieve unemployment, the CCC was responsible for more than half of the nation's reforestation. This public works project successfully promoted environmental conservation, fulfilling its mission of "building good citizens through vigorous, disciplined outdoor labor."

This living environmental education center sports facilities for picnicking, hiking, nature studies and primitive camping on a slope of the Pinnacle, known also as Pinnacle Mountain. By mid-March, when the park reopens each year—before anything else blooms in the wild—a blanket of yellow and speckled green emerges from the forest floor: thousands of trout lilies (*Erythronium americanum*), known also as dogtooth violets. Beneath the canopy of trees planted by the CCC, wildflower enthusiasts also discover tiny spring beauties (*Claytonia virginica*), two varieties of lady's-slippers, an arrayal of trillium, May apples, flame azalea, rhododendron, bloodroot, Jack-in-the-pulpit and, on the creek banks, rare Oconee bells (*Shortia*).

Interpretive signs and audio-visual exhibits, including the popular "talking trees," describe, in a self-guided tour, the managed forest, explaining the function, value and historical use of native trees in the area. Guests enter the forest from Crab Creek Road near the Old CCC Road named for the Civilian Conservation Corps.

This was also the site of the Osteen Post Office, established in 1895, where Elisha Osteen (1869–1951) served as its first postmaster.

Joseph O. Hamilton (1854–1933) owned farmland on both sides of Crab Creek Road, just east of the forest at Rocky Ridge Road—land now comprising Holmes Educational State Forest. Recently named Crab Creek Farm, a stained-glass-window studio occupies a portion of the Hamilton acreage on the north side of Crab Creek Road, and the Hamilton home sat on the south side, where, until recently, an orphaned stone chimney stood on the site.

RUSHER-COLEMAN PROPERTY

A son of Alfred Wiley Rusher (1835–1921) and Malissa Misenheimer Brown Rusher (1828–1912)—who came from Rowan County to Henderson County in 1901—Jacob Alexander "Jake" Rusher Sr. (1866–1941) lived and made quite a splash in Henderson County for thirty years. Jake was chairman of the Henderson County Commissioners from 1930 to 1939, during the Great Depression. He married three times, first to Lucy Emma Beaver (1868–1898), next to Cora Lee Plummer (1883–1937) and then to Hannah Elizabeth Jones Anders (1918–1997) of Jacksonville, Florida.

J.A. Rusher, a farmer and land speculator, became one of Henderson County's largest landowners, with much of his acreage in the Crab Creek, Dismal Creek and Shoal Creek areas. Of an 857-acre tract alongside Crab Creek Road, 302.3 acres remained at the time of his death. He had sold

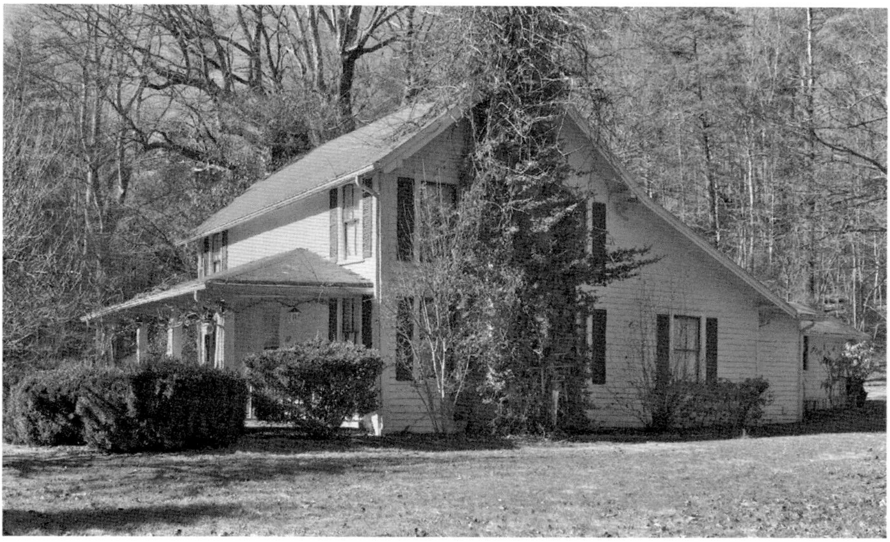

Jake Rusher's house on the south side of Crab Creek Road in the vicinity of Crab Creek Heights Drive and Rocky Mountain Drive.

512.7 acres over time to various parties, including lots in the Hyman Heights subdivision and the old Station Hotel at Hendersonville's Southern Railway station. He bought in the Crab Creek area from D. Wilson Patterson, W.O. Hamilton, Sallie Patterson, Raleigh Patterson, J.B. Patterson, Ella Patterson and more, including Shepherd, King, Ward, McCall and Rhodes, between 1913 and 1931. Besides amassing large tracts of land, Rusher also opened a meat market on Hendersonville's Third Avenue.

The following article appeared in the *French Broad Hustler* in February 1910:

> *A BIG CITY MARKET*
> *J.A. Rusher and Son of Salisbury, on Saturday next, will open their new meat market in the City Market—but it ought to be on Main Street. The place is a revelation to those who have not already seen it, and represents an expenditure of several thousand dollars, possibly by the new firm. Every modern and sanitary device known to the trade has been adopted. The big refrigerator, costing a thousand dollars, has a storage capacity of three tons of ice and 12 dressed beeves. The place is most attractive with its glistening fixtures of steel and polished oak; its plate glass and tiles, and its many interesting devices insuring cleanliness. Mr. Rusher has bought a home here and with his family will prove to be a desirable and welcome acquisition to*

> *Hendersonville, which must be growing surely, to attract so progressive and energetic businessmen as J.A. Rusher and Son.*

The *Hustler* printed another article in May 1910, stating that Rusher had sold the meat business to his son Robert Lee Rusher (1890–1924), mentioning later in that year the several acquisitions Rusher had made "on the right of the Flat Rock road and to the south of the Toxaway railroad" for the purpose of going into a wholesale business. By 1913, the younger Rusher was well entrenched in business in Henderson County, but soon after he joined the circus, working as a concession man, and was killed in an accident in Illinois. He was one of the sons of Lucy Beaver Rusher. In May 1913, the *Hustler* reported:

> *Mr. J.A. Rusher came here from Salisbury a little while back. He stepped off the railroad train at the Southern passenger depot, looked about and then started in to work. Mr. Rusher is an asset to this town and county where he has wisely invested good capital and it is whispered that he is entirely satisfied with his investments. One thing Mr. Rusher has done is to grow more corn to the acre, that is, without the aid of commercial fertilizer, than any other man who ever farmed in Henderson County. He bought that long stretch of bottomland by the Flat Rock road, just beyond the Brevard tracks, and the amount of corn he harvested from that tract last year was a scandal and a shame—so to speak. Mr. Rusher's big dairy barns face this fine piece of bottom and his herd of well-bred cattle graze quietly in adjoining fields. He is the owner of considerable real estate here—both city and county. One of his most recent purchases is a 400-acre tract of mountain land, in connection with which he has certain stock raising plans, which will work out successfully. He has town business interests as well. For that is the way Mr. Rusher always works out his plans—successfully.*

Mr. Rusher's death certificate states that he took his own life with a bullet to the head. Old-timers suggest that he committed suicide after he'd learned that his young wife, Hannah, was engaged in an affair. Records show Jake Rusher's third wife, twenty-three-year-old Hannah Elizabeth Jones Anders Rusher, married five times.

OLD CCC ROAD

The Civilian Conservation Corps began working in the region preparing wilderness land for greater access. Established in 1933, the CCC provided public relief and vocational training designed to relieve unemployment during the Great Depression. The corps performed useful work related to conservation and development of natural resources throughout the United States.

Besides the accomplishments of the CCC at what became Holmes Educational State Forest, other work performed in the region by the corps included construction of the fifty-foot steel lookout tower atop Bearwallow Mountain and, blazing from an old wagon road, the asphalt roadbed between Crab Creek and Sky Valley Roads now named for the corps.

STEPPS ON THE PINNACLE

Snaking up the Pinnacle via the Old CCC Road, the contemporary traveler would never envisage what lay beyond—about a mile on the left, in a cove of Dismal Creek—for nature has all but reclaimed the narrow roadbed leading to Thomas Manders and Fannie Stepp's property.

The story of Frances "Fannie" Stepp (1827–1905) unravels a bittersweet one. A proud and industrious woman, she worked vigorously all of her life, farming, raising four children and making do with only the bare essentials. In her earlier years, she had performed domestic chores for the Memmingers and other prominent families of Flat Rock. Thomas Maudern Manders (1826–1891), the father of Fannie's children, abandoned his family and married Caroline Prideaux Morris (1834–1925) after 1860. Old-timers posited that Thomas and Fannie had never married, for "something seemed odd about the relationship," and what's more, his children took their mother's surname.

Fannie moved with her children to Tennessee after 1861, returning in the 1870s to the farm on the lower slope of the Pinnacle. Manders, in a benevolent gesture, deeded the land to Fannie and their children for one dollar, and Fannie and three of her children remained on the property for the rest of their lives.

Fannie and Thomas's children were Mary (1855–1941), Rebecca (1856–1935), Thomas (1857–1938) and Ellen (1861–1954), with Rebecca the only one to wed, and none of the children was formally educated. Rebecca

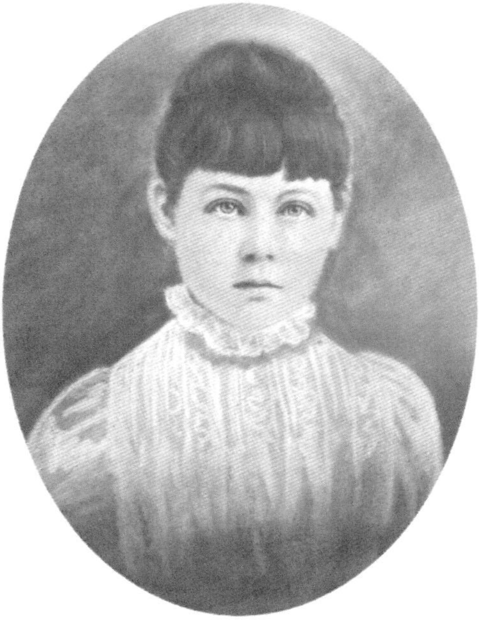

Estelle Stepp. *Photo courtesy of Nancy Harden Dotson.*

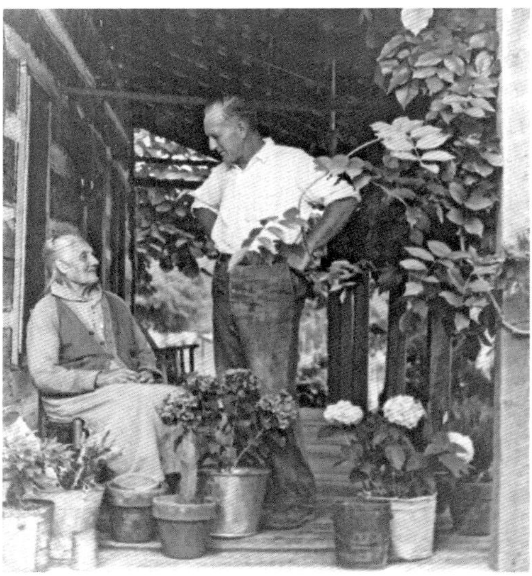

Ellen Stepp with Jim Perry. *Photo courtesy of Nancy Harden Dotson.*

married Bascomb Frederick "Bug" McCall (1857–1921) in 1876. Ellen had a child, Estelle (1881–1903), with Solomon McCrary (1862–1914), and Estelle married Kirkwood "Woody" Campbell Shipman (1878–1932) in 1901. Some say that after Estelle died giving birth to her son Thomas Lavier Shipman (1903), Ellen blamed herself, believing the tragedy was her punishment for having had a child out of wedlock.

Fannie's son Thomas (also known as Bub and Uncle Bubby), a noted storyteller and game hunter, farmed the family plot with the assistance of his siblings. The family kept a vegetable garden, an orchard, some livestock and poultry and also made molasses on the property. Fannie also owned a plot of land in the infamous "Cathead" district, where she grew corn. Bub delivered farm-grown goods by mule-drawn wagon from the Pinnacle to Flat Rock and Hendersonville for barter, and in later years, his sister Ellen walked all the way to town with dressed chickens, butter and eggs to sell or barter.

The Stepps built two homes on the Pinnacle, the first one constructed of logs, referred to by the family as "the old house," with a smaller log structure serving as the kitchen house—both used later for storage after the family moved into a new house on the property. The "new house," though not much larger and finished with weatherboarding, sported two rooms on the ground floor with a central chimney and sleeping quarters in the attic.

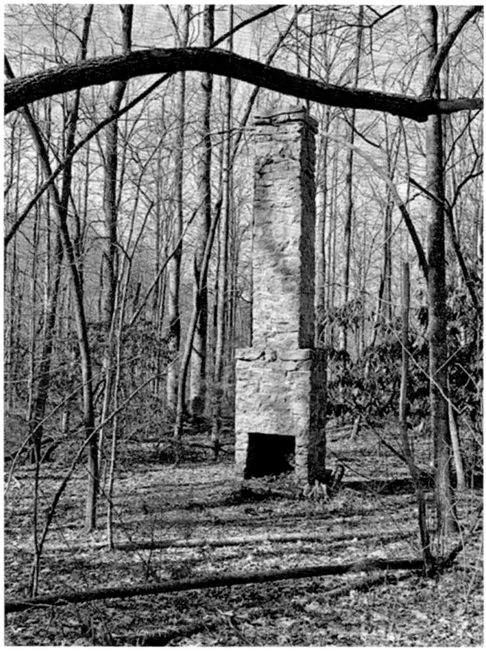

All that remains of the Stepp family's "new house."

Mary Stepp gained regional fame through the writings of Louise Howe Bailey (1915–2009) in books and in Mrs. Bailey's *Hendersonville Times-News* column, "Along the Ridges." While Mary was working at Hendersonville's Hotel Wheeler, Bailey's father, Dr. William Bell White Howe III (1881–1948), hired her as a governess for his daughters Louise and Jennie after divorcing his first wife—a relationship mutually enjoyed by the Howes and Mary Stepp. Dr. Howe looked after the needs of Mary and Bub for the rest of their lives and of Ellen for the rest of his life.

After the Stepps' tenure, Franklin Reginald Neville (1902–1992) owned the 118-acre property, purchased by James Buckner (1931–2012), who sold it in 2002 for half its market value to the Carolina Mountain Land Conservancy to add to DuPont State Forest. Officials plan to carve a trail alongside the homeplace. Over the years, trees have engulfed the farm's rusted barbed wire, and a fine stone chimney with its two-sided fireplace now stands alone on the abandoned site of the Stepps' "new house," as does the large, flat boulder that served as a front step. Nearby, stone foundations of the log house peek through leaf litter and fallen branches. Roof beams of the root cellar have toppled, the stones rest askew in the molasses still, moss enshrouds the old springhouse on the creek that courses below and the roots of an ancient tree have buckled the stack of stones purportedly marking the grave of a Hiram King descendant.

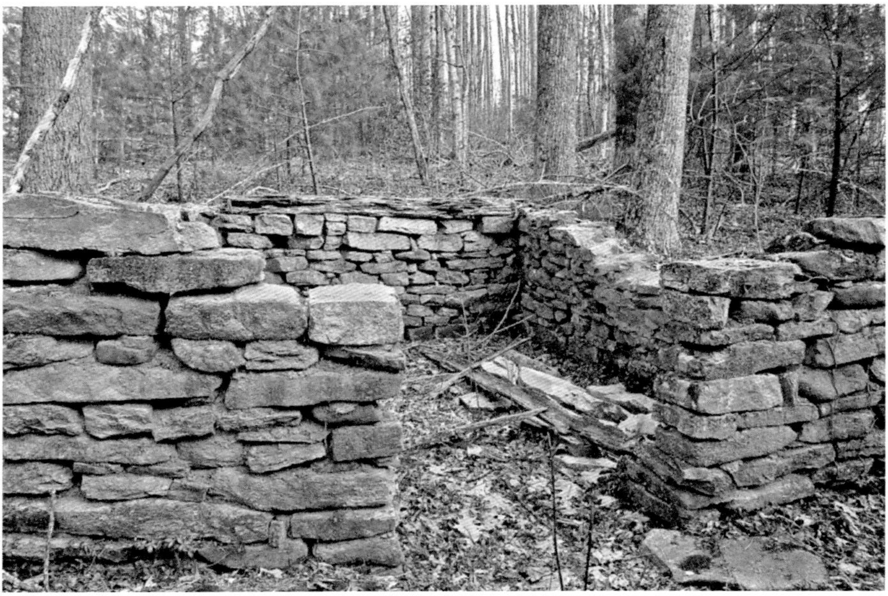

The root cellar on the Stepp property on a lower slope of the Pinnacle.

Back on Crab Creek Road, just past Raven Creek Drive on the left, we find Bug and Rebecca McCall's white farmhouse and across the street from it the home of Frank Edney (1911–1993) and Alice Caroline Justice Edney (1909–1994). The Edneys owned the Hot Spot and Blue Bird Cafés in downtown Hendersonville. Decades ago, local folks enjoyed a brilliant display of lights and their reflections on the sizable pond between the Edney home and Crab Creek Road.

Crab Creek Baptist Church, Cemetery and Community School

From a knoll near the northeast-facing base of Jeter Mountain, in the midst of tombstones, an unobstructed outlook sweeps to the Pinnacle and beyond—perhaps one of Henderson County's most breathtaking vistas. On this land in 1834, the Reverends William Kimzey (1784–1864) and Jacob Cantrell (circa 1780–1854) constituted from Mud Creek Baptist Church a new place of worship they named Crab Tree Baptist of Christ, with Jacob

Cantrell serving as the first pastor. Kimzey moved to Alabama in 1864, and Cantrell moved to Gilmer County, Georgia, where he founded Goshen Baptist Church in the 1840s.

Malinda Shipman Jones (1812–1884), one of the charter members, and her husband, John Jones (1816–1893), helped build a meetinghouse of logs, which hosted services from 1854 until a more substantial sanctuary was erected in 1857. During that era, the church and the Crab Creek School across the street formed the heart of the Crab Creek community.

The 1857 church of clapboard was bricked over in 1969. In 1935, a brick monument was constructed on the site of the old meetinghouse, inset with marble plaques commemorating organizing members and all the church's pastors in celebration of the church's centenary events. The adjacent, larger brick sanctuary was completed and dedicated in 1986.

In 1922, workers finished the road from Crab Creek Road to the church and cemetery. In that same year, an article in the *Hendersonville Times* stated that Crab Creek boasted "one of among the best-kept cemeteries and church grounds in Henderson County," yet another article with a Crab Creek member's lamentation also appeared:

> *We have a nice church house and school building, but the people do not pull together to increase the efficiency of these institutions. Cooperation is necessary. In our community some of the people take an interest in keeping their farms in a good state of cultivation, their homes painted, their lawns mowed and planted in bright blooming flowers. When a religious meeting is called for the improvement of the community, a few go but can't accomplish much. Recently a prominent preacher delivered a very interesting sermon here at our church house, and about twenty members of the church were present while there are almost two hundred members on the church roll. The members had other plans, letting nothing interfere with their own personal lives and pleasures. A small audience of young people goes to Sunday school while the older people seem to have gone to sleep and don't pull together to increase the attendance at Sunday school and church meetings.*

In what could be considered the hub of the Crab Creek community, the church continued to grow as officials added classrooms and restrooms to the back of the 1857 sanctuary in the 1940s. A building housing the fellowship hall, additional classrooms and library were completed in 1987.

The Crab Creek community grade school stood on a knoll across Crab Creek Road from the church. Teachers included Nannie Justice Mitchell

(1882–1964) and her daughter Irene Mitchell (1904–1994). Irene taught in the Henderson County school system for forty-eight years. Nannie also taught Sunday school classes at Refuge Baptist Church, and Irene also taught at Mountain Home, Edneyville and Hendersonville elementary schools. Both women were members of Refuge Baptist Church.

In 2001, *Hendersonville Times-News* columnist Louise H. Bailey wrote of Crab Creek School based on an interview with James King (1915–2009), who attended classes there. King described the schoolhouse as small—approximately twenty-four by forty-eight feet. In its early years, sessions were held from August to February, later expanded to eight months and then nine. King also remembered the potbellied stove and Virgil McCrary (1889–1957) digging a well on the property. The girls had a basketball team that played against girls' teams at Little River and Pleasant Hill Schools. According to King, the Crab Creek team never won a game. Crab Creek School was vacated in 1930, and it burned to the ground at a later date.

BLUE STAR CAMP

Herman Popkin (1918–2002) and his brothers, Henry and Ben, bought the old farmstead of John Jones and his wife, Malinda Shipman Jones, and established a coed camp there in the foothills of the Pinnacle in 1948—the same year the state of Israel was established. The mission of the Popkins' year-round camp was to provide "a safe haven where Jewish children can learn about their shared culture and values." Popkin also co-founded Hendersonville's Camp Judaea.

Besides cultural amenities such as a Living Judaism Program and the on-site Elmore Solomon Chapel, the five-hundred-acre Blue Star Camp proffers myriad outdoor activities, including yoga, a high-ropes course, a bouldering wall, a climbing tree, archery, trails, ten campsites, hiking, biking, horseback riding, water sports and the dramatic arts under the direction of third-generation Popkin heirs. Camp directors also arrange for off-site activities in DuPont State and Pisgah National Forests.

Resuming the journey, eastward bound…

PREACHER JESS OSTEEN'S FARM

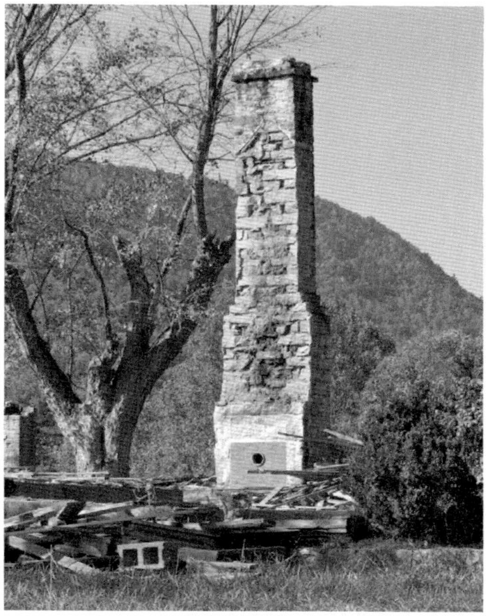

All that remains of the Jesse E. Osteen home.

When workers began dismantling the old farmhouse in 2012, the intrepid visitor would have glimpsed shelves of dusty mason jars in the cellar. Seen too would have been the logs of the original Osteen home, possibly built by Montiville F. Osteen (1865–1934). Now only a stone chimney marks the home site of Montiville's son "Preacher Jess"—Reverend Jesse E. Osteen (1888–1978) and his wife, Emma Mae Corn Osteen (1892–1970). Jesse and Emma's granddaughter Jean Osteen Orr (1940–), who called her grandfather "Papa" and her grandmother "Mama," said, "For some reason his parents didn't give him a middle name, so he just picked the initial E." Mrs. Orr also remembers, "As a little child, if I wanted Papa to do something for me and he was busy reading the Bible and didn't want to get up, he would say, 'I can't. I've got a bone in my leg.'"

Osteen cultivated the land on that tract and also the acreage across Crab Creek Road where he had his barn, sheds and a large horse named Ginger that pulled the plow and powered the molasses mill in what is now the Pinnacle View subdivision. Many local farmers grew patches of sweet sorghum cane for the purpose of making molasses, and some of them milled and boiled the commodity on-site. Other farmers would take their cane to a neighbor who kept a mill on his property, as was the case with Reverend Osteen's neighbors. Jean Osteen Orr recalls:

> *Papa bought or more likely was given some of his father's land. He had almost nine acres on the left* [north] *side of Crab Creek Road with the house, garage and crop fields, with Crab Creek Road as a natural boundary line on one side. He also had 14 acres on the other* [south] *side of the road. That was where the molasses mill, chicken house, barn, pigpen,*

> *strawberry patch, pasture, saltlick, and a little creek that had real clay were situated. Mama said she couldn't keep a cat alive because they all got run over crossing the road from the house to the barn and back. Papa had one horse, Ginger, after old Maude died, at any given time one to four cows, a bunch of pigs and lots of chickens. Papa farmed for a living and tended to the animals. I thought it was wonderful how he could squirt milk in the cat's mouth while he was milking the cow. Mama canned vegetables and dried fruit, and made sausage and liver mush, sewed her own clothes, made quilts, and was the best cook in the world—at least my world. I was grown before I thought they were anything but perfect.*

Self-sustaining farmers preserved fruit and stored root vegetables, honey and molasses "to do a winter." In preparing molasses, the maker would first strip fodder from the canes, cut off the seeds and then chop down the stalks before the first forecasts of frost in October. The next step entailed feeding the canes into a milling device consisting of large cast-iron rollers attached to a driving shaft—a log-pole sweep hitched to the harness of a horse, mule or ox. The beast would circle the press, thus crushing the canes and extracting the straw-colored juice, which trickled into barrels. The resulting squeezings were dipped from the barrel and into a boiler set on a wood furnace, and helpers would use strainers to skim the mixture as it boiled. The first skimmings, generally green in color, would be discarded until the remaining infusion turned red and viscous, and this, the desired product, was ladled into jugs to be stored for up to two years.

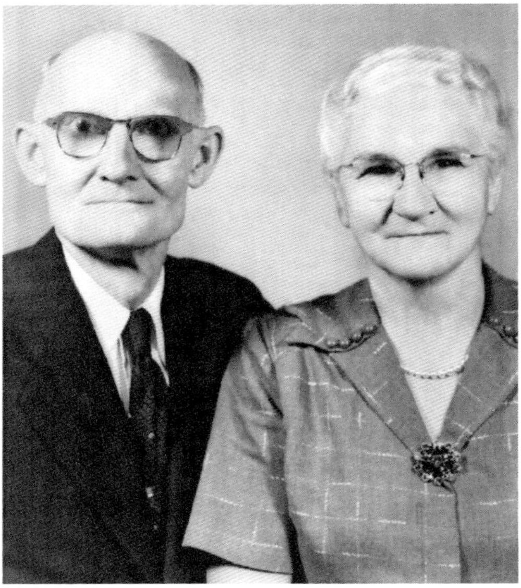

Reverend Jesse E. and Emma Corn Osteen. *Photo courtesy of the Osteen/Orr family.*

The Osteens' nephew Edgar Dwight Osteen (1944–) recalled childhood days spent on the farm. "Like a Norman Rockwell setting," he said of his uncle and aunt's place. The classic white farmhouse encompassed by meadows back-dropped by blue ridges surely evokes such imagery—

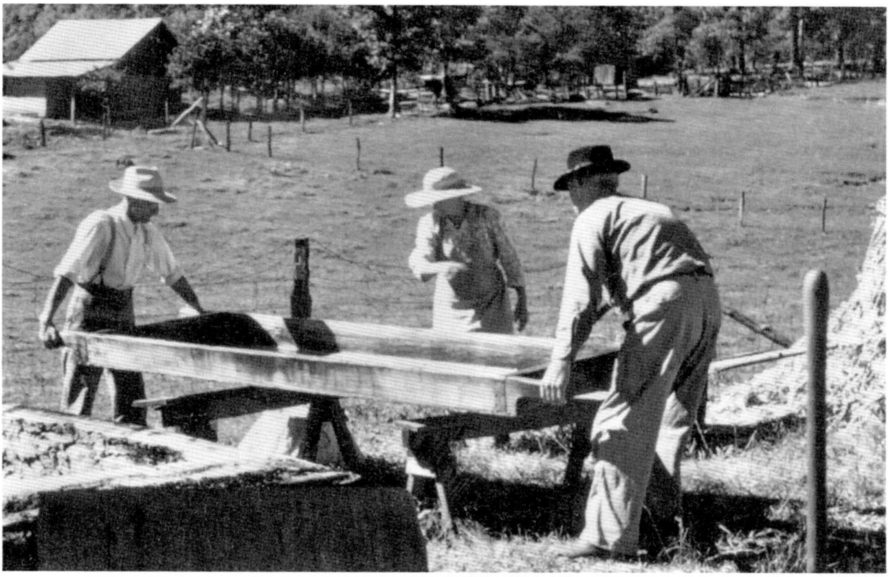

The Osteens operating their molasses mill. *Photo courtesy of the Osteen/Orr family.*

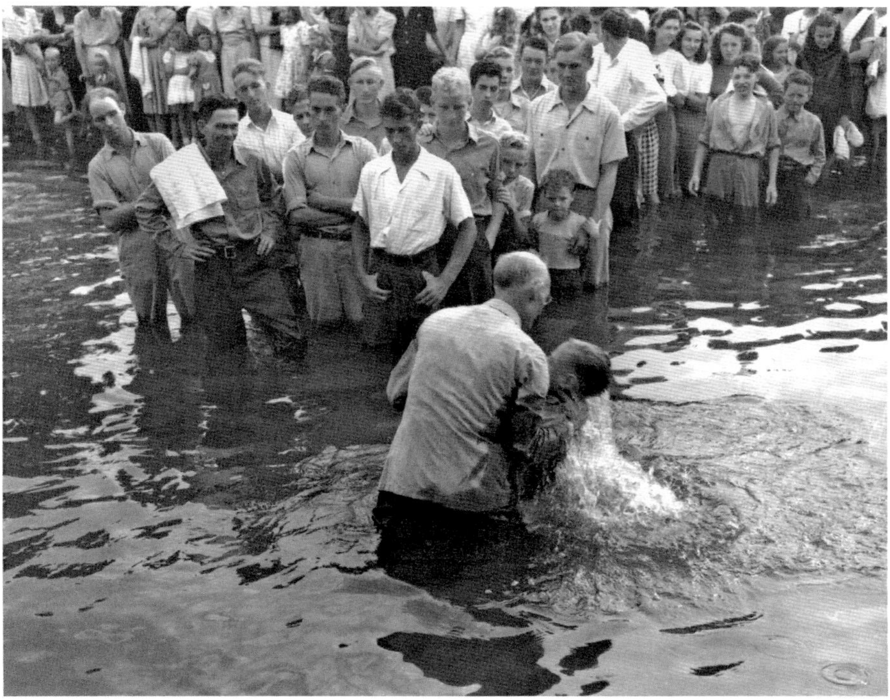

Reverend Jesse Osteen performing baptisms in the Green River, Tuxedo, North Carolina. *Photo courtesy of the Osteen/Orr family.*

and the Rockwell analogy rings even more fitting, considering the countless artists and photographers who, over the years, have painted or snapped this all-American scene.

The Osteens were blessed with three sons: John Seldon (1910–1976), James Melvin (1913–1987) and Melton Alonzo (1915–1994). Dwight Osteen described the family as a musical one. "All had excellent singing voices," he said, "with myself the exception."

Beginning his career as a minister at age twenty, the Reverend Osteen preached over the ensuing decades at a number of regional Baptist churches, including Catheys Creek in Transylvania County; Peniel and Coopers Gap in Polk County; in Henderson County: Berea, Beulah, Green River, Holly Springs, Mount Olivet, Mountain Valley, Pleasant Grove; Flat Rock Missionary Baptist Church (founded 1960 and built 1961–65), which he organized; and Crab Creek, where he served as pastor from 1929 to 1930 and 1944 to 1947.

"A charismatic man," Dwight Osteen said of his uncle, "and much adored by all who knew him. As far as I know, he never took a salary, but at times congregations would take up love offerings to pay for his gasoline."

The *Hendersonville Times* of July 3, 1934, reported:

> *The Reverend J.E. Osteen preached at Crab Creek Church Sunday morning, using as his text Genesis 45:24, "See that you fall not out by the way." Mr. Osteen very forcibly applied this scripture to the Church of today showing how necessary it is for the Church to dwell together in union and what it would mean to fall out by the way.*

MORE FARMS AND A SAWMILL

Just east of the Osteen property and Diamond Mine Lane stands a colossal hangar jam-packed with racecars—Petree Racing Inc., owned by Andy Petree, former NASCAR team owner. Before Petree's occupancy, hang-gliding devotees launched from the Pinnacle, soaring on currents known as ridge-lifts and putting down in the field near the site of the hangar. At one time, this property belonged to Sam Sosebee (1933–) and his wife, Helen Moore Sosebee (1936–), who farmed the acreage stretching between Crab Creek Road and nearly to the bordering ridge to its north. Sosebee also served as a managing partner for Franklin Reginald "Frank" Neville (1902–1992), who owned the two hundred acres known as Shadow Mountain Ranch with a dairy and large herd of Holsteins. Sosebee's father, Ross Sosebee (1905–1982), and mother, Fannie Mae Freeman Sosebee (1909–1995), farmed in the area, as did his uncles and aunts H. Porter Sosebee (1900–1981) and Cora Lee Freeman (1910–2006) and William Benson Freeman (1880–1966) and Alice Lena Moore Freeman (1879–1967).

Today, the Solar-Vista subdivision, alongside Shadow Valley Drive, occupies the former Shadow Mountain Ranch where Joseph Neville's son Frank ran a sawmill. A dwindling number of old-timers remember this operation, which, like the farm across the road, has slipped into the dusk of history.

Across the road, just east of Valley Hill Fire Department #2, the shambles of an old farmstead litter the landscape. Erstwhile also the farmland of Joseph Neville, this property later belonged to James L. Sexton (1913–2005) and his wife, Polly Lewis Sexton (1917–1989), who expanded their dairy operation to the north side of the road, where stands a rusty wire silo abutting a dilapidated barn—the remnants of the Sexton Dairy Farm, owned since 2004 by Larry Holbert, who operates the property as the Crab Creek Catfish Farm. Across the road, the main house, barn and outbuildings on the old Neville-Sexton property have collapsed into ruins. In its heyday, this site was home to Lakeside Dairy, owned by Joseph Reginald Neville (1866–1939) and then by his son Frank Neville in 1939. The two worked the dairy as partners until Joseph's death, after which time Franklin carried on the business of farming. The Sextons later owned the farm under the name of Sexton Dairy, at the time one of the largest dairy operations in the area. Barbara Simpson currently owns the property, where she operates a roadside produce stand.

Joseph R. Neville was a remarkable chap, having crisscrossed the world after his rough beginnings in Ohio. His mother died when he was a child, and his father turned him over to relatives for his rearing. As a young man, he sought fortune, panning for gold in Alaska. He served in the United States Army, lived for a time in Chicago, served as a missionary in the Belgian Congo, worked in England as a master grocer and preached in Hamburg, Germany, where he met and married Jessie Brereton (1878–1971) of England in 1899. From there, the couple moved several times, to Delaware, New York, Pennsylvania and Florida, before finally settling in Henderson County, where they bought land in the Crab Creek community in 1929. Neville spent his remaining years as a farmer and dairyman.

Just eastward, the Kanuga Forest subdivision lies adjacent to the former farms of the Freemans and Sosebees. Up the road, just before

Redden Road, stands a white frame house trimmed in green, which served as the Patterson Store owned by Herman "Harmon" Patterson (1895–1950) and his wife, Kathryn Sumner Patterson (1902–1998). After Herman's death, Kathryn married Robert S. Newman (1907–1997) and continued operating the country store for a number of years, catering to area campers.

Evans Road cuts south and then west off Crab Creek Road. Not far up on the left was the property of George W. Harden (1872–1944) and Mary Eloise Shepherd Harden (1872–1948), including the nicely maintained Harden Family Cemetery.

Between the Patterson Store and the aforementioned farms, Walnut Cove Road cuts northwest off Crab Creek Road—one of the entry points to the legendary Cathead community.

Cathead

Off Walnut Cove Road (County Road 1125) lies a covert corner of the southwestern county known at least somewhat secretively as Cathead,[7] which at one time spawned a preponderance of illegal distilling, with purportedly more stills than families, and called by some "the moonshine capital of Henderson County." Even today, few families populate this small farming community in the shadows of a bald known as Tater Hill.

According to Ted Hamilton of Hendersonville, North Carolina:

> *Everyone around here has always called it Cathead. My father was in the Philippines in World War II and another soldier from some other state asked him where he was from. My father told him, "Crab Creek, southwest of Hendersonville, North Carolina." The soldier replied, "Is that close to Cathead?" So apparently, Cathead was better known than Hendersonville among certain clients of the area's product.*

From Walnut Cove Road, one glimpses from the right a shell of a rock house—past Bear Rock Road near the Stonewood subdivision—resided in last by Slim Rutledge, according to Henderson County native James Preston

7. Whether oral or written, "Cathead" has been pronounced and spelled in various ways, including "Catshead" and "Cat's Head." This text includes the more popular spelling of "Cathead."

"Tooley" Ward (1927–). Rutledge wintered in Florida and summered there with a servant nicknamed "Buttermilk."

One enters the depths of Cathead as Walnut Cove Road transitions from hard surfaced to rugged, unpaved, potholed and twisty. Not far within stands a red springhouse and, just beyond it, a set of concrete steps approaching a now-abandoned plot. This was the home site of High Runimus "Runer" Ward (1871–1958) and Nettie Brown Ward (1884–1984), parents of Tooley Ward.

Other early residents of Cathead, mostly before the asphalt ends on Walnut Cove Road, included John Bates Brown (1861–1943), Rufus W. Brown (1892–1968), Ward Hamilton "Hamp" Brown (1918–1991), Charles Cecil Brown (1921–2012), Elzie Floyd (1906–1958), Sam King (1909–1988) and Reverend Albert P. Jones (1920–2002) and his father, Phillip Jackson Jones (1891–1987). James Crawford Beddingfield (1899–1995) kept a chicken farm there, and other farmers cultivated beans, squash and tomatoes—and corn, of course. Old-timers insist that stills laid concealed within pockets up the sides of the mountain near Sam King Road.

In the midst of this setting, a small log house stands on a knoll alongside Walnut Cove Road. Some local folks believe this was originally the home of Eli "Squire" Shepherd (1815–1896) and Martha "Patsy" Osteen Shepherd (1814–1890), who farmed about fifty acres in the vicinity of what is now Camp Tekoa. Shepherd tilled the soil with an ox named Buck and killed wild game with a rifle, which he called Bean. The Shepherds were forebears of Hendersonville merchant Milas Monroe "M.M." Shepherd (1867–1929). John Bates Brown later moved the Shepherds' log home to his property in Cathead, and according to Brown descendants, he and his wife, Adeline "Addie" Drake Brown (1868–1959), and their children lived in it until they finished a new house across the road. At the time, Brown owned ninety acres in Cathead. Some residents of Cathead speculated that Brown built the cabin. Others maintain that a member of the Drake family built it near Wolf Shoals, saying someone moved it to its current location alongside Walnut Cove Road in the early 1900s.

Legendary distillers, the Browns and others living in Cathead frequently found themselves in trouble with tax collectors and the law. Punters whispered the password "Cathead Lane" upon entering the proscribed property, until snitchers and revenuers caught on and the bootleggers changed the code.

Thomas Stepp (1867–1955) and his family lived amongst the blockaders, operating a steam-powered sawmill known as Stepp's Mill near Justamere Lane off Walnut Cove Road. Stepp's sons William, Arnold and Walter

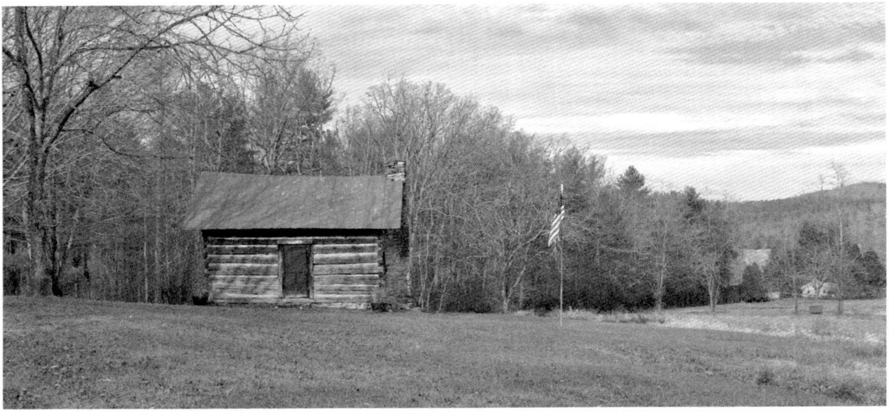

The log home of Eli "Squire" Shepherd, owned by Betty Brown Mullis Lakey of Winston-Salem since 1939.

participated in the milling operation, and his son Nick ran the Valley Hill Grocery Store on Willow Road. According to V. Leon Pace of the Pinnacle, the Stepps were first to have telephone service in the small community, and Thomas was generous in allowing neighbors to use his phone, "except," Pace explained, "when the borrowing party spent more time listening than speaking. Old man Stepp expected people to *talk* into a telephone."

Thomas Stepp was married to Alice Shipman Stepp (1872–1900) and to Elizabeth Sarah Blackwell Stepp (1878–1953). Between the two marriages, Thomas had nine children: Flora, Ida, Walter, Ella, William, Verda, Arnold, Nicholas "Nick" and Annie.

Thomas Stepp acquired a powerful steam engine from the City of Hendersonville—a Farquhar Company machine employed in the building of city roads. Stepp used it to drive his sawmill. When the Stepps fired up the old steam engine, onlookers partook of the fragrance of green wood and a spray of sawdust. The chugging, the piercing whir and then the penetrating scream as the circular blade ripped through the logs were noises they surely could feel. The engine, willed to the Maybin family of Rock Creek, currently sits on Theron Maybin's property.

On April 18, 1930, federal Prohibition raiders—including a chauffeur for the Federal Prohibition Raiding Squad of Hendersonville, Clarence Grady "Fatty" Howard (1902–1930) of Tuxedo—visited Cathead and seized and destroyed a sixty-five-gallon still and twenty-six gallons of moonshine. Edgar Clarence King (1904–1999) and Arthur Case Saltz (1900–1962) were arrested at the still. The next day, John Brown and his

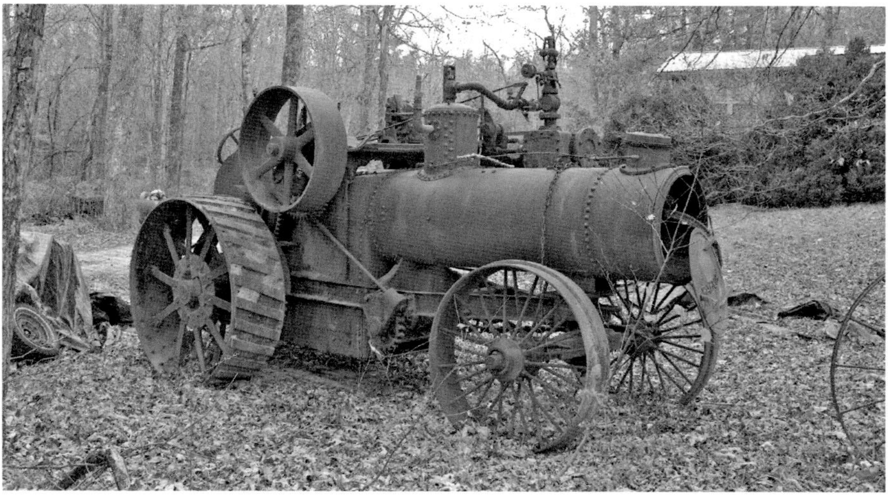

Thomas Stepp's Farquhar steam engine.

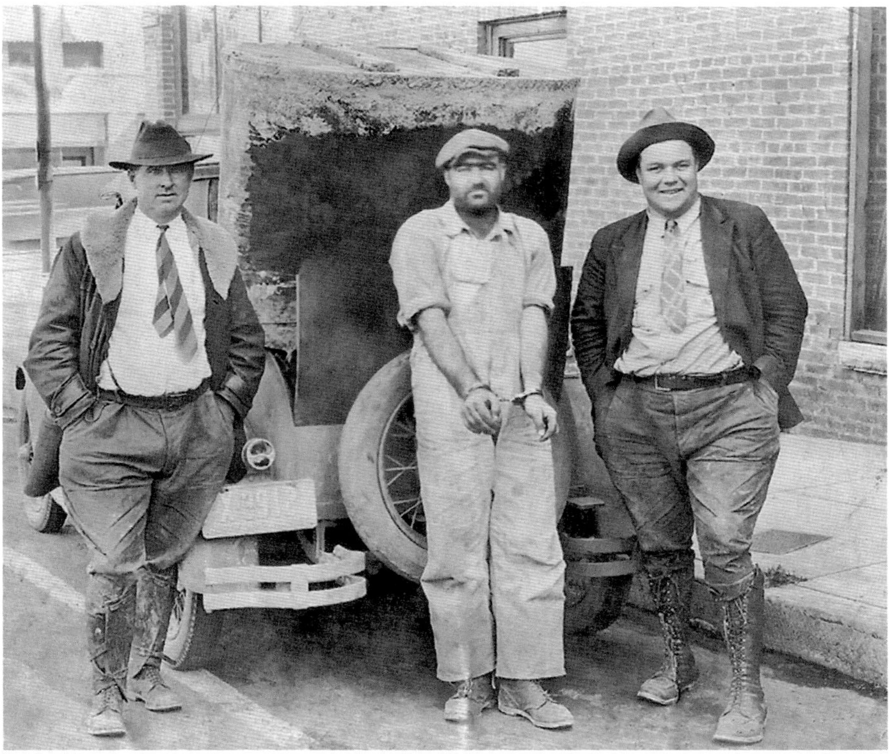

An unidentified convict flanked by Prohibition agents Will Owens (left) and Clarence "Fatty" Howard (right). *Photo courtesy of John Paul Jones.*

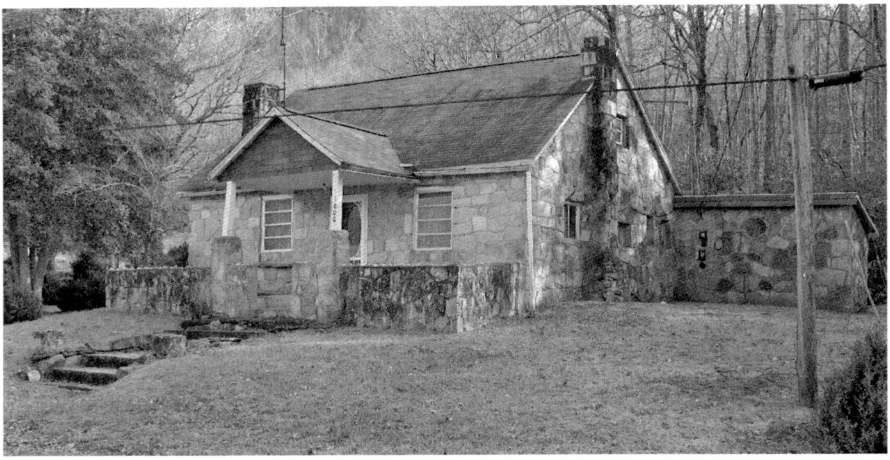

Fred Schwarz's house on Walnut Cove Road in Cathead.

son Jim and Cathead resident Frederick C. Schwarz (1884–1949)[8] were also arrested at the site. Among those implicated, Schwarz managed to escape. On Monday morning, April 21, 1930, near the Justus Pharmacy on Hendersonville's Main Street, Schwarz shot Howard in the head. Howard died at Patton Memorial Hospital the following afternoon.

Ironically, Clarence G. Howard was the son of James Holland "Hol" Howard (1872–1924), a deputized South Carolina constable, killed during a raid on a distillery on Hogback Mountain in 1924.

Schwarz was indicted on October 10, 1930, and charged with first-degree murder. Witnesses testified to Schwarz's having threatened Howard with, "Big boy, I'll get you if it's the last thing I ever do."

"Fred was a coppersmith who moved here from New York and married a local girl," said Sammy Williams. "He was a customer of our store, and he bought a good deal of copper. One day he gave us a miniature copper still he had made. We kept it on display in the store until someone stole it."

On October 18, 1930, in less than five hours, the jury on the Schwarz case reached a verdict of second-degree murder. Judge W.F. Harding sentenced Schwarz to fifteen years in the state pen at Raleigh. The judge closed his

8. Records show different spellings of Schwarz's surname and even his given name, in some cases as "Frederick Charles Schwartz Jr." and as "Raul C. Schwarz, German-born, merchant" in the 1920 Henderson County Census. Several *Times-News* articles from 1930 consistently used the spelling "Swartz." Schwarz was married to Rose Brown Schwarz (1894–1987).

remarks with, "Since the jury found that Schwarz did not kill in self defense it might as well have found him guilty of first-degree murder."

Judge Harding also remarked, "Liquor will get every man who fools with it. Regardless of how mildly a man drinks it will get him sooner or later, and all violations of the law are for the benefit of the people who drink."

Frank L. FitzSimons, in his book *From the Banks of the Oklawaha* (Vol. II) wrote:

> *They honestly felt that it was their inalienable right to make it. Their fathers, grandfathers, and even great-grandfathers had turned their corn and rye into this valuable product that they could so easily exchange for the necessities of life. They thought the government was unreasonable and tyrannical for sending law enforcement officers to search for and destroy their copper stills and arrest those they caught operating them.*

IN THE STILL OF THE NIGHT

Distilling liquor was not unique to Cathead. Old-timers tell of "nearly everyone" having made the magic elixir in days of old. Most folks made hooch for their own use, and others made a serious business of it.

"Moonrunners" and "blockaders," they called them—distillers who transported their illegal grain liquor at breakneck speeds through the mountains' dangerously serpentine roads, outsmarting and outdriving revenuers. In the earlier decades of the twentieth century, North Carolina's Wilkes County gained infamy as the blockade liquor capital of America. By the late 1940s, runners further souped up their vehicles, repurposing them for sport and profit—the precursor of NASCAR. Frank L. FitzSimons wrote:

> *Nearly everyone who lived in the area, though, made illegal whiskey...the clear potent whiskey that was distilled from the grain grown on the patches of corn and rye that dotted the area, and it found a ready sale. It was generally referred to as white lightning because of the speed with which it struck the imbiber. Some called it moonshine because it was said to be distilled at night by the light of the moon, and some who drank it spoke of it as white mule because of its color and its kick, which was comparable to the kick of a mule.*

Whether intended for recreational or medicinal use, the illicit production of liquor once prevailed deep within the wooded slopes and vales of Henderson County. Back in the day, local folks whispered about Dark Corner, a locale notorious for its production of the spirituous beverage. Situated at the foot of Melrose, Rocky Spur and Hogback Mountains, Dark Corner actually lay secreted within the thickets of a territory where Henderson and Polk Counties, North Carolina, and Spartanburg and Greenville Counties, South Carolina, joined. Lake Lanier and the Greenville Watershed now mostly cover the region. The runners, known as the "Dark Corner Boys"—generally the sons of distillers—ran blockade liquor to buyers, fending off intruders, including the law, as necessary. Folks generally avoided such places, sensing the danger of accidentally trespassing upon them.

The August 1912 *French Broad Hustler* reported:

> *One of the largest stills ever captured in North Carolina was put out of business Saturday morning by Revenue Agent Will Harkins, Constable T.B. Conner, Mack Bryson and Will Hudson in Chunn's Cove, 12 miles southeast of Chimney Rock. Constable Conner states that the raiders visited the place Friday night and began the devastation about daylight Saturday morning while the still was hot from Friday's operation. He states that the still was of 240-gallon capacity; that 7,000 or 8,000 gallons of beer, ten bushels of meal and five bushels of corn malt were destroyed in addition to the complete outfit representing an outlay of about $300. The copper still was so large that the raiders were unable to take it away, but they punctured it to the point of uselessness. Constable Conner saved the cap and worm as a relic, and has them at the courthouse on exhibition. It required nearly two hours to play havoc with the plant, which, it is understood, had been in operation for about two years. No arrests were made as no owner was found.*

The inherent chemistry of blockade liquor—simply the conversion of grain into sugar—involves a process of boiling, vaporizing and distilling and then distilling again. In essence, junior high school science teachers tutor the basics of concocting a still with a glass retort flask in which a liquid or liquid mixture boils over a flame. Attached to the retort, a condenser collects the vapor and recondenses it, and the distillate disperses into a receiving flask—the condenser consisting of two tubes between which a current of cold water flows in an upward direction or opposite the flow of the distillate.

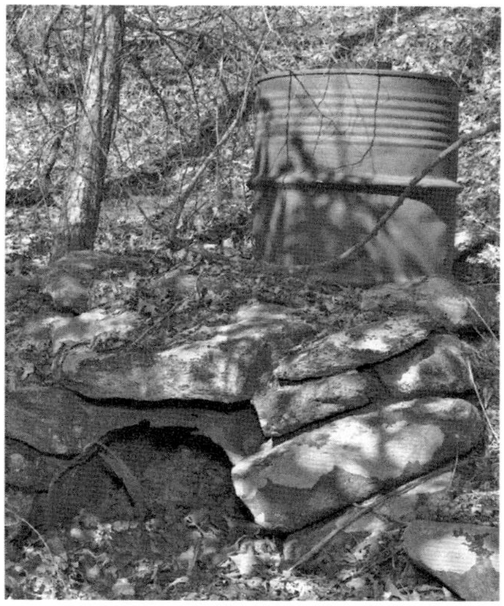

The ruins of a still in Dark Corner, 2013.

In the heyday of blockade liquor, backwoodsmen employed similar principles, but in lieu of sophisticated laboratory glassware and Bunsen burners, they applied more rustic measures: a vessel such as a soap kettle or another large metal container set on a primitive wood-burning furnace. On the kettle, the blockader placed a lid with a cap arm or "horse's head," which stretched to another vessel called the "worm box." Some distillers also used a vessel between the still and the worm box—a steam chest or "thumpin' chest." From the steam barrel, a stretch of copper tubing—coiled at its other end and called the "worm"—conveyed vapors to the worm box, where cold water passed over it. A spigot toward the bottom of the worm box dribbled the finished product into a holding container—ordinarily a bucket, crockery jug or canning jars.

Such a crude apparatus lay concealed deep within a laurel hell or wooded hollow within reach of a running creek or spring-branch. Blockaders sometimes built crude sheds over their stills, and at other times they simply felled trees or planted quick-growing bamboo to conceal their illicit operations.

Manufacturing "mountain dew" entailed the steeping of grain—traditionally, corn and/or rye—in water, which slowly percolated through the grain over a period of two or three days. As water leached through the mix, the distiller replenished the supply until the grain sprouted—a process converting starch to sugar—a method used as a substitute for malt. Next, the sprouted grain would be dried, ground and added to boiling water, resulting in mash, which required stirring. At this point, rye malt may have been added, and at times distillers added sugar or molasses. If available, yeast may also have been added, at which point the distiller carefully managed the temperature of the mash so as not to kill the yeast microbes.

When yeast was not readily available, distillers allowed their mash to stand for eight to ten days, effecting a fermented sour mash or "wash" (beer), essentially a suspension of carbonic acid and alcohol. The wash would then be returned to the still for the condensation process, during which time the fire was kept stoked under the kettle. What dribbled from the condenser—the first distillation—would be redistilled to refine and intensify the resulting product, known as "doublings."

At this point, the blockader tested the bead of his liquor to determine its proof, watching for a soapy appearance—bubbles rising to the top of a tilted vial of the sampling. Once approved, the distiller might run the liquor through a charcoal filter to rid it of any residual fusel oil. The average yield from a bushel of corn equaled about two and a half gallons, and a typical backwoods blockader was capable of producing between ten to fifty gallons a day.

As if all of this were not in itself complicated and time-consuming, maintaining a distillery posed further problems. That certain nighttime glow and the sheer aroma of simmering mash lured whistle-blowing neighbors, regional sheriffs and revenue agents and their spies who would routinely riddle the equipment with bullets. Blockaders were fined and arrested, and they in turn occasionally wounded or killed government agents, informers and local law-enforcement officials. Stubbornly proud, distillers refused to pay a governmental tax on their homemade spirits. Their ancestors had fled from Scotland, Wales and Ireland to avoid taxation, and their Celtic roots fiercely resisted such foolishness as levies and tolls.

In his book *Our Southern Highlanders*, author Horace Kephart (1862–1931) maintained the prevalence of distilling liquor throughout the mountains of the southeastern United States. Henderson County historian Jennie Jones Giles concurs. "Nearly everyone did it," Jennie said. The "water of life" was viewed as a divine creation due to its curative powers and economic value, and the making and selling of it was nigh on the only way most early settlers could make money in a society based on bartering.

A 1908 referendum made North Carolina the first southern state to prohibit the production and sale of alcoholic beverages, after which time the blockade business became even more stealthy, and attempts to enforce laws prohibiting the distilling and sale of contraband spirits instigated frequent cases of violence and murder. Henderson County native John Paul Jones claims that more revenuers were killed in a valley called Reedy

Patch (originally named "Read a Patch"), off Hog Rock Road (County Road 1703) in Edneyville, than in any other place in North Carolina. Another such place, in the hollows of Pleasant Grove, was known as the Follies. Much of this activity occurred after the enforcement of Prohibition and with the temperance movement.

For the most part, home distillers produced liquor for their personal recreational and medicinal use, including brandy distilled from peaches, apples or berries. With a dearth of drugstores or traditional doctors available, granny women (unlicensed country doctors) dosed their patients with blockade liquor as a curative or temporary relief from the symptoms of upper-respiratory disorders and other ailments. Such doctors, some of them illiterate or semi-literate, memorized cures passed down to them or to their ancestors from Native Americans. Such medications and treatments included poultices and tonics formulated from wild herbs, roots, bark and berries, and largely the antiseptic and pain-numbing, anti-inflammatory qualities of liquor counted among the home remedies. Aging or "chartering" the distillation rendered it smoother and better tasting.

In some cases, blockaders tainted their formulas, resulting in dangerous concoctions known as "pop-skull." These brews sometimes proved fatal,

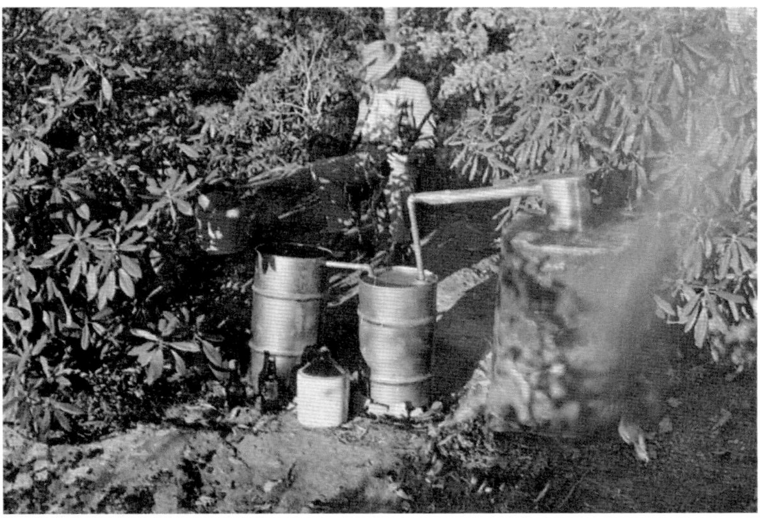

Vintage postcard of a classic still once on exhibit in Laurel Park.

particularly when distillers contaminated the blend by adding lye products to the spirits. On the other hand, unadulterated liquor proved dangerous only to those who consumed too much of it. The double-processed liquor, after all, could yield a proof of 140 to 170 (70 to 85 percent alcohol purity).

In addition to illicit blockading, blind tigers—known also as speakeasies—existed in Henderson County. The *French Broad Hustler* mentioned occasions of arrests at downtown Hendersonville's Dixie Café and Central Café in the early 1900s. North Carolina Supreme Court records cite several instances of convicted distillers in Henderson County. One such case—*State v. John Blackwell*, filed December 15, 1920—involved Blackwell and his still at Big Hungry. Sheriff M. Allard Case made the arrest, even though Blackwell told him he "was fixin' to make some whiskey for my own use, and you got me before I made any."

According to an August 1912 *French Broad Hustler*:

> *The latest proposed addition to Laurel Park is an artificial one and will be unique. Those parts of the gigantic still captured in Polk County brought to town by Constable T.B. Conner, will be set up in Laurel Park as a curiosity. Manager Walter Smith announces that arrangements have been made to install the equipment somewhere near Crystal Springs. A complete outfit will be rigged up and the plant put in operation but the depressing side of the situation—as viewed by thirsty souls—is that Crystal Springs water will be the strongest liquid that will be allowed to issue from the coil.*

BEREA CHURCH ROAD AND OLD CAPPS CEMETERY

Farther up the pike would be another entry point to or exit point from Cathead. Leaving Cathead from Walnut Cove Road and facing Berea Church Road, one finds a lone chimney near Gilbert Cove Drive. Alec Capps (1856–1950) built a house on this site in the late 1800s, which later was owned by Harvey Franklin "Frank" Gilbert (1886–1967). The abandoned dwelling deteriorated and was razed.

Picture-perfect Berea Baptist Church stands right up against the northeastern edge of Berea Church Road. Locals claim that Cornelius Capps (1792–1860), son of William Capps Jr. (1764–1847), founded the community, and his family conducted worship services in the family's home until a church was organized in 1920. The current sanctuary replaced two others, which burned in the 1940s and 1958. A neatly kept cemetery occupies a prominence behind the church.

Backtracking to Crab Creek Road, at Kanuga Valley Lane, Case Paint & Body distinguishes the site of a farm once owned by Frank McCrary, father of the famous McCrary twins (more on them later), and just north of Kanuga Valley stands an abandoned white cinderblock building. This, the 7 to 11 Market operated by William D. Gurkin (1943–), counted among the country stores that served local farmers and campers. Gurkin lived on West Chestnut Drive on the outskirts of Hendersonville.

Delmont/Pleasant Hill

Where Little River Road empties onto Kanuga and Crab Creek Roads and across the way from Pleasant Hill Baptist Church, vines, weeds and saplings all but envelop a wooden structure on the brink of extinction, standing adjacent to the T of the three roads bordered to the north by Kanuga Lake Road and to the south by White Squirrel Lane. In the early 1900s, the Jonathan Singleton Drake family lived in this abode and also operated a store from it. The Drakes sold feed and dry goods and ran a milling operation behind their home and store.

Sifting through the history of a tiny population center such as Pleasant Hill—once known as Delmont—presents certain perplexities and challenges. Properties swapped hands, and roads changed names and became rerouted. Schools consolidated and moved, a church burned and people passed away—people who, for the most part, left few or no chronicles of their habitat and lifestyles.

The *French Broad Hustler* in October 1906 noted: "Bill Drake is erecting a handsome six-room house on his place at Pleasant Hill." On March 1912, it reported: "Pleasant Hill News—Mr. S.A. Hefner is having bad luck raising hogs for Kanuga Club. He has lost four during the past week. Mr. Roy Brown shot and killed a fine duck on Kanuga Lake the other day."

THE DRAKES OF PLEASANT HILL

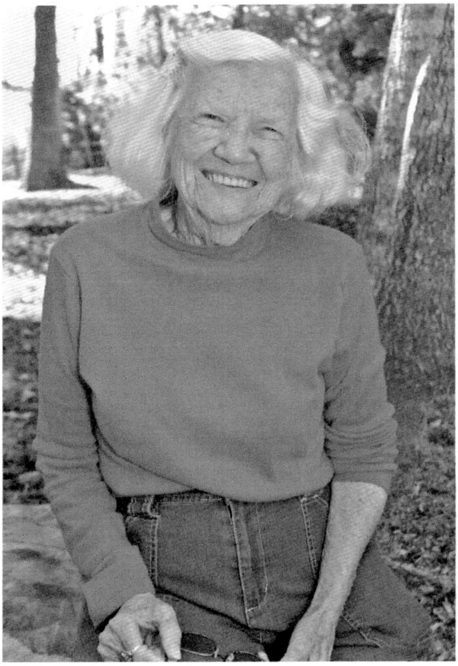
Sindy Drake Jones Justus Hamilton, 2012.

Sarah Lucille "Sindy" Drake Hamilton (1925–) recalls selling iced soft drinks and snacks to golfers at J.C. Smoot's nine-hole course when she was growing up alongside Crab Creek Road west of Little River Road. Phyllis Brown Nanney (1906–2007), another Pleasant Hill resident, caddied on the course in the days when cars or horses brought players—including vacationers from Camp Pinnacle—to the creek near the first hole. Acres of the subdivision named Sugar Hollow Farm now cover the course.

Sindy was one of Jonathan Singleton "Sing" Drake (1885–1957) and Sarah Theresa Drake's (1887–1971) seven children reared in the dwelling that now falls into disrepair near the junction. Sindy's great-uncle John Tyler Drake (1876–1927) built the house in the late 1800s for his wife, Altha Attie Anderson Drake (1883–1977), and their family and was a son of Richard Theodore Drake (1844–1930) and Elizabeth Brown Drake (1840–1888).

About her family's store, Sindy explained, "Just one large room on the ground-level. Besides the kitchen and living room, we also had one bedroom downstairs and the rest of the living quarters upstairs."

The family ran a gristmill, kept a vegetable garden and operated glass-top gasoline pumps in front of their home/store in an era before the county paved Crab Creek, Little River and Kanuga Roads. Sindy's uncle Hezekiah Elezer "Skin" Drake (1890–1964), who operated H.E. Drake Groceries on Hendersonville's Main Street and First Avenue East, sold some of the grain milled at her father's property on Crab Creek Road. Sindy explained that her uncle's "skinny frame led to his nickname 'Skin.'"

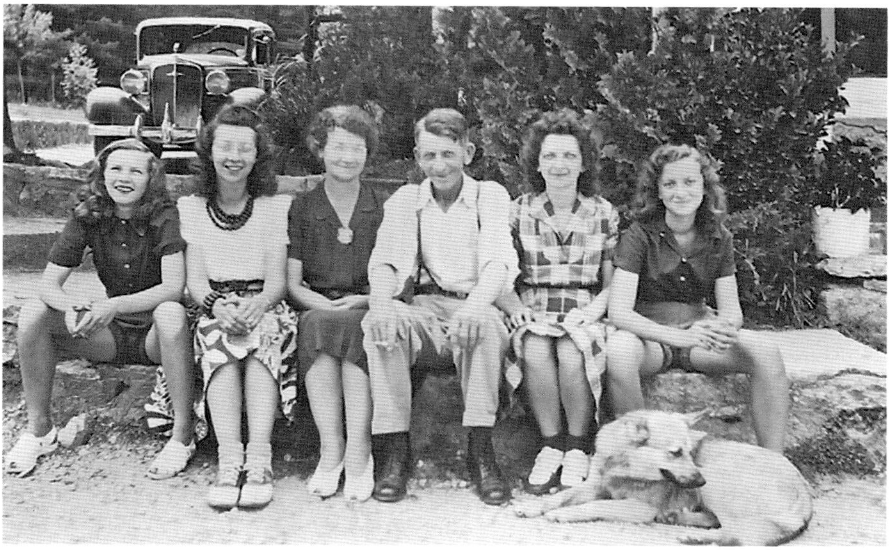

The Drake family at home in the early 1900s. *From left to right*: Sindy, Adge, Theresa, Sing, Midge, Gracie and Pal the dog. *Photo courtesy of Sindy Drake Hamilton.*

"I can still see myself standing on a chair," Sindy reminisced, "using a wall telephone, calling my brother Preston and asking him to bring me a banana from Skin Drake's store where he worked.

"Although we were poor, we had a good life. We grew most of our own food, and Mama canned, so we always had plenty to eat."

Sindy's eyes sparkled as she recalled her oldest sister, Margaret "Midge," playing a pump organ and her brother Edwin strumming a guitar in the parlor of that old house. "We'd all sing," she said, "and we held street dances and played ball out there before the roadbed was paved over. There wasn't much traffic when it was a narrow dirt track."

In his book *Postmarks*, Lenoir Ray, one of Henderson County's early rural postal carriers, mentioned the Delmont Post Office having been established in 1881 with Lawrence Earle Turpin (1860–1905) as its first postmaster. When mail service was discontinued at Knight in 1894, its mail went to Delmont. Ray also explained, "While the exact location of the post office is not known, in later years it was in the store building on the Crab Creek road opposite the Pleasant Hill Baptist Church."

Kirkwood King (1850–1928), son of Jason King (1825–1906), was appointed postmaster at Delmont in 1882 and served for twelve years before Adina Anderson (1873–1896) succeeded him in 1894. When Adina died at twenty-two years old, her sister Clelia replaced her. Clelia's uncle Joel M. Anderson succeeded her when she moved to South Carolina to marry in 1900. Joel moved to the East Flat Rock Post Office in 1901, and Margaret J. Wilkie (1854–1930) replaced him, acting as postmistress until 1904, when rural service out of Hendersonville supplanted the Delmont office.

PLEASANT HILL BAPTIST CHURCH

Originally known as Antioch Baptist Church, organized as a missionary Baptist church (circa 1869) on a different site, Pleasant Hill Baptist Church stands on a knoll at the corner of Little River and Crab Creek Roads. Its founders, Martha Buckner, Sarah Buckner and James B. Drake (1870–1955), deeded "one-half acre, more or less" in 1882 (*Henderson County Deeds*, Vol. 54), and F.C. Abbott and Annie B. Abbott of Charlotte, North Carolina, deeded "one acre, more or less" in 1908 (*Henderson County Deeds*, Vol. 61). As were so many small country churches, Pleasant Hill's sanctuary was sheathed in clapboard painted white, with a large belfry relative to the scale of the church—a tower featuring Gothic apertures and a rose window.

In January 1907, the *French Broad Hustler* printed the following:

> *Kindly allow me space in your valuable paper for a few words in regard to my work at Pleasant Hill Church, where I have been serving as pastor for the past year. My work with these good people has been very pleasant. We had a glorious meeting last Sunday. After preaching to a large congregation, in company with J.R. Wilkie, I went to the home of brother L.E. Rackley, where we partook of his hospitality. We then went to Mud Creek Church, where I preached to an attentive audience. After preaching I went to the home of J.S. Hefner, where I united in the bonds of holy matrimony S.D. Capps of Shaws Creek and Miss Rachel Hefner, daughter of J.S. Hefner. Many friends and relatives were present. I am glad to know there are so many kind and generous hearted people in Henderson County. Yours in the work, C.D. Cole.*

Dedicated in 1901, Pleasant Hill Baptist Church then supported 231 members under the guidance of Reverend Elijah Marion Allison (1839–1923). Early congregants included Andersons, Coles, Drakes, Freemans, Gosses, Huntleys, Masons, Orrs, Stanleys, Stepps and Wilkies, with E.A.

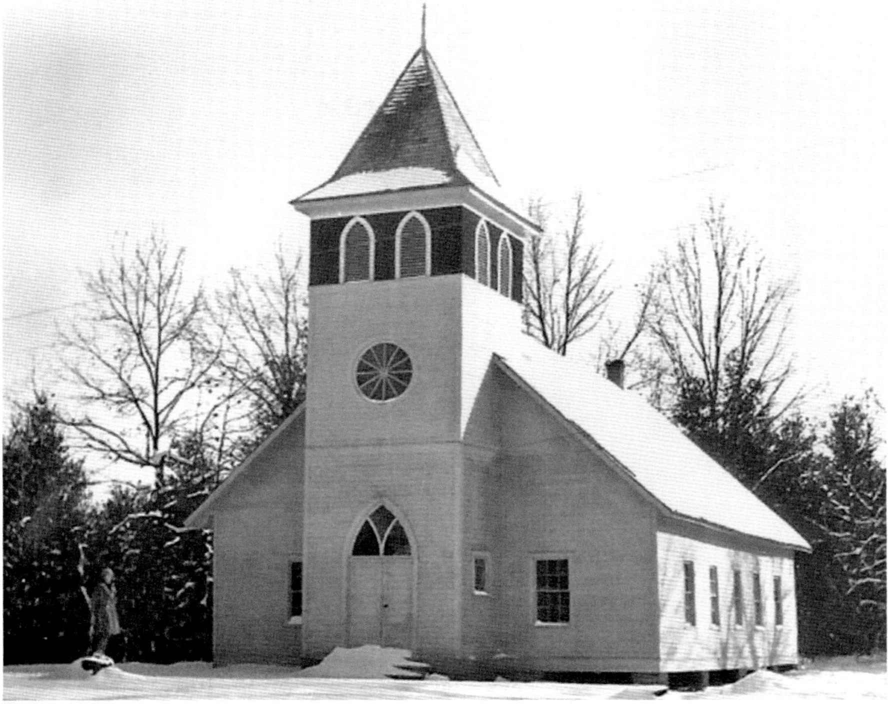

The 1901 Pleasant Hill Baptist Church. *Photo courtesy of Sindy Drake Hamilton.*

Drake (1847–1909) and his wife, Eugenia Foulds Drake (1856–1922), two of its oldest members. For several years, the church offered services on the last Saturday and Sunday of each month. Other former pastors included the Reverends Robert F. Hamilton, Oscar Orr, R.R. Mahaffey, Lawrence Anderson, C.D. Cole, Dan Willis, Albert Jones, Lawrence Rhodes, Jesse E. Osteen and Harold L. McKinnish. In October 1913, the *French Broad Hustler* reported:

> *The annual session of the Carolina Baptist Association, composed of 36 churches of Henderson and Polk Counties, met with Pleasant Hill Church near Hendersonville Thursday and Friday of last week. Reverend R.N. Pratt preached the annual sermon, which was interesting and helpful, following which, Reverend. A.I. Justice perfected an organization as moderator with F.D. Brown serving as clerk. Reverend K.W. Cawthon and Mr. Brown made reports from churches.*

In 1957, several members of the church filed suit against supply pastor Julian Edward Corn (1925–2011)—after Corn withdrew Pleasant Hill Church from the Carolina Baptist Convention—stating that Corn had departed from the characteristic doctrines, practices, usage and customs of the church. The case, *State v. Edward Corn*, read in part:

> *...defendant Edward Corn has also had many of the above named plaintiffs wrongfully and illegally expelled from the membership of said Church for no other reason than their refusal to follow his leadership in his efforts to destroy said Church as a Missionary Baptist Church. In the conferences and in his preaching, he often becomes very bitter against those who do not follow his leadership, and on one occasion provoked an altercation between one of his followers and one of the plaintiffs herein, and on another occasion he stated that he was glad that the members who were not attending were gone and "he hoped the fire had gone with them." During the church services he dances, jumps and hollers, leaps over benches and chairs, and many of the above-named defendants who are following his leadership do the same thing, and such conduct creates so much noise and confusion that there can be no Christian worship in any of said services, and very often the noise and uproar are such that they disturb people living in the immediate vicinity of the church and the services amount to no more than solemn mockery.*

Zeb V. Nettles, judge of the Twenty-eighth Judicial District of North Carolina, heard the case. The law firm of Redden, Redden & Redden and J.E. Shipman acted as attorneys for the plaintiffs. The plaintiffs won their case, and Corn was dismissed.

The clapboard building burned to the ground in a suspected arson fire on June 23, 1971. Phil Grose III and Mike Grose reported the fire, to which Valley Hill, Blue Ridge and Etowah-Horse Shoe Fire Departments responded. At the time, membership had dwindled to forty regular attendants. Today, the original church bell stands atop a brick platform facing Crab Creek Road, and the members rebuilt a brick sanctuary in 1972. Reverend Jonathan Rackley of Rosman currently leads the small congregation. In mid-December 2012, the church sponsored its first live Nativity and plans to continue the tradition on an expanded basis.

James Robert Arrowood, volunteer firefighter with the Valley Hill Fire Department and twenty-six years of age at the time, was convicted of four arson fires in 1971: Flat Rock Junior High School on August 18, Balfour Elementary School on August 21, Fruitland Bible School on August 30 and the

Herbert Merrill residence on Terry's Gap Road in Fruitland. Other suspected arson fires at the time included Pleasant Hill Baptist Church and the attempt to burn Hillandale Elementary School, a hay barn on Kanuga Road, Jones Gap Baptist Church and the Stepp family's café at Dana. Arrowood, a self-employed carpenter and contractor, lived at Osceola Lake. According to Valley Hill Fire Department battalion chief Tim Garren, after serving time, Arrowood moved to Chapel Hill and married a woman twenty-two years his senior. His body was found in the trunk of a car in Biloxi, Mississippi, the cause of death determined as "a blow to the head with a blunt instrument."

THE HEMLOCKS/WOODHAVEN

Martha Connell Grose (1939–), retired Hendersonville city clerk and tax collector (1958–72), grew up on her family's ancestral farm near Pleasant Hill Baptist Church, where her husband, P.H. Grose Jr. (1925–), once served as a deacon. Martha's great-grandparents were William Coubro Connell (1833–1918) and Agnes McNee Connell (1838–1923). After Lady Agnes McNee fell in love with her family's gardener, William Coubro Connell, her parents banished the couple from Scotland. They married, moved to Henderson County in the mid-1800s and bought a house on a tract of forested land named the Hemlocks, in what was then considered a part of Flat Rock, from Matthew Richard Singleton (1817–1854), one of the original stockholders of the Farmer Hotel Company in Flat Rock. Izard Middleton built the house in 1838, described by author Blanche Marsh as "grand and spacious with Tudor-style chimneys." It has been written that the farm boasted perhaps the largest hemlock tree east of the Rocky Mountains. Matthew R. Singleton, a member of St. John in the Wilderness Church at Flat Rock, bought the property in 1847. Singleton helped collect funds to enlarge the church. As late as the early twentieth century, an original painting of Queen Victoria hung in the house at the Hemlocks, a portrait given by the queen to the family of Lady Agnes McNee Connell.

The Connells operated a self-sustaining farm in the Hemlocks within what is now called Woodhaven, a modern subdivision off Little River Road across from Camp Pinnacle, entered via Woodhaven Drive. Mr. Connell was an officer in organizing the first Western North Carolina Fair, which was held in Laurel Park. Elected as representative of Flat Rock in 1907 to a prohibition campaign, he also worked for the cause of temperance in Henderson County.

By the late 1900s, the Connell home had fallen into disrepair and was razed. The property was overgrown by the time Carl B. Fisher (1920–) of Connecticut and his cousin Charles Barker Jr. (1947–) of Hendersonville ventured to develop eighty acres of it in 1977. The partnership led to Woodhaven Homes, Inc., and Fisher had the first house built there for himself and his wife, Mary B. Fisher. Fisher, a U.S. Air Force colonel, later worked in the aerospace industry. He was also an assistant to President Eisenhower for aviation and a director of research and development for the Federal Aviation Administration.

The Fisher-Barker venture later purchased sixty-nine acres from contiguous Pleasant Hill Farms, including the historic house Pleasant Hill (circa 1839). Fisher had the granite pillars that marked the Old Town Way entrance into Pleasant Hill removed and placed at the entrance to Woodhaven on Little River Road. As there was no Little River Road in the days of the building of Pleasant Hill, could Old Town Way have been the "Dark Valley Road" connecting Beaumont and Pleasant Hill, referred to by Sadie Smathers Patton and other writers of the earlier history of Henderson County? According to Patton, this was a quarry road passing through the Mud Creek swamp. Christopher Gustavus Memminger (1803–1888) and Andrew Johnstone (1805–1864) were those attributed to having opened Little River Road.

The Fishers named the subdivision Woodhaven after an area where they lived in McLean, Virginia. An enormous stump is all that remains today of the namesake hemlock.

The *French Broad Hustler*, in September 1906, noted: "J.C. Connell of Pleasant Hill has sold 100 acres of his farmland in that section for $4,000. Mr. Connell is one of the most progressive farmers of Henderson County."

Just east of Woodhaven lies a road named for the historic home of William Johnstone, entered via Pleasant Hill Drive. William Johnstone (1829–1893), son of Andrew Johnstone, sold the property and home known as Pleasant Hill to a relative, Dr. Means of Parris Island, in 1858. The property has since passed through numerous hands.

PLEASANT HILL, VALLEY HILL AND ATKINSON SCHOOLS

Little has been written and recorded about the elementary school at Pleasant Hill. Though it opened as recently as the turn of the twentieth century, only one photograph seems to exist, with records nonexistent. We do know the

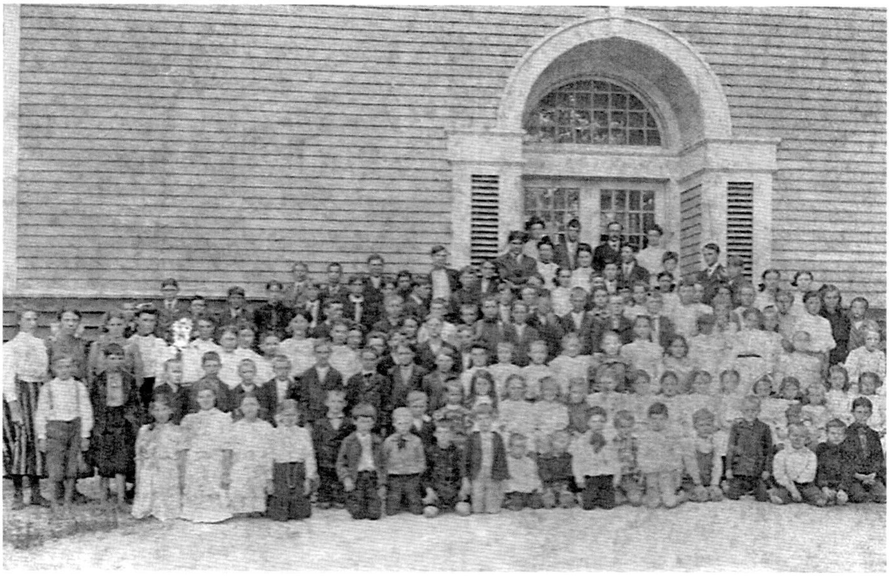

Pleasant Hill School. *Photo courtesy of Henderson County Genealogical and Historical Society, Inc.*

one-room school stood on Kanuga Road north of Little River Road near the junction of Old Kanuga Road, where a house stands today. The student body outgrew the capacity of the schoolhouse, and in 1938, the pupils joined Valley Hill School.

Enie Pace, a student at Pleasant Hill, recalls an unpleasant incident. "They heated the schoolhouse with a potbellied stove," she said. "Rufus and Margaret Brown's daughter Evelyn was a student there, and one day little Evelyn stoked the stove with a wad of papers, which backfired and burned her severely."

Sketchy accounts mention that in the early 1900s, A. Ficker[9] gave an acre of land with a log structure on it for the purpose of establishing a school. This would become known as the Ficker School.

In 1908, Dorothy "Dollie" Philpot Morris Osborne (1858–1928), part-time resident from Ohio, gave funds to build a new educational facility on the Ficker property, and shortly thereafter men in the community built a three-room school named Valley Hill. A five-classroom building replaced it in 1919, and in 1928, Valley Hill's student body included grades one through eleven. The school's five rooms made it of a size to earn an accreditation

9. Some texts state that "Arnold Ficker" donated the land and cabin for the beginning of Valley Hill School, but research suggests it was likely Adolf Ficker (1864–1955).

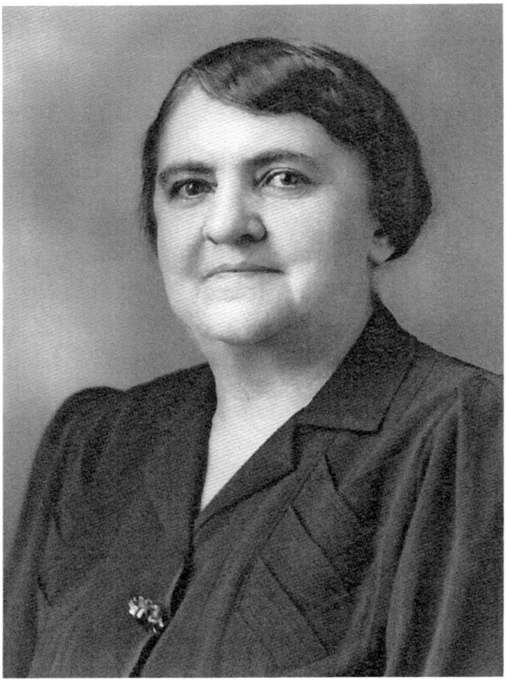

Julia Trimble Redden. *Photo courtesy of Valley Hill Baptist Church, Reverend Danny Pridmore and Virginia Laughter Hamilton.*

standard. Laboratory facilities increased to the point of offering equipment and facilities for all high school science courses. The school's library has been described as outstanding, for its time, in the county system—the last step required for its full accreditation, and in 1930 Valley Hill was deemed an accredited high school. Further accounts state that "through the efforts of Mrs. Julia Redden and Mrs. Bennison the school's music department flourished." Redden, a charter member of and organist for Valley Hill Baptist Church, was Valley Hill School's first principal, succeeded by Clara Mae Capps Babb (1906–1999) and then Ted Warren Reed (1933–2002). In 1934, Valley Hill's high school students transferred to Flat Rock.

In front of the empty Valley Hill School stands a granite monument with a bronze plaque bearing a tribute to Julia Sophronia Trimble Redden (1878–1951), originally from Louisiana and wife of John Lewis Redden (1865–1944). Mrs. Redden's commemorative plaque reads: "In loving memory of Julia Trimble Redden who served Valley Hill Community forty-three years. She fought a good fight and finished her course."

Mrs. Redden, known affectionately to hundreds of pupils as "Mother Redden," was among the first women to earn prestige as a principal in North Carolina, "for in those early days only men were considered strong enough to cope with the strong and sturdy mountain youth," according to a September 4, 1969 article in the *Western Carolina Tribune*. The subheading of the *Tribune* article stated, "She was the epitome of the immortal schoolmarm who made a nation great; made men of boys and mothers of girls." Mrs. Redden—whose motto was "not teaching subjects, but teaching boys and girls"—saw Valley Hill School grow from the one-teacher facility of Pleasant Hill School to an accredited high school. A big move for consolidation reduced Valley Hill to an elementary school, and Mrs. Redden worked to make it accredited.

When Redden's son Monroe Minor Redden (1901–1987) was elected to Congress of the United States, she was quoted as having said, "I know he will do what he thinks is right; but that doesn't make him any better than anyone else. He has a great responsibility." Mrs. Redden retired in 1945.

With its construction begun in 1981 and completed in 1983, Atkinson Elementary School opened on Old Kanuga Road, and Valley Hill School was closed; its four hundred students, together with Principal Reed and the teachers, transferred to Atkinson, two miles distant but closer to the old Pleasant Hill School location. Named in honor of Mr. and Mrs. Jack Atkinson, who donated the property to the children of Henderson County, the school was designed by Six Associates, Inc., of Asheville—a firm established in 1942 by Erle G. Stillwell and five other prominent western North Carolina architects. Plans entailed preserving the natural surroundings, including a branch of Perry Creek that runs through the property. Atkinson Elementary School was one of the first green buildings in Henderson County, designed with skylights and atriums and rigged for solar panels. The architects planned solar IV in their original design, but budgetary matters precluded these features. Margaret Jane Pardee (1940–), daughter of Ivor and Jane Pardee, donated land abutting the Atkinson property, bringing the property to a total of twenty acres.

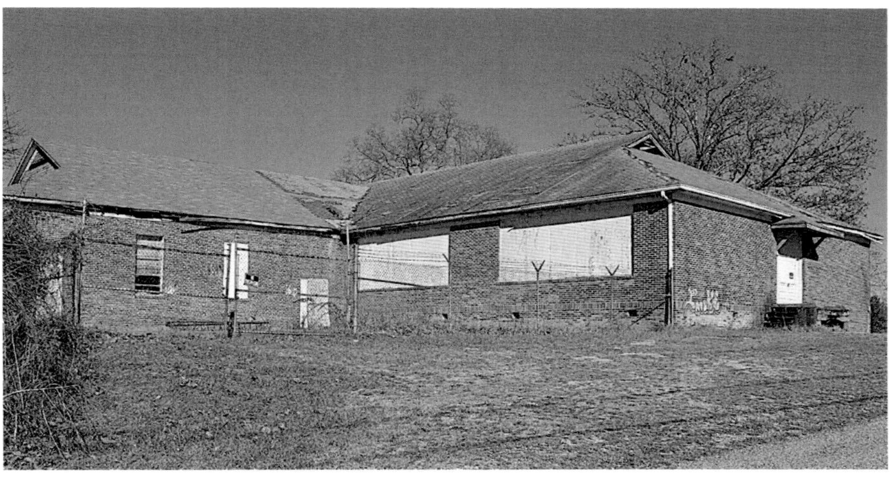

The abandoned Valley Hill School.

Much of the playground equipment from Valley Hill School was moved to the new Atkinson playgrounds for the enjoyment of students from kindergarten through sixth grades. The old Valley Hill School served as Pathway Christian Academy from 1999 to 2007.

KANUGA, A PLACE OF BRIARS

Just north of the old Drake store, a tall triangular kiosk once stood atop a rock foundation at the corner of Kanuga Road and Kanuga Lake Road, directing retreatants and campers to the summit of the hill. Small brown signs now guide the way to the wooded sanctuary—providing white pine fronds have not blurred the white lettering from view.

ARROWHEAD HILL

Making the turn west at Kanuga Lake Road, one passes the subdivisions of Sugar Hollow Farm and the Wilson Farm on the right and Nighthawk Lane—a private driveway—on the left. This driveway wends its way—through a gatehouse—to a soaring elevation where perches a nine-thousand-square-foot, half-timbered, stone-and-stucco mansion. Walter Boyer Gillican (1874–1954) and his wife, Lucile Reynolds Arndell Gillican (1884–1976), of New Orleans, visited and became enamored of the location in 1916 and bought the property in 1918 for a summer home, for which they hired architect Erle G. Stillwell. The property encompassed views of Kanuga Lake before the woods matured, and Stillwell designed the house to take advantage of cool mountain breezes, incorporating open porches and interior stone facings. The Gillicans named the property Arrowhead Hill because of the numerous Indian artifacts unearthed there. Arrowhead Hill included a gatehouse with servants' quarters, barn, greenhouse, pond, tennis court, apple orchard and vegetable and flower gardens. Gillican, a partner in Gillican-Chipley Company and owner of New Orleans Naval Stores Company and Fort Bayou Turpentine Company, amassed enormous wealth from his lumber, turpentine and railroad interests. He owned miles of pine forest along Florida's Gulf Coast, and some say Gillican cornered the world market on turpentine production.

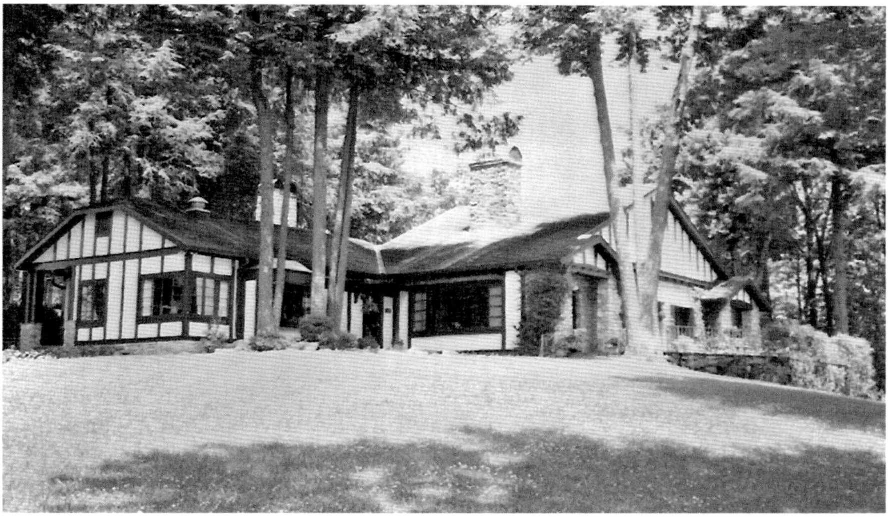

Arrowhead Hill. *Photo courtesy of Sally Walker Hughes.*

The Gillicans hired local farmer Zollie M. Prince (1903–1978) as a caretaker. Before they sold Arrowhead Hill, they bought Mr. Prince a property in the Little River community. Sindy Drake's sister Anvalie "Adge" Drake did domestic chores for the Gillicans.

"We liked them," Sindy remarked. "They were friendly and very good to my sister. A lot of kids got jobs that way, working part time for summer residents."

James Clinton Smoot Jr. (1900–1987) of the Parish of Terrebonne, Louisiana, and president of Smoot-Beeson S.A. of Panama City, Republic of Panama, purchased the Arrowhead Hill property and additional acreage in what is now Sugar Hollow Farm, including its golf course, in 1943. J.C. and Jeanne Locke Smoot (1899–1993) enlarged the residence, enclosed its porches, enswathed the living room's walls and fireplaces of native stone with sheetrock and paneling, concealed hand-carved beams and lowered the ceilings. J.C. Smoot in turn sold the house and twenty-five acres of the estate to Radford Crane (1911–1981) of Florida in 1960.

Hassan Abdulla Mansouri (1931–), formerly of Bahrain, purchased the property in 1995—which was renamed Arrowhead Farm. He felled a number of trees and replaced the original shingle roof with one of metal. Mansouri also bought the Woodfield Inn at Flat Rock—built in 1852, known then as Farmers Hotel—and renamed it Mansouri Mansion.

SUGAR HOLLOW FARM AND THE WILSON FARM

Adjacent to Arrowhead Farm—and accessed via Kanuga Lake Road—lay two subdivisions, once parts of the Kanuga Lake Club and later sold to James C. and Jeanne Smoot, who in turn sold 220 acres in 1959 to Robert Lawrence Rickel (1920–1987) and Helen Ogle Rickel (1924–2011) of Broward County, Florida. Rickel operated a beef-cattle business on the acreage. Charles Douglas Wilson (1895–1973) and Lois Wilson (1897–1988) of Greenville, South Carolina, bought the property from the Rickels in 1965 in the name of W&W Land Company. (The deed mentions "property of Margaret Drumbarh Shaffer and M. Lee Shaffer, 1948," *Henderson County Deeds*, Vol. 284.) Wilson, the principal owner of a South Carolina statewide mortgage lending and servicing company, also operated insurance and real estate concerns in Greenville and a cattle farm near Travelers Rest, South Carolina. The Wilsons used the W&W Land Company parcel in Hendersonville for pasturing cattle and harvesting hay.

The Wilsons' grandson John Walker (1953–) described the ranch as "studded with numerous barns, and the land fenced and cross-fenced from the Rickels' tenure there. The fertile soil and mild weather—usually wet in those days—yielded top-quality pasturage, and each year the calves produced were amazingly large, healthy and uniform in size. The herd won

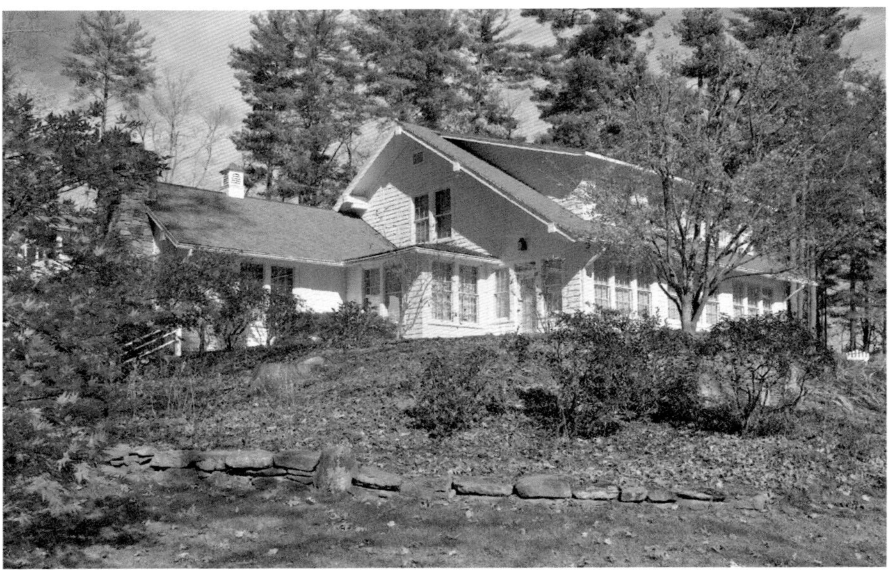

The farmhouse at the Wilson Farm.

the Greenville County Beef Cattle Association's award for best weights of calves on two occasions. Clemson University selected members of the herd for bio-stimulant experiments because the uniformity of the cattle provided excellent test-and-control samples."

The Wilson family kept Angus cattle on the property until 1982 and sold twelve acres of it, including the farmhouse, to Jeffrey E. and Alicia H. Boyle in 1992. The Boyles added a barn, fencing and paddock near the pond at the entrance to the community.

John Walker and his brothers, J. Herman and Douglas, inherited part interest in the farm, acquired the rest of it with another ten acres and began developing it as the Wilson Farm subdivision in 1983. The Walker brothers sold ninety acres of the land to Pete Green in 1986, which Green developed as Sugar Hollow Farm under the name of the Green Company. Both farms were outfitted with underground utility lines. In 1997, James Earl Thompson (1933–2012) and Janet T. Thompson (1937–) purchased the Boyles' twelve acres and farmhouse in the Wilson Farm.

Brigadier General Frank B. Blazey Jr. (1924–) currently owns and lives in the farmhouse (circa 1909) in the Sugar Hollow Farm subdivision, and Mrs. James E. Thompson lives in the farmhouse (circa 1909) in the Wilson Farm. Although we find nothing on the architect for the two aforementioned farmhouses, one can only assume that Richard Sharp Smith designed them, since George Stephens, who hired Smith's services for his Kanuga Lake Club, owned the

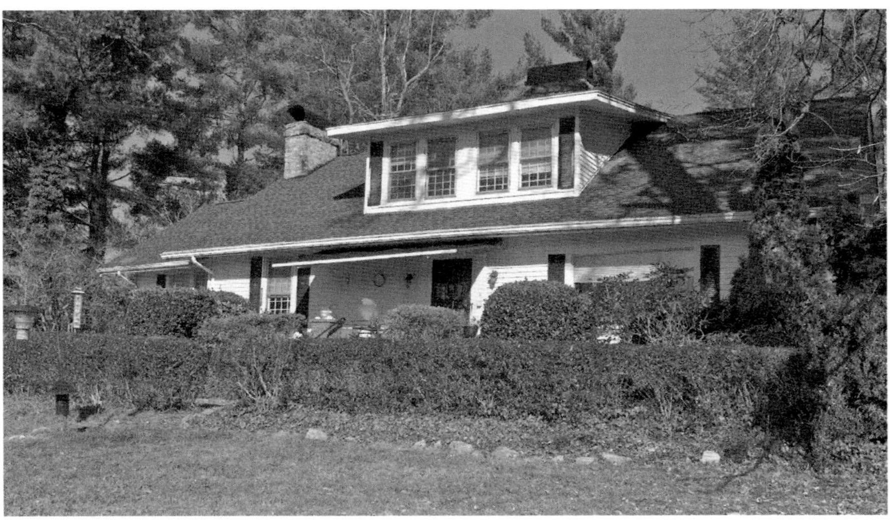

The farmhouse at Sugar Hollow Farm.

land under the houses during the dates of their construction, the period when Smith designed the cottages and clubhouse for Stephens's facility.

The lineage of ownership of the farmhouse and associated property in Sugar Hollow Farm includes, in order of succession: Walter Lambeth, George Stephens, Charles C. and Margaret G. Krumbhoor, Margaret Minor Krumbhoor Shaffer, James Clinton Smoot Jr. and Jeanne Locke Smoot, William Gardner, H.B. Owsley and David C. Howard and Christine H. MacMartin, who sold to Frank B. Blazey and Joy Drew Blazey (1924–2013) in 1971.

Each of the Sugar Hollow and Wilson Farm farmhouses, once covered in shake shingles, has been modified and enlarged, including the enclosure of sun porches. The Blazey property includes its seven original stone fireplaces, a log-constructed icehouse and separate servants' quarters.

CAMPS

The woods were my Ritalin. Nature calmed me, focused me, and yet excited my senses.
—*Richard Louv, author of* Last Child in the Woods

The region of Pleasant Hill is rife with recreational facilities. Besides those at Kanuga Conferences, the neighboring girls' Camp Ton-A-Wandah (at Lake Falls Road off Little River Road), United Methodist Camp Tekoa (at Thomas Road off Crab Creek Road) and Camp Pinnacle at the Wolf Lake reservoir (at Wolfe Lake Drive off Little River Road) count among nature's local playgrounds.

Tekoa

Established as Camp Bar-H by Henry Bartol Jr. of Tryon, North Carolina, in 1947, the facility with its spring-fed three-acre lake was renamed Camp Tekoa under the ownership of the Western North Carolina Conference of the United Methodist Church when the organization took it over in 1980. Henry George "Skipper" Bartol Jr. (1908–1974), a former lieutenant commander, USNR, and part owner of WTYN in Tryon from 1956 to 1971, served as director of the camp.

Originally, Henry Bartol and Baxter Morgan Haynes Jr. (1909–2002) owned the property in partnership, adding cabins, a water storage tank,

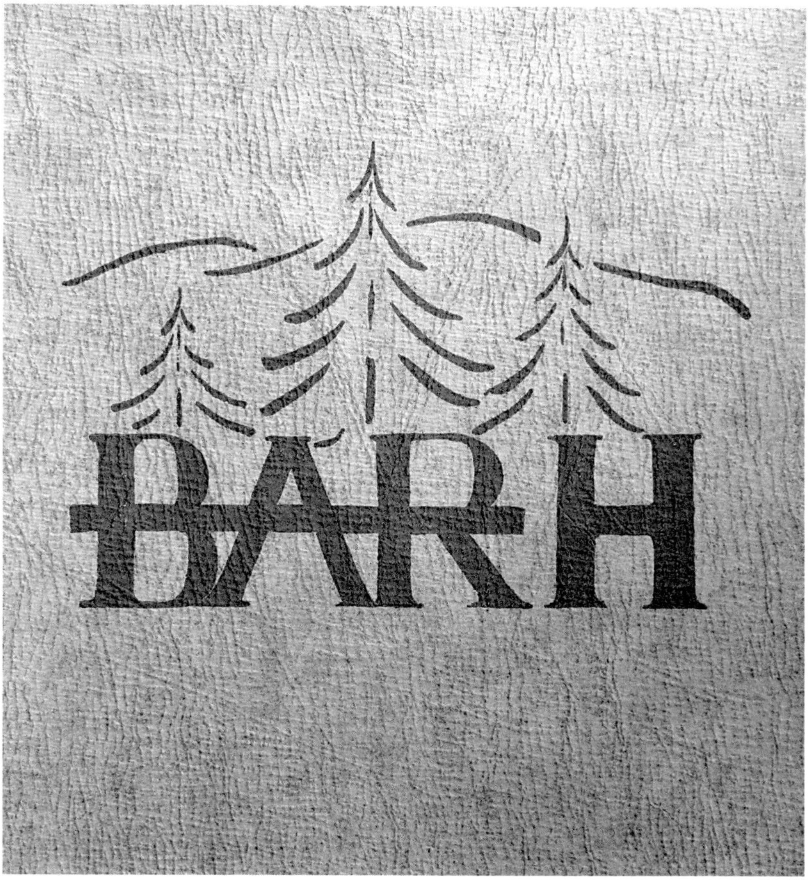

A 1940s Camp Bar-H brochure. *Courtesy of James Johnson, Camp Tekoa.*

a bathhouse, septic facilities and a barn and ran it as a private summer camp for boys in the 1940s. At the end of the first season, Haynes sold his interest to Bartol, who continued to run it until the Board of Education of the Methodist organization bought it for $57,500 in April 1949. The group made it a year-round coed camp and retreat center, with the mission: "Touching hearts, changing lives, sharing the light of Christ."

The name Tekoa is the biblical name of a city in south Judah most famous for being the home of the prophet Amos. In Hebrew, the prénom Tekoa means "trumpet," or "sound of the trumpet," and in days of old was most often used as a boy's name. Other sources suggest that Tekoa originally meant "the pitching of tents."

Pinnacle

Near what is now Wolf Lake, the Pinnacle Post Office opened in 1875 with Jason King, a miller, as its first postmaster. Now a nondenominational destination, its wooded campgrounds swathe the shores of eighteen-acre Wolf Lake between Little River and Crab Creek Roads. Unlike other area camps with all-boys, all-girls or coed formats, Pinnacle operates with a "brother-sister" format: separate programs for each gender, with concurrent dates.

In 1927, Hubert Ray "Red" Dobson (1900–1959), a football coach from South Carolina, brought a group of boys to the mountains of western North Carolina for the coming football season, and the assembly camped at Wolf Lake. The following year, Dobson established Camp Pinnacle for Boys. In 1929, Dobson formed a partnership with Van Carl Kussrow Sr. (1899–1988), a business leader from Miami Beach, Florida. Kussrow had seen the property while vacationing in the area, and at the recommendation of Reese Combs, his former Miami scout master, Kussrow agreed in a joint venture to purchase the property. Kussrow's business acumen combined with Dobson's athletic ability and teaching skills provided for a highly successful and complementary partnership. The affiliation endured for thirty years until Dobson's death in 1959, after which a series of directors served both the boys and girls camps at Pinnacle. Camp Pinnacle was chosen as the site for the films *Heavyweights*, released in 1995; and *Secrets of the Fall*, released in the spring of 2013.

Kussrow also bought the nine-hole golf course built for George Stephens during his Kanuga Lake Club tenure. Guests of Camp Pinnacle played the course also available to local residents. The facility closed in 1942. James C. Smoot purchased the course and several surrounding acres in 1943.

In 2011, the Kussrow family leased Camp Pinnacle to the partnership of Adventure Treks and Camp Champions. Activities include water sports, trails, archery and riflery, mountain biking and crafting.

Ton-A-Wandah

A cascade bestows an awe-inspiring focal point for this campground, founded in 1933 by Alice Grace Ballenger "Donnie" Haynes (1879–1961). With a dream in her heart, Haynes leased 42 acres with an 8-acre lake within what was known then as Lake Falls Resort from W.P. Bane (1883–1959), who also had a quarry on the property. Haynes later bought the site for $24,000.

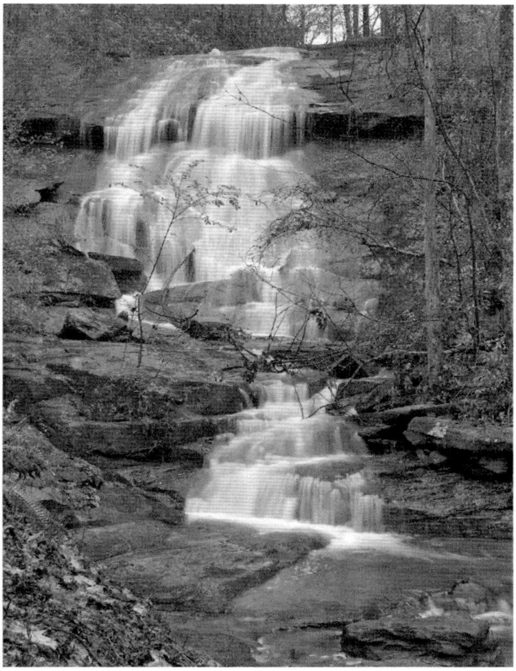

Ton-A-Wandah Falls.

Contemporary promotional materials for the camp describe it as having 365 acres and a 10-acre lake, suggesting that *ton-a-wandah* means "by the fall of water" in a Native American language, with Iroquoian sources suggesting *tahnawá-teh* as meaning "confluent stream."

For more than eight decades, Ton-A-Wandah has served as a private residential camp for girls ages six to fifteen. The facility's lake, part of which flows under the dining hall, provides outdoor activities, including canoeing and swimming. On-site stables and three riding rings offer campers a program based on the principles of hunter-seat equitation, with emphasis on safety and respect for the animal. Unlike some of the area's faith-specific camps, Ton-A-Wandah offers an interdenominational environment with optional services on Sundays. The camp's ties to nature and deep respect for Native Americans who originally inhabited these mountains invoke the inspiration behind the alliance of the camp's Three Tribes theme (Cherokee, Mohawk and Navajo) and a Tribe Day celebration. Today, Bill and Judy Haynes, third-generation owners, serve as co-directors of the camp.

YONHOLME AND THE BARROWS

Just up the way from Arrowhead Hill, hidden nearly a mile off Kanuga Lake Road via a lengthy, unpaved driveway through the woods, stands the summer compound called Yonholme. Originally the part-time home of the Hanckel family, the grand estate exudes an aura of mystery.

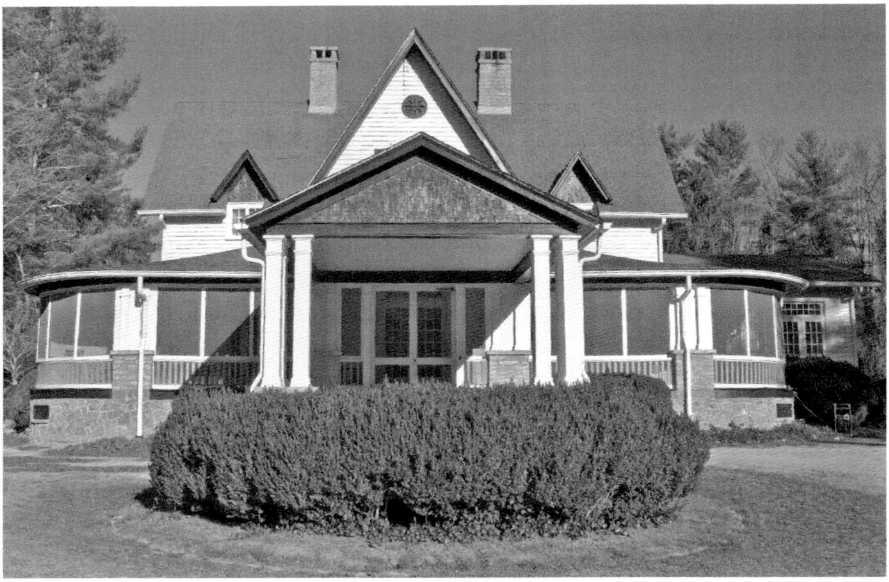

A hidden architectural treasure: Yonholme.

Following the Hanckels' tenure at the secreted property, George Stephens of Charlotte—developer of the Kanuga Lake Club—owned the tract for a short while before selling to Dr. Craig Barrow (1876–1945) and his wife, Elfrida De Renne Barrow (1884–1970). Frank L. FitzSimons Sr., register of deeds at the time, signed the deed. The Barrows owned Noble Wimberly Jones's Wormsloe Plantation near Savannah, Georgia, and summered at Yonholme in Henderson County. Craig Barrow, a descendant of Georgia colonist and Whig leader Noble Jones (1723–1805), was chief surgeon of the Central Georgia Railway, and Elfrida, also a descendant of Jones, authored several books about the history of Savannah. Their daughter Muriel Barrow Bell (1913–2011) and her husband, Malcolm Bell Jr. (1913–2001), inherited the Yonholme estate. Malcolm Bell was a banker, historian and civil rights advocate.

THE KANUGA CLUB

Continuing west up the hill past the aforementioned subdivisions and Arrowhead Farm and Yonholme, the driver, hiker or cyclist passes between hundreds of acres of dense forestland on an asphalt swath called Kanuga Lake Road. The national meeting center of Kanuga Conferences, with its associated campgrounds, currently surmounts 1,365 acres at the promontory of this 2,306-foot elevation.

In the early nineteenth century, Charlestonians and other lowlanders initiated the social custom of summering in the mountains of western North Carolina. By the early twentieth century, land speculation boomed throughout the region, including Henderson County. Although most speculators hailed from Florida, Charlotte banker, capitalist and newspaper publisher George Stephens also began buying land in Hendersonville. County deed books show Stephens's having purchased lots in Hendersonville and at Osceola Lake as early as 1899, when he also purchased 410 acres above Delmont, including what was referred to at one time as the Hanckel estate, from John H. and Margaret J. Williams of Buncombe County for $3,000. Stephens then aggressively added to the Hanckel/Williams property, acquiring contiguous plots of land from owners, including Shepherd, Brown and Merrell.

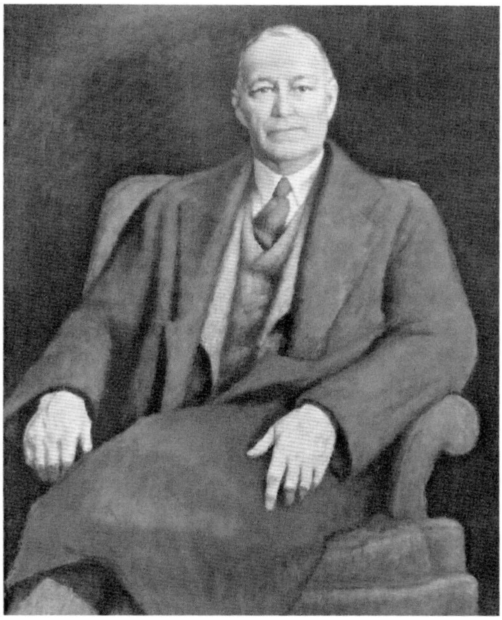

George Erwin Cullet Stephens, founder of the Kanuga Club. *Oil on canvas by American artist Wilford S. Conrow, 1943; photo courtesy of the Duke Mansion, Charlotte, North Carolina.*

FOR ONE REASON OR ANOTHER, early scribes of Henderson County history merely skimmed over the prominent Lowcountry family of Hanckels in their writings, yet the family deserves more mention here. Henderson County deed records show that land purchased by George Stephens for the nucleus of his Kanuga Lake Club at one time belonged to Reverend Christian Hanckel (1790–1870), with Annie Maxey Hanckel (1859–1937), Mary Bull Hanckel (1875–1951), Charles Francis Hanckel (1829–1898) and James Stuart Hanckel (1817–1892) recorded as Hanckel heirs. Charles's wife, Anne Matilda Heyward Hanckel (1833–1915), was daughter of Daniel

Heyward (1810–1888) of Cotton Hall Plantation in Yemassee, Beaufort County, South Carolina. Reverend James Stuart Hanckel of St. Paul's Episcopal Church of Charleston was a visiting minister to Calvary Episcopal Church in Fletcher, North Carolina, and ministered three times at St. John in the Wilderness in Flat Rock, North Carolina. Reverend Christian Hanckel's daughter Ann Stuart Hanckel Means (1812/13–1899) is buried in the churchyard of St. John in the Wilderness.

Before Transylvania County was formed, Reverend Christian Hanckel's son Reverend James Stuart Hanckel of Beaufort, South Carolina, built a Greek Revival frame-style summer residence in 1856 for his family at Dunns Rock, near what is now Brevard. Pennsylvania banker Joseph Kuhns Barclay (1864–1938) later owned this historic home, known today as the Hanckel-Barclay House.

Henderson County deed records from 1883 show that James Stuart Hanckel sold "286 acres more or less" in the area of Crab Creek to Henrietta M. Heath for $1,350. Records indicate that Solomon West (1811–1886) owned part of the property in 1857, and sections of the Crab Creek land acquired by the Hanckels once belonged to Francis Withers Johnstone (1813–1882), brother of Andrew Johnstone of Beaumont, and to Franklin Brevard Hayne (1857–1918) of New Orleans—known as one of the "Cotton Kings."

Sadie Smathers Patton makes brief mentions of Hanckels in her book *Flat Rock: The Little Charleston of the Mountains*. Patton wrote, "Dr. Christian Hanckel settled some four [five-plus] miles from the center of Flat Rock...Dr. Hanckel remained at his place until the end of the war, when it was acquired by other owners. This property of later years has been known as the Craig Barrow estate, off the road leading to the Kanuga Conference grounds."

But for the most part, the history of Hanckels in Henderson County remains sketchy.

George Stephens also purchased right of way easements—for the creation of vehicular access to his club—from Woodson Drake, N. Drake, J.S. and M.G. Hefner and J.H. Fisher, among others. His vision for the hilltop above Delmont (Pleasant Hill) was a private organization, which he named Kanuga Lake Club. At that time, 950 acres comprised Stephens's holdings for his club.

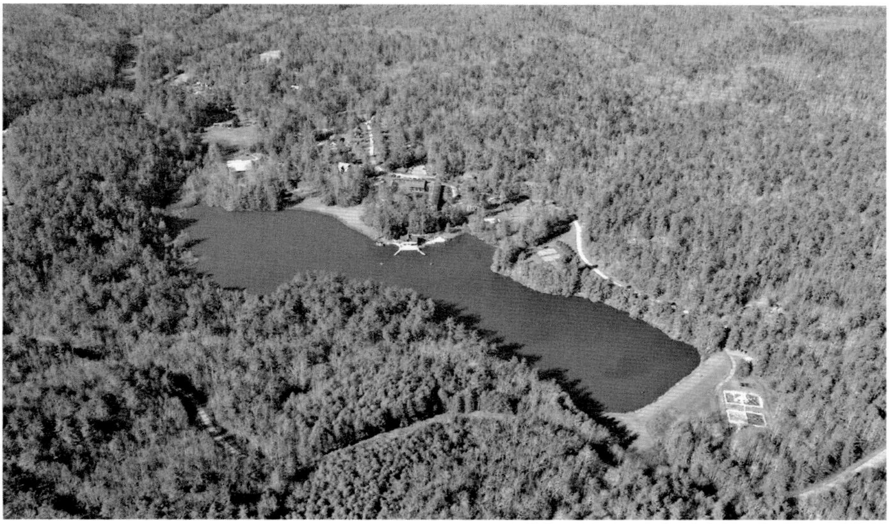

An aerial view of Kanuga Conferences. *Photo courtesy of Tim Culberson, Aerial Photo Professionals.*

An extract from the Henderson County Road Petitions and Protests minutes dated 1906–11 reads: "The establishment of this road would only do injury to private citizens without any resultant benefits to the public." One of the signers was Solomon Jones (1844–1938). The document also refers to the "Hanckel old mill place" and "the Jones store place on the Crab Creek road." Evidence of a mill on the property would include the waterfall and dam off Evans Road at the edge of Kanuga Conferences and millstones on the Arrowhead Farm property.

To fulfill his vision for Kanuga Lake Club, Stephens employed eminent southern architect (English-born) Richard Sharp Smith, as well as top American designer of the time, the Boston-based landscape architect and city planner John Nolen (1869–1937), who had studied under Frederick Law Olmsted. Nolen designed the lake, roadways and landscaping features, and Smith drafted the plans for a clubhouse/hotel and guest cottages. Nolen added stands of white pines among the volunteered evergreen and deciduous trees and bushes that included dogwood, sourwood, rhododendron and kalmia. When Stephens developed Myers Park in Charlotte, he hired Nolen as designer/planner.

Eight of the Craftsman-style cottages—the first to be built—boast stone chimneys, the others having brick. Most of the bungalows are sheathed in board-and-batten, the first six in shingles, all painted hunter green with white trim, hip roofs, multi-pane casement windows and screened-in porches and furnished with Mission-style oak furniture designed by Richard Sharp Smith, crafted from trees felled on the property.

With fellow University of North Carolina–Chapel Hill alumni, Stephens established the Kanuga Lake Club in 1907, after which the group had Little Mud Creek dammed in 1908, impounding its waters to create a one-hundred-acre lake as the centerpiece of the club. Architect Smith defined the character of the woodland setting with rustic one-story frame Craftsman cottages, planning the architecture so as not to mar the beauty of the lakeside village.

Stephens sold memberships mainly to alumni and other colleagues of Mecklenburg County. The cost of membership: $150 for a period of ten years, with funds raised through memberships to be used to erect facilities. Members of the privately held club—called Kanugans and Tribesmen as a promotional effort—would enjoy the privileges of lake sports, tennis and shuffleboard courts, baseball grounds, golf links, trails, a lakeside pavilion and clubhouse and bridle paths. Charles Gilmore Tatum (1877–1964) supplied horses from his livery stable in Hendersonville.

Hendersonville's early newspaper, the *French Broad Hustler*, made several mentions of the progress of the Kanuga Club. In an October 1908 article, the *Hustler* wrote that W.W. Bell of the *Charlotte Observer* spent time in Hendersonville to gather information for his paper about

> *Mr. George Stevens'* [sic] *gigantic development proposition of the old Hanckel property near this city. Work is now actually beginning on the lake, a large group of men, with teams and machinery, being actively at work.*
>
> *Really, the plan is to form a cooperative summer colony in the mountains. A membership for 10 years will cost $100* [sic], *payable in monthly installments of $15 each. The money derived from the first two hundred members, $20,000, will be used in the development of the property. The lake and buildings will be completed by next season.*
>
> *A member's privileges are: the dispensation of residence; he may board at the clubhouse at actual cost. The clubhouse will mostly be a high-class summer hotel; or he may live in one of the modern cottages to be built and take his meals at the clubhouse. These cottages will have a bath, telephone, electric lights, etc. Then there will be the use of tennis courts, baseball grounds, golf links, the drives and bridle paths of the estate.*
>
> *To each member of the first colony of 200 will be given a lot, 200 x 50 feet. An attractive six-room house will be built on this lot for the member*

> *for $1,000, the actual cost, there being no desire to make any profit on any building for the membership.*
>
> *No cottage costing less than $400, or more than $2,500, may be built. There will be the rental stable, where horses may be boarded at cost, the electric lighting from waterpower of the dam and a telephone system. The water for the clubhouse and cottages will come from far up in the mountains.*
>
> *There will be a resident physician, Dr. C.S. Mangum, of the University of North Carolina. There will be a kindergarten, and a "boy's leader."*
>
> *Only those personally known to Mr. Stevens* [sic] *or recommended by some member of the colony are eligible for membership.*
>
> *The lake itself is 125 feet higher than Hendersonville and comprises 1,000* [sic] *acres, and is about four miles from this city as the crow flies. A new gravel road will be built to the lake from this city.*
>
> *Mr. John Noland,* [sic.] *a noted landscape engineer is in charge of that feature of the work. Mr. R.S. Smith of Asheville will approve all plans for clubhouse or cottages, that "jarring contradictions in design" may not disturb the beauty of this lake village.*
>
> *Among those already members are the following: Dr. Francis Preston Venable, president of the University of North Carolina, and 42 gentlemen from Charlotte, the home of Mr. Stevens* [sic].

A 1908 *Hustler* article titled, "BEAUTIFUL KANUGA LAKE AND SOME LOCAL STOCKHOLDERS" stated that construction of the clubhouse had been started and would cost over $10,000. At the time, Stephens remarked that the club had received—even surpassing his expectations—much encouragement. Local members at that time included J.H. Justus, druggist; W.A. Smith, lawyer; Captain M.C. Toms, farmer; K.G. Morris, banker; J.G. Waldrop, physician; Charles E. Pless, stationer; M.G. Ewart, lawyer; Sam T. Hodges, traveling salesman; Dr. J. Steven Brown, physician; Dr. J.L. Egerton, physician; Dr. A.B. Drafts, physician; A.F. Baker, photographer; and Wiltshire Griffith, pharmacist.

In the same year, the *Hustler* covered the development of Osceola Lake, with contractor Henry Jordan in charge. A sixty-room hotel was planned for Osceola, with thirty rooms charted for completion by its next season. A January 1909 article in the *Hustler* reported:

> *Hendersonville, next summer, at Kanuga Lake, will have golf links unsurpassed in this country, amidst surroundings of such wonderful natural beauty that no other place in the world may be compared with them. This*

> *is but one feature of the greatest enterprise now under way here—Kanuga Lake—Mr. George Steven's* [sic] *gigantic proposition near town, which will result in bringing hundreds of the best known bankers, editors, doctors, lawyers, and professional men in the state to Hendersonville. An army of men is now employed at Kanuga Lake, which, with its big clubhouse and many cottages will be ready by next season. Some of the best known players of this country will be here next summer for the great golf tournament to be held at the lake during the week of the mid-summer horse show, and the nine-hole course will be the equal of any in the country.*

Henderson County certainly was poised as a tourist destination.

By March 1909, Stephens's "army of men" and one hundred mules continued work at Kanuga Lake, the clubhouse coming well along, cottages started and roads being laid out. An electric bus with a capacity for sixteen passengers would carry visitors from the Southern Railway depot to the lake along a new road to be built. At the same time, Osceola Lake was filled.

As water rose at Kanuga Lake, the *Hustler* mentioned a flock of fifteen wild ducks having been spotted there. The article also mentioned twenty-five miles of roads and trails being completed at Kanuga and one mile of the private road from town having been finished. Contractors paneled the interior of the clubhouse with oak, and twenty to thirty cottages would be ready for the upcoming season. With the harvesting of on-site lumber for the purpose of constructing buildings and furniture, and with its own hydroelectric plant, the facility would operate sustainably—"green" way ahead of its time.

In April 1909, the *Charlotte Observer* reported:

> *Kanuga Club, the cooperative residential colony near Hendersonville, will open for the season July 1. Mr. George Stephens, of Charlotte, who devised the scheme, launched it and who has brought it to its present stage of development, has just issued a concise description folder in which all the information members may desire is to be found.*
>
> *The idea is, summer living on the cooperative plan at the mere cost of maintenance. The plan includes a clubhouse where the members may board, and colony cottages, which may be rented at low cost, in lieu of which the resident may build and occupy a cottage of his own.*
>
> *The electric plant is now being installed, power being secured from the falls below the dam; the central clubhouse and the cottages are being given finishing touches, the grounds are being dressed again, and work on the*

> *roads is being pushed. The tennis courts will be in fine shape and also the golf links, ball grounds, bridle paths and roads.*
>
> *The terms are reasonable. Board will be $8 per week for adults and $4 per week for children.*

The *Observer* article went on to include information on Mrs. K.G. Whistler of Flat Rock, North Carolina, and Camden, South Carolina, who was among the first to join Kanuga Club. George Stephens induced Mrs. Whistler to take the management for the 1909 season at Kanuga Lake Club, as she had experience in accommodating select guests in her homes. Mr. Addison Lambeth was chosen to be estate manager of the club, Catherine Thomson of Charlotte would lead the kindergarten students in nature work and medical student W.P. Jacocks was elected boy's leader.

Less than a month before the Kanuga Club opened for the season, a headline in a June 1909 issue of the *French Broad Hustler* read, "Kanuga Lake Waters Claim Its First Victim." The casualty involved Sheldon Stepp, a carpenter employed at the club. Furman Bane and a boy named Robert McCall accompanied Stepp. The three had gone out on the lake in a boat that capsized. Thereafter, George Stephens forbade the use of all boats or rafts on Kanuga Lake, with the exception of those crafts owned by the company, which he asserted were "perfectly safe."

The Kanuga Club opened as planned in July 1909 even while construction of the clubhouse continued. Other features included a pavilion with auditorium, boathouse, billiards room, a telephone line to Hendersonville and an ice-and-refrigeration plant. The club featured weekly themed events and had a baseball team. Stephens was well on the way to meeting his initial objective of selling lots to purchasers for the purpose of building summer homes or cottages within his summer cooperative residential colony incorporated as Kanuga Lake Club.

Success of the club led to more building. The *Hustler* announced the addition of 150 rooms at Kanuga, mentioning also that Stephens expected six hundred visitors for the season of 1910.

Gully Washer

All was going swimmingly for Stephens until the forces of nature squelched the success of his mountain cooperative. As the season was getting underway at Kanuga in the summer of 1916, a cyclone spun in the Gulf of Mexico. The storm moved northeast, reaching and stalling over the Blue Ridge by July 5, when it rained unremittingly for six days straight, oversaturating the ground with more precipitation than had been recorded in the region's history. Meanwhile, another hurricane brewed in the Atlantic, moving westerly, making landfall north of Charleston on July 14. When the center of the Atlantic storm reached western North Carolina the next day, carrying with it twenty-four hours of pouring rain, pandemonium swept the region. As lakes, reservoirs, creeks and the French Broad River continued rising and then surpassed flood-stage levels, the massive volume of water burst dams, including Henderson County's largest at Kanuga Lake. Houses jettisoned downstream from Marshall and Bat Cave, and railroads, bridges and roads washed out, leaving thousands of people stranded. The Great Flood of 1916, Henderson County's worst natural disaster on record, left Kanuga in ruins, as it did much of the surrounding region.

Kermit Edney, in his book *The Kermit Edney Weather Book* (1986), wrote:

> *The flood was due to a period of daily local rains, augmented by a heavy general rainfall attending a storm, which advanced slowly northeastward from the Gulf and remained nearly stationary over the mountain region from the 8th to the 10th followed on the 15th and 16th by an excessive downpour in connection with a hurricane from the South Atlantic coast, which moved northwestward across South Carolina over the mountains. The course taken by this hurricane was very unusual. Tropical storms generally re-curve to the northeast upon reaching higher latitudes, but this disturbance was prevented from taking this course by the high-pressure area overlying the northeastern states, and so practically exhausted itself against the mountains. This resulted in an enormous rainfall ranging from 10 to 23 inches.*

Stephens sold his summer home in Henderson County and moved back to Charlotte in 1918. He offered the Kanuga property for sale in 1920, and in 1922, he relocated to Asheville, where he was co-publisher of the *Asheville Citizen*. He bought Biltmore Village from the George Vanderbilt estate for resale to individual purchasers, and he was the first chairman of the Asheville City Planning Commission. With Kanuga Lake Club on financial rocks, Stephens reorganized his holdings as Kanuga, Inc., and then as Kanuga Estates, Inc., in 1925. In an attempt to cash in on the land boom, he hired H. Walter Fuller (1865–1942), a Henderson County resident who was in charge of the publicity for Laurel Park Estates. County deed records from 1920 to 1926 show several citations of Stephens having bought back the shares of his Kanuga Lake Club. Forever the optimist, Stephens ordered the sand-clay paving of Kanuga Lake Road, the first such road thusly paved in North Carolina. He also added gaming tables and promoted the inn to non-members. But perhaps more so than the overwhelming effects of the 1916 flood, the popularity of automobiles opening more diverse travel opportunities led to the demise of destination resorts such as Stephens's club. Stephens had based the concept of his project on a community of members who would travel to the resort by railroad for longer stays.

George E.C. Stephens—celebrated as an athlete at the University of North Carolina–Chapel Hill, from which he graduated in 1896—was named a trustee of the university in 1901 and remained a trustee until his death in 1946. He was married to Sophie Converse Myers Stephens (1875–1958) and had developed the 1,200-acre, upscale neighborhood Myers Park in Charlotte, previously a cotton plantation owned by his father-in-law, John S. Myers. Stephens was a partner in the real estate firm Abbott and Stephens, with F.C. Abbott—developers of Charlotte's Piedmont Park. In 1901, Frederick C. Abbott, George Stephens and Word H. Wood formed the Southern States Trust Company. Stephens's bank holdings, which began as the Southern States Trust Company—later, the American Trust Company—became Bank of America. George and Sophie Stephens are buried at Calvary Episcopal Churchyard in Fletcher, North Carolina.

KANUGA CONFERENCES—EVOLVED ON FAITH

It has been written that George Stephens chose the name Kanuga for his club because of the Cherokees who were said to have gathered at the great flat rock about five miles to the east. Stephens believed that *Kanuga* meant "meeting place of many peoples" in Cherokee. In his book *Kanuga: Story of a Gathering Place*, author Jack Reak suggests that Kanuga means "a gathering place" in Cherokee, and officials of the conference center use Reak's subheading to theme their facility. Reak also suggested that *Kanuga* in Cherokee referred to a scratching device fashioned from briars. The phrase "gathering place" translates as *unadasgisdiyi* in Cherokee, and in the same language—according to Cherokee linguist Garfield Long—*kanuga* (usually *kanugali*) means briars, place of briars or blackberry briars.

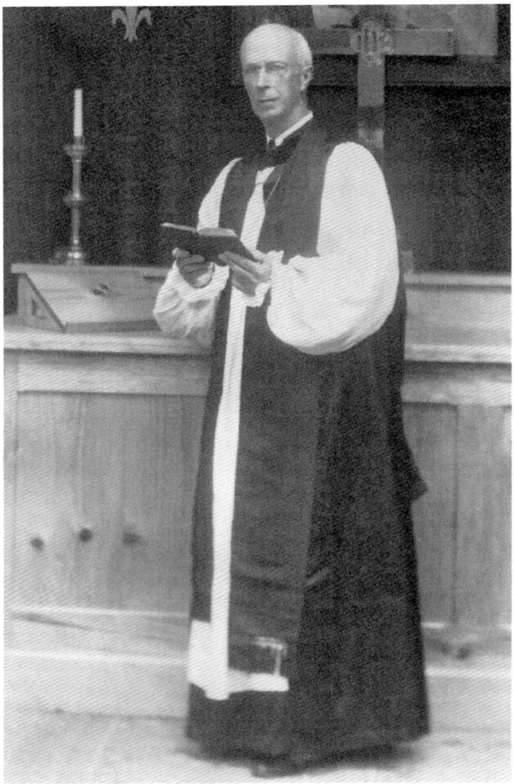

Bishop Kirkman George Finlay. *Photo courtesy of Kanuga Conferences, Inc.*

Whatever the case, had it not been for George Stephens's vision for a lakeside resort in the mountains—and if not for the Great Flood of 1916—there would likely not be a four-season denominational retreat and conference center above Pleasant Hill in central Henderson County today. In 1923, Stephens put the Kanuga property up for sale. With the support of the Episcopal Dioceses of Upper South Carolina, the State of South Carolina, East North Carolina and Western North Carolina, through Episcopal bishop the Right Reverend Kirkman George Finlay (1877–1938), began negotiating with Stephens on price and acreage.

Finlay was bishop coadjutor of the fledgling Diocese of Upper South Carolina and previously the rector of Trinity Church in Columbia, South Carolina, and an original member of Stephens's Kanuga Lake Club. Having explored locations for a summer camp, Finlay announced his plan in an address to the annual convention of the new Diocese of South Carolina in 1923. His mission: "A summer vacation colony to further Christian life and education, Christian love and leadership."

At the time, nine hundred acres of Stephens's property at Kanuga had been appraised at $300,000, an unrealistic price considering the dioceses' bankroll. Stephens offered the property to Finlay for $186,000. After much discussion, Stephens offered four hundred of the core acres and all of the buildings on it to Finlay for $95,000. Finlay set about working arduously with North Carolina and South Carolina dioceses and private backers, and he traveled extensively to raise the funds necessary to underwrite his vision for an Episcopal campground in the mountains. Finlay sometimes lodged in Cottage No. 1 at Kanuga for summer residency but lived full time in a house called Perth at Bonclarken, the conference center of the Associate Reformed Presbyterian Church, on the Greenville Highway.

In 1928, Stephens agreed to loan four hundred of the acres and its lake and buildings to the Episcopal diocesan group of four until the asking price could be raised, and he pledged $5,000 toward the goal. In 1929, the dioceses purchased the four-hundred-acre property for $104,000 (including back taxes and expenses), naming it Kanuga Conferences Association, to be run as an Episcopal camp. (The Diocese of the State of North Carolina would become a participating member in 1938.) Alan Wood, it was later discovered, had anonymously gifted $45,000 toward the cause.

Finlay could not be stopped, even from the capricious forces of nature. The 1928 flood broke the dam, in spite of the lake having been reduced—after the 1916 flood—to one-quarter of its original capacity. The ice storm of St. Patrick's Day 1936 downed a number of pines like so many matchsticks. Finlay had the dam restored and repurposed the fallen timber, storing it for future use. He also involved himself in the building of a boys' camp with log buildings in 1929. Kanuga Conferences Association purchased an additional 400 acres in 1932 and 390 more in 1934, and still more acreage at later dates, bringing the total to 1,365 acres. The North Carolina Forestry Department later provided hundreds of white pine saplings to fill in for what had been lost in the ice storm. Today, those trees soar to nearly sixty feet.

Although warned by his doctor that he should not push himself too hard, Bishop Finlay labored untiringly to jumpstart his pet project, continuing his fundraising efforts, leading hikes, working in the stables and proffering hands-on labor in the construction and maintenance of the property. In the midst of a project, he suffered a heart attack and died with his boots on at the age of sixty-one.

Finlay's death occurred in the midst of planning and fundraising for an enclosed chapel to be constructed at the conference center. Since 1933, religious services were held at an open-air venue, which members named "Chapel of St. Francis of Assisi" in 1941. Only a month before Finlay's death, the Kanuga board of managers selected a site for the long-proposed chapel.

A Kanuga committee, impressed with his work in rebuilding Fletcher's Calvary Episcopal Church after it burned in a 1935 fire, hired Asheville-based (Scottish-born) S. Grant Alexander, OBE, to design and oversee the construction of its Chapel of the Transfiguration. Alexander worked with the timber Finlay had stored since the ice storm of 1936, having it milled on-site, adding to the required lumber with additional trees from the property. Members laid the cornerstone on June 30, 1940, and upon completion, the new chapel was dedicated to Bishop Finlay on July 19, 1942. Some of its furnishings included those from the 1887 Chapel of the Gethsemane of Bowman's Bluff, disbanded in 1907, after which its fixtures had scattered.

Kanuga buildings-and-grounds superintendent Rufus Franklin Huneycutt (1882–1952) oversaw the fabrication of other furnishings for the chapel on-site, including the pews. Huneycutt had cautioned architect Alexander about white pines lacking the tensile strength of English oak—a warning left unheeded. With the roof in place, Huneycutt's admonition bore out when the chapel's walls began to buckle outward. Engineering consultants solved the predicament with steel tie bars stretching from wall to wall. Additional steel supports were added under eaves and through transepts in 1957 to stave off further movement of the walls. The chapel features the Tudor arch, Gothic Revival tapering buttresses and siding of board-and-batten, its interior finished with knotty pine paneling. Aside from the 1997 narthex extension, the cross-plan frame chapel appears much as it did upon completion in 1942.

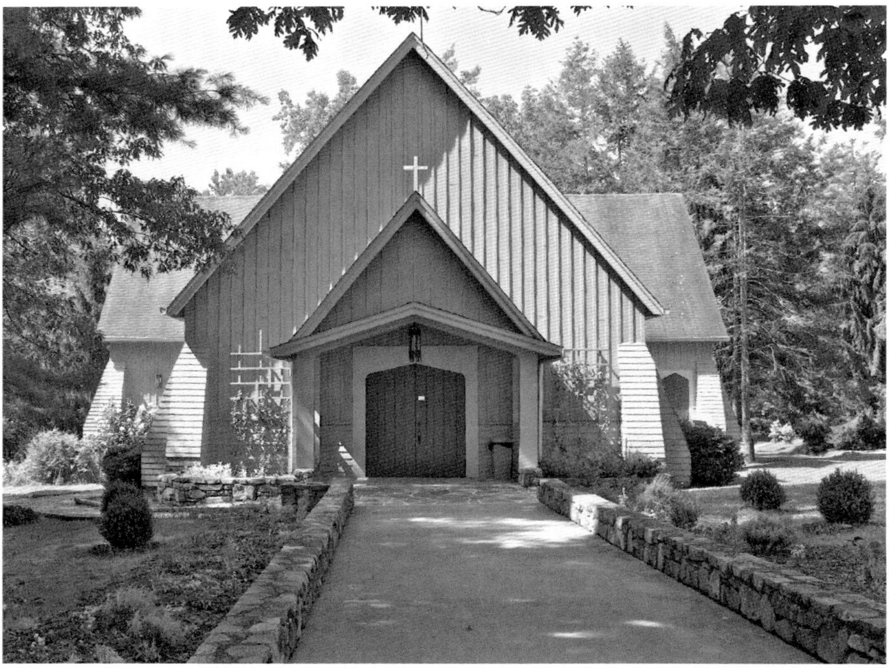

The Chapel of the Transfiguration.

The Kanuga Conferences Association reorganized as Kanuga Conferences, Inc., in 1950, and added the Boys Camp in 1962. Earlier in its history, the separate Girls Camp was known also as the "Midget Camp."

In the mid-1960s, Asheville architect J. Bertram King designed a new building of stone, glass and wood to replace the old clubhouse with a modern inn, dining hall, meeting rooms and service facilities. Three bungalow-style cottages were added, having been relocated from Hendersonville, and three more were built. The old pavilion was taken down and replaced with the Cunningham Pavilion in 1991.

Much more than a mountain oasis for religious retreatants, campers and hikers, Kanuga Conferences also hosts members of the "Hotshot" Unit of the United States Forest Service who have trained there since 1989, and the National Wildlife Federation has leased camp facilities at Kanuga since 1974. Botanists, both amateur and professional, frequently hike the trails in search of indigenous lichens and mushrooms, wildflowers, shrubbery and trees. The grounds also feature trails, including High Rocks and Daisy's Lake Trail; Camp Kanuga, a campground facility for boys and girls; and a meditation labyrinth. In 1950, the progressive board of Kanuga opened the facility to an African American Boy Scout troop, years before the civil rights movement. In 1988, the conference center formed Session Six, a no-charge camp for underprivileged children, which evolved into Camp Bob.

Estimable campers have included Reverend Dr. Robert Emmet Gribbin Jr. (1917–2004) of Tuscaloosa, Alabama, who attended Kanuga's Youth Camp, where he served as bugler. Reverend Gibbin was known to say, "At Kanuga everything moved by bugle call." Another Youth Camp member, L. Mendel Rivers (1905–1970), became a South Carolina congressman. Noted speakers at Kanuga have included Dr. Billy Graham; lawyer, activist and President Clinton advisor Vernon Jordan; and author, humorist and publisher of the *Carolina Israelite* Harry Golden. Kanuga has also hosted the annual meeting of the Primates of the Anglican Communion, and the House of Bishops continues to meet regularly at the center.

John F. Gibbs (1871–1960) of the Pinnacle worked at Kanuga as a caretaker. Sindy Drake Hamilton's cousin Julia Elizabeth Drake (1888–1972) was in charge of housekeeping for more than thirty years. In 1988, Melinda Pilgrim Lowrance (1951–) became the first African American to work the front desk at Kanuga Conferences—from 1993 to 1994. Lowrance remembered her first years at the center, working in the mailroom, and the palpable lack of air-conditioning during the summer. "I kept after them until they allowed us to wear more comfortable clothes in the mailroom," she said.

Lowrance now owns her own janitorial services business headquartered in downtown Hendersonville.

The National Register of Historic Places describes the Kanuga Lake Historic District as "comprising some 100 acres including Kanuga Lake and 53 buildings, structures and sites in an oasis-like church-related conference center in central Henderson County." Historic structures include the Kanuga Lake Inn (on the site of the original Kanuga Lake Club) and thirty-nine cottages, thirty-seven of which occupy their original positions.

Stephens survived the crash and the impending Great Depression. It may be safe to assume, however, that had it not been for the flood of 1916, the Episcopal conference center—the largest in the United States—would be in another locale, and there would likely be no Sugar Hollow Farm or Wilson Farm subdivisions.

PLEASANT HILL CEMETERY/ DRAKE FAMILY CEMETERY

Old Kanuga Road branches west from Crab Creek Road, another route completed by the CCC during the Great Depression years. Alongside Old Kanuga, the surname Drake predominates the inscriptions in what we now call Pleasant Hill Cemetery, known as the Drake Family Cemetery in days of old. Bootleggers from Cathead share this burial ground with the multiple Drakes.

BEAUMONT (CIRCA 1839)

Many have read and heard the story of the murder of Andrew Johnstone by bushwhackers in the banquet hall of this historic site and of Johnstone's son Elliot shooting some, and killing one, of the assailants, yet few have had the privilege of reading an eyewitness account written in a letter tucked away in a private Flat Rock home. What follows is an extract from that letter written by Lucy, with no surname listed, dated June 11, 1864:

> *My dear Otey, the startling information your doctor gave you last night of our dear friend Mr. Johnstone's death is 100* [percent] *true. He did not live an hour, said to his wife, "My dear, I am very sorry to leave you so soon but in a few minutes I am to appear in the presence of my maker.*

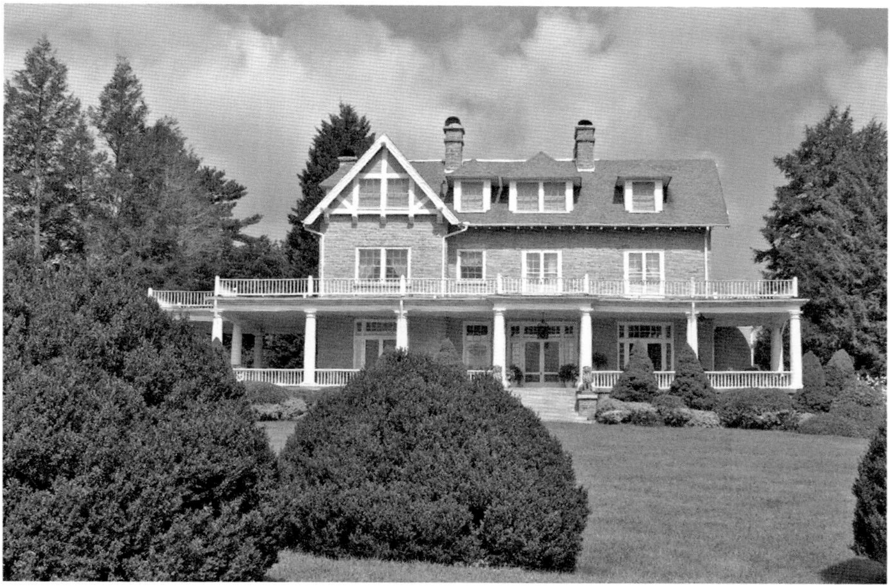

Historic Beaumont.

> *I trust His mercies in a crucified Savior. Bring the children each to me to bid good-bye, not together for it is more than I can endure but one by one."*
>
> *What a fearful tragedy! What a commentary upon the truth—in the midst of life we are in death.*

Another little-known aspect of Beaumont would be its general appearance as distinct from the way Andrew Johnstone knew it. Referred to as the "rock mansion" when Franklin Brevard Hayne bought the property in 1909, the house did not sport its wraparound porch and other graceful details during the Johnstones' tenure. Hayne hired Richard Sharp Smith to remodel and enlarge the mansion in the Tudor Colonial Revival style, reminiscent of the English country estates with which English-born Smith was familiar. At the same time, Hayne hired professional landscape architects to add terracing and what were referred to as "sunken gardens" on the 800-acre estate—land purchased by Johnstone from Samuel Allison—257 acres of which were purchased by Allison from Benjamin King (1777–1841) and James Kuykendall (1781–1846) in 1829.

Today, the historic home, which was considered to be in Flat Rock when constructed—serves as a centerpiece for the exclusive subdivision known as Beaumont Estates alongside the eastern boundary of Kanuga Road.

OUT IN THE COUNTY

Early residents considered the regions of town outlying the city limits of Hendersonville "out in the county" when what are now city lots of an acre or smaller took in several acres with gardens, livestock and poultry. By the early 1900s, with an influx of year-round and summer residents, the automobile gaining in popularity and the need for housing becoming a priority, additional opportunities arose for building houses farther away from the core downtown area. Numerous farms were subdivided to meet the growing need for housing. Early deed records describe this real estate as "just outside the corporate limits of the City of Hendersonville."

PINEBROOK

In springtime, Bradford pear trees frame a Neoclassic mansion with a profusion of white blossoms, which may be glimpsed from Kanuga Road, between granite pillars, about 160 feet up a winding driveway. In 1910, Alfred W. Wheeler (1876–1954) and his wife, Leslie Priedy Wheeler (1878–1955), had this stately pile built with granite quarried from the site. Five two-story

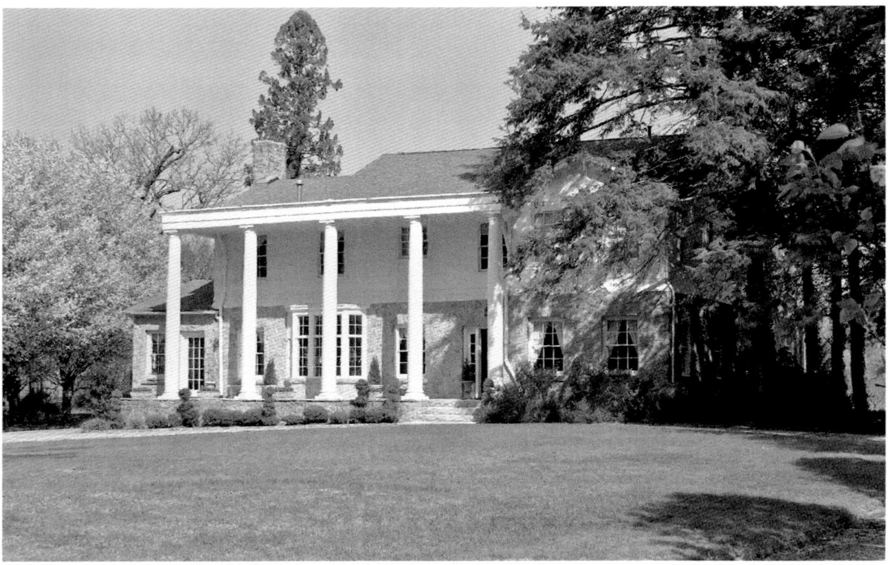

Pinebrook.

columns carry the roof of the broad front porch, cut granite defines the first-story façade and white siding sheathes the second story. The Wheelers named this estate Pinebrook, now called Pinebrook Manor by current owners Terry and Melanie Welton, who restored the home and guesthouse in 2004 and operate the buildings as a fine bed-and-breakfast inn.

The 4,700-square-foot Pinebrook stands in the midst of 4.93 acres of formal gardens under the shade of oak trees described as nearly two hundred years old. Boxwoods, hydrangeas, topiaries and rose gardens planted by the Wheelers lend added grace to the setting. The guesthouse once garaged the Rolls-Royce of Ivor Robert Pardee (1902–1965) and his wife, Jane Isadora Johnston Pardee (1914–1992), who owned the property after the Wheelers' tenure. Ivor's aunt Margaret Roberts Pardee (1869–1941) had left him $100,000 to donate to a worthy cause, and this bequest was the seed money for Hendersonville's Margaret R. Pardee Memorial Hospital, dedicated in 1953.

The Pinebrook estate once included more extensive acreage. Henderson County deed records cite the Pardees purchasing 31.63 acres from E.L. and Jessie P. Newton in 1938. The Wheelers bought the core of the property from James Theodore Gibbs (1875–1952) and Lucretia Elsa Saltz Gibbs (1891–1958), land originally belonging to Carrie Nelson (1875–1950), who sold to the Gibbses in 1919. Much of the original property has recently been developed as the àVirea subdivision.

SARAH OPHELIA COLLEY CANNON—AKA MINNIE PEARL

One could say the character Minnie Pearl took root in Henderson County. After all, Sarah Colley developed the name and persona after her theatrical dealings at Hendersonville's Skyland Hotel.

Sarah Ophelia Colley (1912–1996), an American country star and comedienne, became most famous for her more than fifty years of appearances on the Grand Ole Opry stage and on the television show *Hee Haw* from 1969 to 1991. Born in Centerville, Tennessee, Colley studied theater and dance at Nashville's Ward-Belmont College. After graduation, she taught dance for several years before accepting a position with the Wayne P. Sewell Production Company in Atlanta, Georgia. Based from this company, she recruited local talent, supplied costumes and produced and

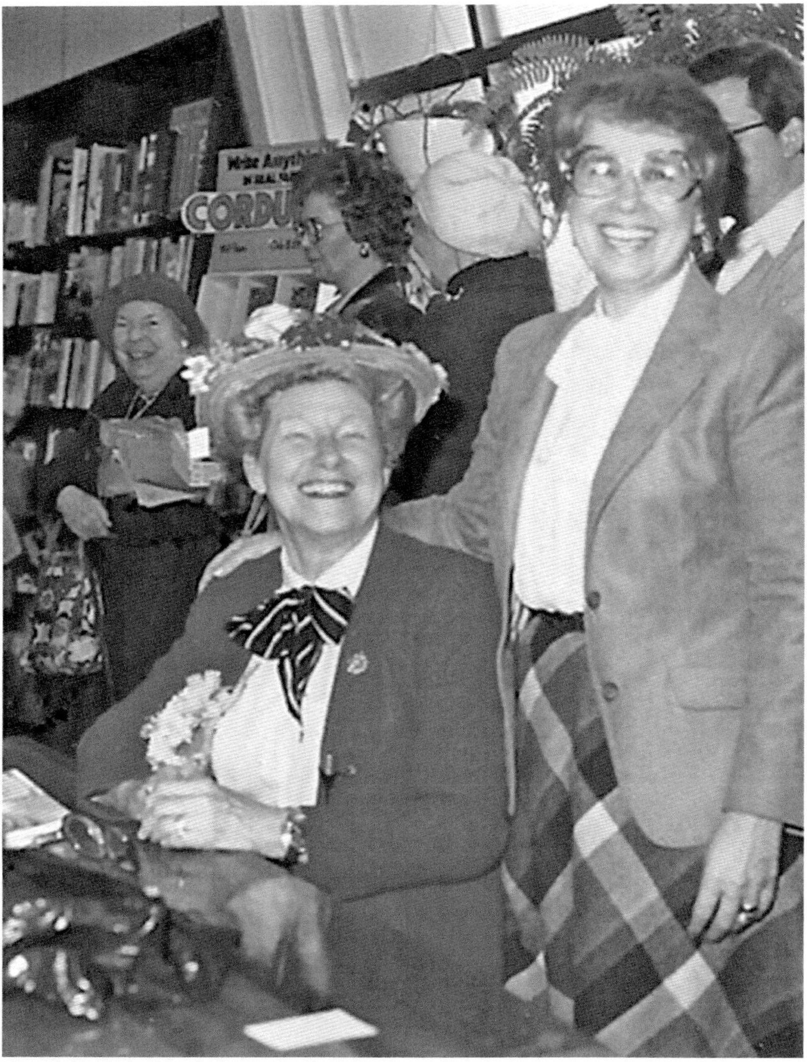

Minnie Pearl at Carolyn's Book Shop, 1982. *Photo courtesy of Gayle Hamilton Stepp.*

directed plays and musicals in small towns throughout the United States, including Hendersonville, North Carolina.

Hendersonville radioman Kermit Edney wrote that Minnie, at the age of twenty-one, got her start working up her act with the help of Sally Stokes in the Skyland Hotel in the 1930s. In his book *Kermit Edney Remembers* (1997), Edney quoted Minnie as saying:

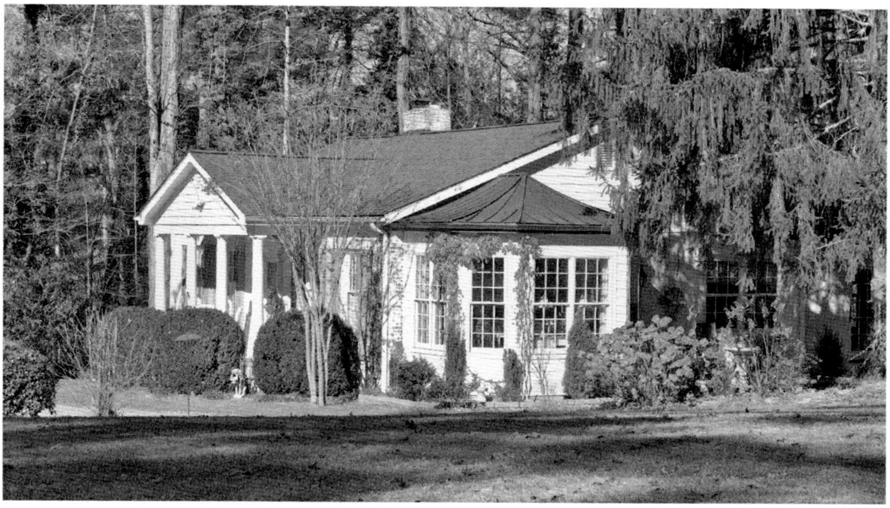

The home of Mary Colley Kershaw near Kanuga Road.

> *Every time I come to Hendersonville to see Mary, my sister, I drive by that hotel and I thank the Lord in all reverence. I am not being flippant. I'm being serious, 'cause it was through that company that sent me here to Hendersonville to train, to go out and coach these plays that I found Minnie Pearl in Northern Alabama in 1936.*

In 1947, Colley married Henry R. Cannon who took over the management of the Minnie Pearl character, his clients also including Elvis Presley, Eddy Arnold, Hank Williams and Colonel Tom Parker.

Minnie frequently visited her sister Mary Colley Kershaw, who kept a home on Kanuga Road in the outskirts of Hendersonville. She also signed copies of her books at Carolyn's Book Shop on Main Street.

Minnie Pearl, a member of the Grand Ole Opry Hall of Fame, was awarded the National Medal of the Arts in 1992, and artifacts pertaining to her career may be viewed at the Grand Ole Opry Museum.

THE MCCRARY TWINS

Billed during their professional career as the McGuire Twins, Henderson County natives Billy Leon McCrary (1946–1979) and Benny Loyd

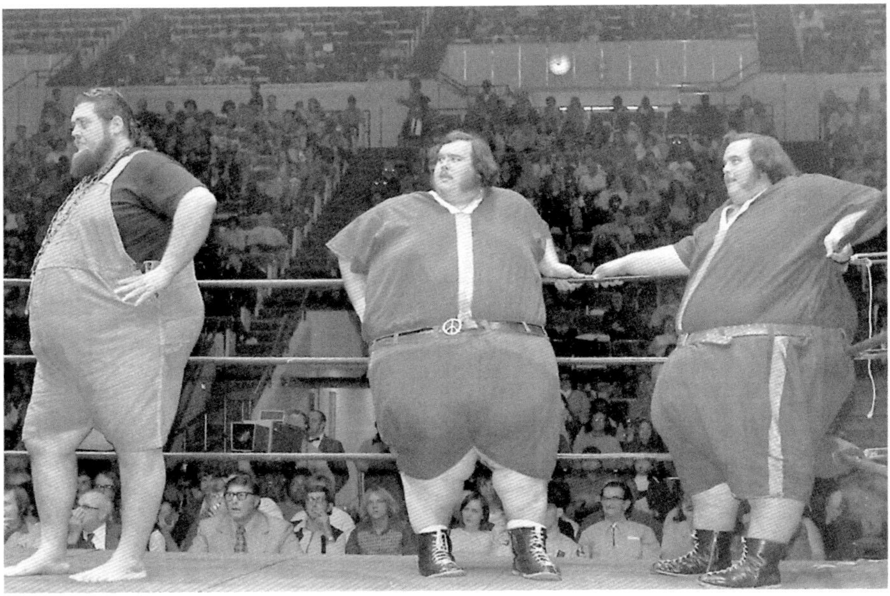

The McCrary Twins with William Dee "Haystacks" Calhoun at Cobo Arena, Detroit, Michigan, early 1970s. *Photo courtesy of Brian Bukantis, Arena Publishing, Inc.*

McCrary (1946-2001) are listed in the *Guinness Book of Records* as the world's heaviest twins, a distinction unchallenged to this day. In November 1978, Billy and Benny weighed 743 pounds and 723 pounds, respectively, and each sported waists measuring eighty-four inches. Benny at one time weighed in at 814 pounds.

Upon miniature trail bikes, the twins would leap a parked toy bus. Billy and Benny McCrary counted among the attractions in Henderson County's King Apple Parades and also in Asheville's holiday parades, and local and regional cycle dealerships clamored for their sponsorship.

Each weighed only five pounds at birth; then, at age four, German measles damaged their pituitary glands, after which time the McCrary boys gained enormous poundage, each weighing 200 by age ten. They reached 450 pounds each during their time at East Henderson High School, from which they were both expelled at age sixteen for arguing with the principal.

Their father, Frank B. "Throttle Boy" McCrary Jr. (1922–1991), bought farmland on Kanuga Valley Lane alongside Crab Creek Road and kept horses there in an attempt to provide the twins with a means of working off weight. The boys quickly lost interest, much to the relief of the horses.

Henderson County native V. Leon Pace remembers when Billy and Benny's father, Frank, ran a produce stand on the Spartanburg Highway. "Not for long, though," Pace said. "Those boys ate most of it before they could sell it." Pace also remembers the twins riding swaybacked horses. "Swaybacked from all that weight," Pace added. Other Henderson County old-timers shared stories of the twins' mother, Virginia G. McKinnish McCrary (1928–2009), frying up pounds of bacon each breakfast time for her boys. Mrs. McCrary was a clerk at Hendersonville's Robotyper Corporation.

Sammy Williams remembered the McCrarys as regular customers at his hardware store on Seventh Avenue. "We were able to order special shoes for the twins," Sammy said. "And their father, Frank, bought car parts and hardware from us."

Ted Hamilton said, "When they were old enough their father gave them a 1955 Chevrolet to drive. He took out the back seat and moved the front seat way back so they could fit behind the wheel. They liked to drag race that Chevy. Billy and Benny were my distant cousins. I'm glad their condition was not genetic."

The twins' portliness presented certain problems, including having to buy custom-tailored clothing and paying for structural enhancements to their vehicles. Billy once found himself wedged in an airplane lavatory and had to wait for landing to be freed. The twins also traveled with portable jacks to bolster their motel beds.

Benny and Billy began their show business career as a wrestling and comedy team. When discovered by *Life* magazine, the McCrary brothers went on to achieve national fame as tag-team wrestlers and in carnival stunt shows. They worked their first show business gig as rodeo clowns in Texas. The twins appeared in Las Vegas, where they played trumpets and told jokes with four-hundred-pound go-go dancers. They trained for two months in Juarez, Mexico, fought their first fight in a bullring in the same city and then took their show on the road, wrestling across the country in locales including El Paso, Las Vegas, Detroit, Los Angeles and beyond. In Montreal and Japan, after announcers mispronounced their surname with what sounded to them like "McQueery," they complained, "We ain't no queers" and chose the name McGuire for their act.

Promoters typically pitted up to twelve other wrestlers against the twins, and the twins always won. In Detroit, the McCrarys beat pro wrestlers William Dee "Haystacks" Calhoun (1934–1989) at 620 pounds and Man Mountain Mike (1940–1988) at 610 pounds—with their "Tupelo Splash," a technique where they would throw themselves on their opponents, landing on top and pinning them down. They remained undefeated for years.

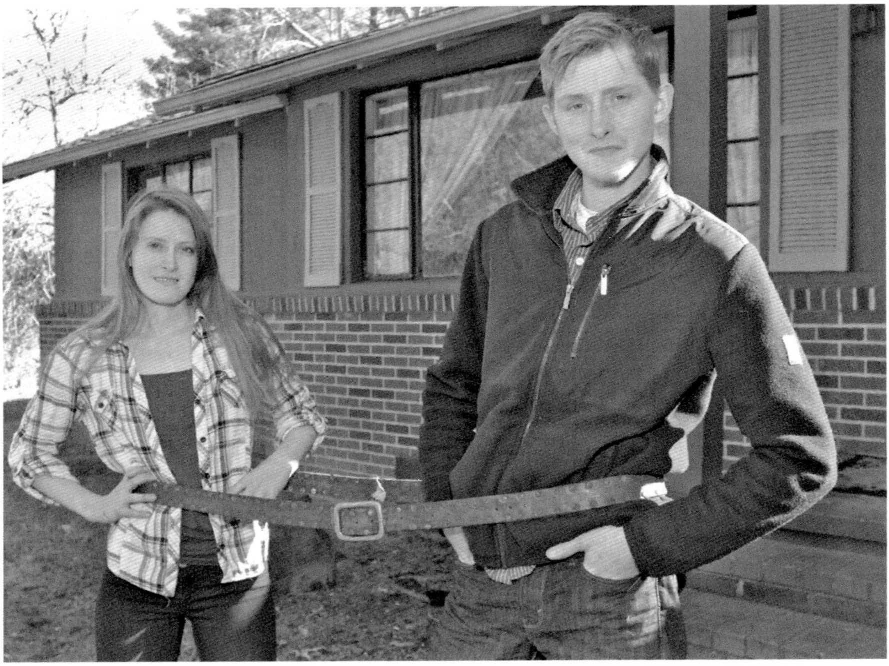

Twins Amanda and Peter Leonard currently live with their parents and siblings in the McCrarys' house on Kanuga Road. Pictured here, the Leonard twins within Billy McCrary's eighty-four-inch belt hand-tooled with the words, "THE WORLD'S LARGEST TWINS. BILLY."

In a double wedding in El Paso, Texas, on November 30, 1971, the McCrary twins married French-Canadian sisters Danielle and Tina Jarry. Benny and Tina divorced, and in 1977, Benny married amateur wrestler Tammie Elaine Alley, to whom he remained wedded for the rest of his life. Each of Billy and Benny's wives was normal in size.

Traveling between wrestling-circuit and carnival bookings, the twins paid 50 percent surcharges on airfares, each of them requiring two seats. They appeared on *The Tonight Show* and *The Merv Griffin Show* and at the Circus Circus Casino in Las Vegas and performed daredevil stunts on mini Honda motorcycles.

Billy died in 1979 from respiratory failure stemming from injuries sustained in a botched stunt at Niagara Falls, Canada. As a solo act, Benny—aka Benny McGuire—appeared during the summer of 1981 at Ripley's Believe It Or Not Museum in Myrtle Beach, South Carolina. He retired from show business, shed half his weight and established McCrary's

Pawn Shop & Auctions, Inc., at 403 Kanuga Street at the "Busy Bend" in Hendersonville, currently occupied by a consignment emporium. Dr. William Askew Lampley (1920–) was his physician.

Benny and his wife Tammie lived in the family home on Kanuga Road. In 1998, the couple moved to Walkertown, North Carolina, and Benny began working for the Christian Golfers Ministry at the Pine Knolls Golf Course. Evangelism through golf combined Mr. McCrary's religious beliefs and his love of the sport.

Benny died of heart failure in 2001. Shortly before his death, his uncle Reverend Harold McKinnish (1933–) visited him. Benny said, "Unc', don't pray for me to get better; pray for me to get out of this ol' body." Even in death, the twins set another record, buried beneath the world's largest granite tombstone at Crab Creek Baptist Church Cemetery in southwestern Henderson County. Benny commissioned the thirteen-foot-wide, three-ton monument after Billy's death. The inscriptions read:

A BIG MAN WITH A BIG HEART, LOVED AROUND THE WORLD, WITH A LEGEND AS BIG AS THE MOUTAINS AROUND HIM.
Billy

"A KIND HEARTED MAN SPREADING GOD'S WORD IN A BIG WAY! AN INSPIRATION AND A SOURCE OF ENCOURAGEMENT FOR US ALL."
Phil. 4:12
Benny

Hallowed Ground

For more than 160 years, countless acts of faith have transpired on the land framed by Kanuga and Price Roads, Patterson Street and West Chestnut Drive. This site, home to churches—two current and one former—hosted religious camp meetings in the mid-nineteenth century.

COVENANT PRESBYTERIAN CHURCH

Although the building has stood for but a few decades, its windows strike a chord of bygone familiarity, harkening back to turn-of-the-twentieth-century Hendersonville—as well they should. Members of the fledgling Covenant Presbyterian Church broke off from First Presbyterian Church of Hendersonville in 1979 to found their own church and completed phase one of their new facility in 1983. It had come to the attention of the members that Gladys Krause Pursley (1909–1994) rescued the magnificent windows from the 1905 First Presbyterian Church when that part of the sanctuary was being razed in the early 1960s, and Pursley had stored them in a corncrib off Sugarloaf Road. Forgotten for decades, the windows remained, for the most part, salvageable, so when the new Covenant membership's architectural committee discovered them, the group decided to restore them and design its new sanctuary around them.

Only two of the large windows remained mostly complete, so with pieces from a third window, restoration experts at Statesville Stained Glass of North Carolina were able to make necessary repairs and replacements to missing and broken pieces in the two mostly intact windows, which, when installed in new aluminum frames, added a blaze of light and color to the north and west walls of the sanctuary after the second phase of the church was completed in 1993.

FAITH TABERNACLE AND REVEREND SHERMAN T. PATTERSON

Only scant traces remind us today of what may have occurred on a property alongside Kanuga Road: a small, log-veneered building between West Chestnut Drive and Patterson Street now used for meetings and a bronze historical marker on a granite boulder fronting the Universalist Unitarian Church.

The plaque memorializes the Boiling Springs Baptist Camp meetings held on this site in summers, where the Baptist Convention organized in 1845 and shortly thereafter disbanded. In 1958, the Baptists erected the marker on the property.

Lieutenant Colonel Lucille Galloway (1908–2002) of the Salvation Army used the log structure—owned now by the Unitarian Church—for her missionary work and lived behind it at 501 West Chestnut Drive. Galloway, of Augusta, Georgia, launched the senior citizens' program for the Salvation Army in Hendersonville, and according to Lieutenant Colonel David Holtz (1931–), retired, Galloway was "an extraordinary evangelist."

Edward Cook and his wife from Pennsylvania also used the log structure as a residence. Other buildings on the neighboring property included a prophet's chamber, a Sunday school and the home of Martin Luther "Calvin" Patterson (1844–1932) and his wife, Louise "Lonesa" Hamilton Patterson (1847–1928). In 1890, Patterson purchased the land—21.5 acres for $322.50—from Ida Ann Slocomb Richardson (1830–1910) of New Orleans and built a log house in 1891 on what would be their farmstead after having moved there from what is now called Shoal Falls Farm on Crab Creek and DuPont Roads. Martin Luther Calvin Patterson, a Union soldier in the Civil War, was a son of Reverend H.W. Patterson (1806–1880) and Elizabeth Moore Patterson (1809–1901). H.W. Patterson was pastor of Little River Baptist Church in 1848–49 and 1859 and was said to be "important to educational movements in the Pleasant Hill community."

Martin L.C. Patterson's son Sherman Tecumseh Patterson (1882–1970) left home in 1903, at age twenty-one, moving to Buncombe County, where he took a job in the Asheville Steam Laundry owned by J.A. Nichols. He married Margaret Lee Jarvis (1888–1968) in 1905, and the couple had three children.

Patterson converted to the Baptist faith in 1908 at a revival meeting in the First Baptist Church of Asheville. After suffering a near-fatal

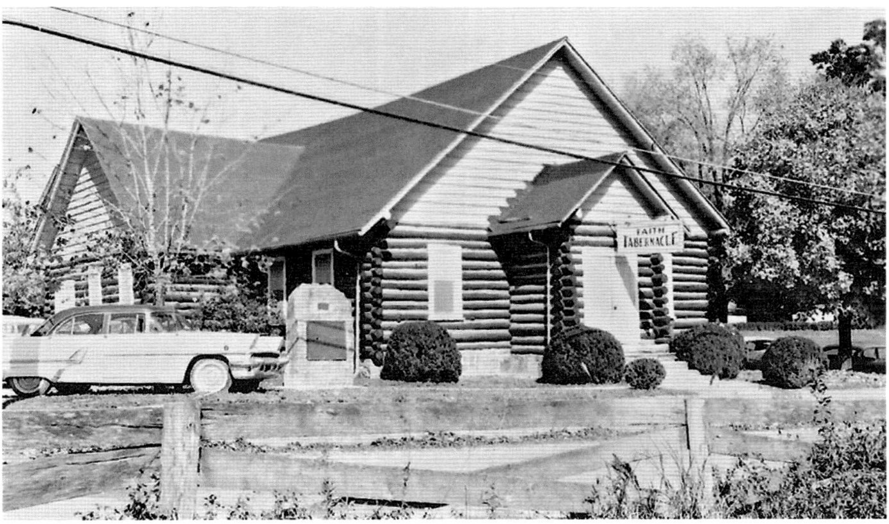

Reverend Patterson's Faith Tabernacle. *Photo courtesy of Nancy Harden Dotson.*

accident at the laundry in 1909—becoming ensnarled in a shaft while changing a belt on a machine—two doctors pronounced Patterson dead of strangulation. As the coroners were about to remove Patterson's body from the scene of the accident, a third doctor, Jerry Cox, managed to resuscitate him. Patterson then witnessed a revelation from God while recuperating in the hospital, telling others that in the vision he saw a log building, mountains and people.

Sherman T. Patterson served as an officer and preacher in the Salvation Army for seventeen years, traveling with his wife throughout the Southeast, having risen to ensign in 1924 and resigning in 1934.[10] He was ordained as a minister at Augusta Road Baptist Church in Greenville, South Carolina, in 1935. When God's vision again appeared to him, he returned to his father's land in Hendersonville—property that his brother Ernest then owned in part. Patterson organized camp meetings on the site, agreeing to build a nondenominational church providing his brother would permit him to do this on the ancestral land. Sherman then constructed a tabernacle of notched white pine logs acquired from John Anders (1918–1975) with the help of neighbors, including George Harden (1896–1960) and Frank B. McCrary Jr., and opened the church in 1937 for the gathering of the Hamilton, Patterson, Osteen and Pickelsimer reunion on the first Sunday of August. Regular services commenced in 1938, including Sunday school lessons and Bible and missionary conferences. Additionally, Patterson led a revival at East Flat Rock Methodist Church and held weekly Bible classes at Holly Springs and Little River Baptist Churches. He was also interim pastor at Grove Street Gospel Church (the "old R.V. Miller church," later Calvary) and Pleasant Hill Baptist Church and led revivals in seven states. The Reverend Patterson and his wife, Margaret, were considered to be gifted singers.

Patterson retired in June 1959. Successive pastors of Faith Tabernacle included Dr. Wendell Evans (until 1960) and Reverend Cleo Winningham. The church sponsored the Christian Service Brigade for Youths aged twelve to fifteen and a full young people's program, including worship, education and two young people's choirs, and became Faith Bible Church for a brief time during the 1970s. "At that time," said local newspaper columnist Chip Worrell (1959–), "the church was being held together with cables strung from wall to wall. It took two men to heave up the windows for a breath of fresh air, and you could stand at the pulpit and see daylight through two sets

10. Husbands and wives share the same rank as a team in the Salvation Army.

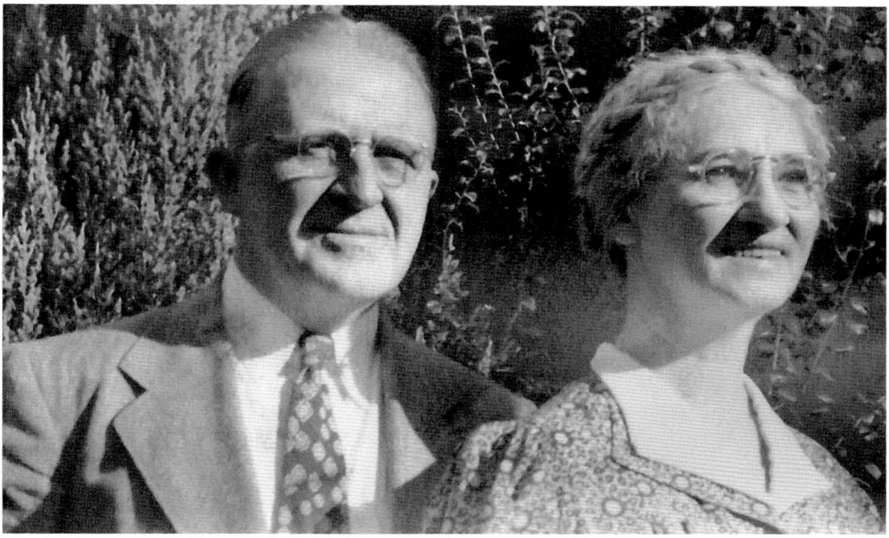

Reverend Sherman T. Patterson and Margaret Lee Jarvis Patterson. *Photo courtesy of Nancy Harden Dotson.*

of foyer doors." Worrell continued, "I have been inside churches from Nebraska to Italy, and Faith Tabernacle was the most beautiful church I have ever seen. The pine plank paneling was virgin-cut and the pine logs gleamed from the thousands of hand-rubbed wax coats." Worrell also pointed out that the seating used in the tabernacle came from Hendersonville's Rex Theatre after it burned.

Before 1980, members of Faith Bible Church razed the old Faith Tabernacle and built a new sanctuary set farther back from Kanuga Road. In 1982, approximately half of the congregation left to start Bethany Bible Church, meeting at Faith Christian School until the completion of their new sanctuary on Chadwick Avenue. When the Unitarian Universalist Fellowship purchased the property in 1994, the remaining half of the Faith Bible congregants moved to a church in Mills River, which dissolved in 2009. The Unitarian Universalist Fellowship continues to occupy the former Faith Bible Church building and renovated it in 2012. The Unitarians organized in 1980 and met at Opportunity House before purchasing the Patterson property in 1994. The Pattersons are buried at Hendersonville's Oakdale Cemetery.

CRAIL FARM/CROOKED CREEK

Passing by the entrance signs to the Crooked Creek subdivision off Kanuga Road, how many would sense the history that lies beyond? Old-timers occasionally speak of Hollywood royalty having been hosted by a studio mogul at Crail Farm just north and west of Flat Rock. At last, a descendant of Captain Marion Columbus Toms revealed the facts behind the story.

The 6,600-square-foot clubhouse at Crooked Creek Golf Club—a rambling one-level structure with an ell apartment joined to it by a slate-floored breezeway, now enclosed as the pro shop—was once the part-time home of Hollywood film executive Abraham Aaron Wonskolaser—more popularly known as Aaron "Albert" Warner (1884–1967) of Warner Brothers Studios. During their brief tenancy at Crail Farm, the Warners hosted such Hollywood icons as Greta Garbo.

According to the *Hendersonville Times-News* of May 27, 2007, "The story goes that the Warner Brothers, living in California, became nervous during World War II living so close to military bases in the West. They came east and constructed the mansion that is now the clubhouse."

Born to humble Polish immigrants, Mr. Warner likely appreciated the general demeanor of Henderson County natives, for it has been written that

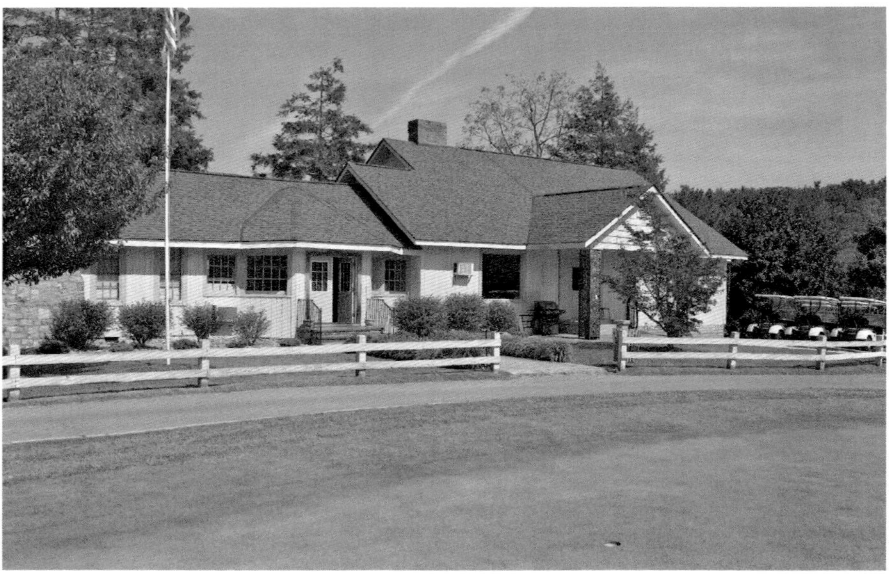

Crooked Creek Golf Club, former residence of Aaron "Albert" Warner.

he never adapted to the "upper-class lifestyle," remaining down-to-earth throughout his life.

According to deed records at the Henderson County Genealogical and Historical Society, Inc., Warner acquired the property in 1943 through his second wife, Bessie Siegel Warner (circa 1901–1970) of New York, who had purchased the tract from Mitchell Campbell King (1879–1959) of Atlanta, Georgia, in 1941. Mrs. Warner also bought contiguous land from Cecil and Fred Camp in 1942 under two separate deeds.

Everett Camp II served as caretaker for Crail Farm. His son Everett "Junior" Camp III remembers the Warners and has saved cards and letters from them. "The Warners kept Guernsey cattle there," Camp said. As a youngster, Junior and his siblings called Mr. Warner "Gramps." The Warners' tenure at Crail Farm was brief. In 1945, Harry D. Blomberg bought the tract and sold it in portions to Frank Odell Sherrill (1922–1983)[11] in 1945 and 1946.

Frank O. Sherrill, a native of Shelby, North Carolina, co-founded with Fred Weber the Charlotte-based S&W Cafeterias in the 1920s, a chain of restaurants located throughout the Southeast and in Washington, D.C. Sherrill also owned Select Foods Company, a restaurant-supply company headquartered in Hendersonville, and raised a herd of Hereford cattle on the Crail Farm tract. Henderson County residents, including Everett Camp III, who remember Mr. Sherrill describe him as a "nice fellow." Everett Camp II stayed on as a ranch manger and caretaker for Sherrill's cattle enterprise. Preston McDowell (1931–2009) served as herd master for Sherrill.

General Electric Company later leased the Crail Farm property and put up corporate guests, including Ronald Reagan when the actor was assigned to make a public relations visit to the GE plant in Hendersonville in 1960.

In 1966, Don and Waverly Broadwell of Fayetteville, North Carolina, and W.F. Sledge of Whiteville, North Carolina, purchased Crail Farm at auction. The partners formed Crail Valley Corporation and developed the subdivision known as Crooked Creek, which opened for sales in 1967. In 1968, for the grand opening of the Crooked Creek Golf Club, promoters brought in Max Baer (1937–)—who played the character Jethro in *The Beverly Hillbillies* television sitcom—and also featured PGA pro/NCAA medalist Larry Hinson (1944–), tour player George Walter "Bunky" Henry (1944–) and the club's pro, Tommy Vargo (1940–).

11. The historic mansion Hopewood, also known as Sherwood, in Flat Rock was home to Mr. and Mrs. Frank O. Sherrill. In 1878, Joe Cox owned the estate, and according to Frank L. FitzSimons, the vicinity of this property hosted a Cherokee camp during the "Trail of Tears."

The course at Crooked Creek, designed by Stuart Gooden (1930–), hosts golf teams from several area high schools to practice and hold matches and is home to the Applejack Golf Tournament and the Western North Carolina Amateur Tournament.

PGA pro William Marcus Gooden (1949–) and his father, Paul Gooden (1927–2008), subleased the course in 1972 from Alec Guionn and Caldwell Hoerter of Charlotte. The Goodens purchased the golf course property and clubhouse in 1986, operating it since as the Crooked Creek Golf Club. Looking back to Frank Sherrill's cattle enterprise on the property, the term "pasture pool" for golf seems fitting.

It should be noted that during the tenancy of the Warners and for decades thereafter, no formal entrance to the property opened from Kanuga Road. Residents, visitors and ranch hands accessed the estate from Crail Farm Drive—a clay swath cut through the woods between Kanuga Road and Middleton Road—a track that remains unpaved to the present time.

OKLAWAHA CIRCLE

North of Crooked Creek, a road named Oklawaha Circle intersects Kanuga Road from the east. Perhaps it was someone's sense of humor that led to the naming of the next avenue north "Oklahoma."

When dealing with the reportage of history, drawing from lore and undocumented accounts tends to perpetuate errors. A glaring gaffe in our local history would be the attributed source of "Oklawaha," albeit it a tempting prospect. In her 1947 book *The Story of Henderson County*, local author Sadie Smathers Patton (1886–1975) referenced "Ocklawaha Creek." In 1958, Hendersonville native and North Carolina Poet Laureate Lila Ripley Barnwell (1863–1961) wrote the poem "Oklawaha," in it implying the name meant "muddy creek" in the Cherokee language. W.A. Smith opened Henderson County's first real estate firm in 1887 and named it Oklawaha Land Company, Captain Marion Columbus Toms chose Oklawaha for the name of his Victorian home perched on a hill overlooking downtown Hendersonville and a street branching from Kanuga Road a mile south of Toms Hill was named Oklawaha Circle. The *North Carolina Gazetteer* perpetuates this misinformation, as does the greenway named Oklawaha at Hendersonville's Jackson Park. Cherokee linguist Garfield Long maintains that mud creek translates to *sawota geyv*, muddy creek to *sawotahi geyv* and muddy stream to *uweyvi geyv*; and the

Dikaneisdi (Cherokee word list) deciphers *tlawotu usdi uweyv* as mud creek—none of these terms bearing the euphony of the attributed *oklawaha*.

The *French Broad Hustler* (October 1906) included a letter titled, "Not the Old Indian Name." In it, A.M. Huger wrote, "Dear Sir: I see in your issue of the 25th that the old Indian name of Mud Creek was "Oclawaha," but I have excellent grounds for believing that this name was not the old Indian name, as the word is from the Seminoles, a tribe that still lives—a remnant of them in Florida; and a navigable stream, a tributary of St. Johns [River], bears this name to this day. The above name was probably given by some of the earlier settlers at Flat Rock, in 1926 or '30, or even earlier."

In 1976, local radioman, teacher, school principal, banker, football coach, U.S. Marine corpsman and register of deeds Frank Lockwood FitzSimons (1897–1980) authored the first in his three-volume series titled *From the Banks of the Oklawaha* in which he perpetuated the Cherokee connection to the misused term. FitzSimons's index lists several references to "Oklawaha" and "Ocklawaha." Ever since, many have posited that the Cherokee people called this region *Oklawaha*, which they named for our Mud Creek. Not so.

In central Florida, a river and an unincorporated town with one of the highest crime rates in the state bears the name Ocklawaha. Recorded as early as 1763 and a derivative of the Creek term *aklawahe*, *ocklawaha* would be a Seminole or Seminole-Creek place name meaning swamp, dark water or muddy water; and *oklowahe* means wild potato in the Seminole-Creek language.

The last stanza of Lila Ripley Barnwell's poem "Oklawaha" reads:

> *Oklawaha, yes I love it,*
> *Lord, I pray my soul to keep*
> *Let me lie near Oklawaha*
> *When I take my last long sleep.*

Lila Ripley Barnwell was in fact buried in Hendersonville's Oakdale Cemetery, and not in Florida by the banks of the Ocklawaha.

O.B. Jones Farm

Omra Burr "Bervie" Jones (1888–1951) and his wife, Sallie Hunter Jones (1890–1973), once farmed a ten-acre parcel of land where Raymond's Garden Center now operates its nursery at 1310 Kanuga Road. Prior to

Carl Raymond and his family's presence at the site, Henderson County Sheltered Workshop—known then as Something Special—once used the land for agricultural instruction for individuals with special needs—a program established by local Kiwanians in the early 1960s.

O.B. Jones, a graduate of North Carolina State University's Farm-life School at Rowan County, graduated in 1920 with a bachelor of science degree. The Joneses married in 1919 and adopted a daughter, Alice. Jones was, besides a farmer, a teacher and superintendant at Rowan County Farm-life School and served as a Henderson County farm agent from 1927 to 1935. O.B. and Sallie Jones are buried in Red Oak Presbyterian Cemetery, Buncombe County.

Frederick Jones mentioned, in his book *Darkness Comes in the Morning*, "Bug" McCall having worked on the Mud Creek Farm near Kanuga Road (Crab Creek Road) and Erkwood Drive. Speculation might suggest the latter was the provenance of the O.B. Jones Farm.

A fine example of a barn occupies the old Jones farm—a barn where Sallie Jones resided in her later years after the farmhouse burned to the ground. At the time, neighbor Robert Lee Whitmire, upon noticing the raging fire, dashed across Kanuga Road to check on Mrs. Jones, who stood safely outside of the burning house.

Old-timers of Henderson County remember the eccentric Mrs. Jones driving a creaking station wagon until it would run no longer. They also recall having seen her walking to town with newspapers bound with string in lieu of shoes. One day, concerned bank patrons, who found her dressed in that manner, contacted social services, and Mrs. Jones was moved to the county home for the indigent.

HILL HAVEN (1941)

In 1940, King Gallileo Justus bought 11.3 acres from Annie D. Jordan (1862–1946) across the road from the Jones farm and built on this hill a house for James Oscar Harley (1883–1959) and his wife, Rosalye Treadway Harley (1888–1951), of Florida in 1941. The story goes that the Harleys liked the house but would have preferred it closer to town, even though their property stood less than half a mile from town. The Harleys sold to Fred W. Young (1886–1955) and his wife, Leona Allen Young (1883–1952), in 1946, and the Youngs sold to Robert Lee Whitmire (1898–1970) in

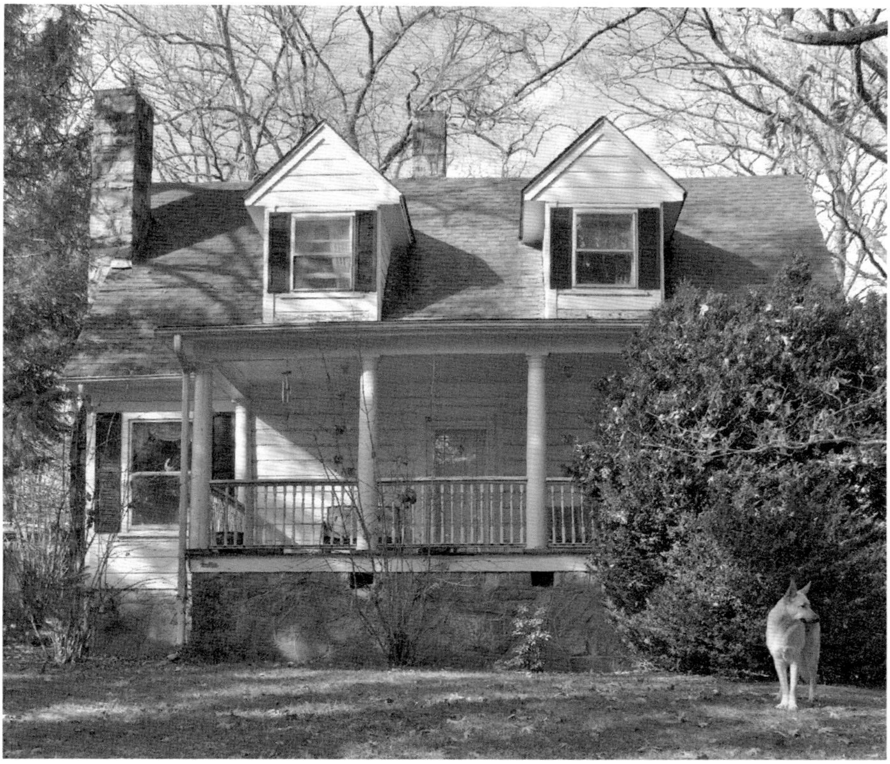

Hill Haven.

1948. Whitmire had married Irene Louise Jones (1905–1932) of Georgia in 1925. Whitmire, an attorney and Superior Court judge, served on the North Carolina House of Representatives from 1945 to 1957 and was elected to the state senate in 1957. He also served on the North Carolina Utilities Commission until 1958. The Whitmires had a son, Robert Lee Whitmire Jr. (1926–1993).

Whitmire sold in 1963 to Cecil D. Foster (1918–2009) and Martha C. Foster (1930–?). The Fosters sold in 1968 to James H. (1934–) and Linda Laird Barnette (1938–), and the Barnettes sold in 1998 to Harry and Barbara Weeks, the current owners.

The Colonial Revival residence with drop-cove (German) siding stands at the summit of a wooded hill, well camouflaged from Kanuga Road. Old-timers remember that one of the occupants kept a chicken ranch on the Hill Haven property.

Of the property, local preservationist-architect John Horton said:

> *This is indeed a sacred property, for it is at the backdoor of this very house that I kissed my future wife for the first time. I went on to spend most of my high school senior year—and most weekends during my first two years of college—in this house trying to have a quiet moment with a pretty girl, but our plans were often foiled by her little sisters and brother spying on us. I also recall the sensation of someone watching me when I went into the kitchen, but it was only one of their goats staring at me through the kitchen window.*

Horton's wife of thirty-three years is the former Kimberly Barnette (1959–), a Henderson County native whose grandfather, James Harold Barnette (1907–1995), painted many of the historic homes in Henderson County.

DRAKE STREET, ERKWOOD DRIVE AND STATE STREET

In the 1950s and '60s, Edgar A. "Eck" Garren (1906–1973) and Addie Lee Corn "Nanny" Garren (1914–2008) operated a roller rink at the end of Drake Street. The shed-style building stands forsaken today, yet some still remember its highly varnished wooden floor and meeting friends after school to rent skates. The Garrens also had the Putt-Putt Golf Course and a pony ride venue on their property.

Not far up Erkwood, at the end of Estate Drive, stands the Count deChoiseul's "castle," known more popularly as Chanteloup. Lieutenant Colonel and Assistant Adjutant General David Urquhart (circa 1828–1900) of New Orleans bought the estate in 1858 and owned it until 1898, after which time it passed between several owners, a foreclosure, abandonment, name changes and, more recently, an impressive restoration. The name Erkwood was a corruption of Urquhart, according to the late historian/author/columnist Louise H. Bailey.

Traveling west on State Street between Kanuga and Willow Roads, one finds a Queen Anne/Classical Revival mansion (1904) on the north side—once the home of celebrated U.S. Army major Frank Egerton Strider (1918–1981) and Ruby Emma Williams Strider (1920–2009). The Striders donated land in 1978 for Maranatha Baptist Church in East Flat Rock. Earlier in his life, Mr. Strider had owned Strider's Self Service grocery store on North

Main Street in Hendersonville, and he also sold cars. The home boasted a library of more than six thousand books. Across the street from the Strider home may be seen a former equestrian facility once owned by business and community leader Clifton J. Shipman (1923–2010). The house was built in 1903, and Shipman added the twelve-stall barn in the 1940s. "Cliff" and his brother, Seldon Edgar "Buddy" Shipman Jr., started the Jaycee Saddle Club on the property, which hosted square dances in the barn in the early 1950s. Cliff owned one of Hendersonville's first drive-in restaurants, the Hasty Tasty, and also Clifton's Cafeteria, the Chicken Shack, the Cedars, the Chariot, Putt Putt Golf Course, Minit Car Wash and the Jump Off Rock Gift Shop.

When Hendersonville Little Theatre (HLT) formed in 1966, Clifton Shipman donated the use of a storage building on Haywood Road for the purpose of the theater group's productions. When quick success of HLT found the group lacking for space, Shipman allowed it to use the barn at his saddle club in 1969; it operated there until 2012, when the group moved to the abandoned sanctuary of the Seventh-Day Adventists on Washington Street. The Adventist church was organized in 1924 and built 1929–30. Succeeding the Seventh-Day Adventist Church's tenure, other occupants included Pentecostal Holiness Church and the restaurants Samovar Café and

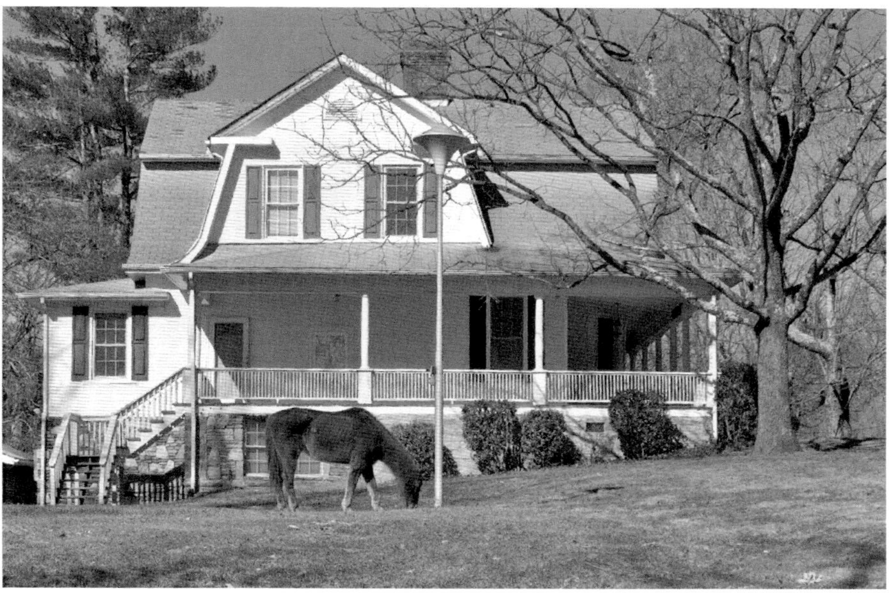

The Shipmans' former home on State Street.

LaCapella Carmella. In the process of converting a church building into a theater, board members of HLT donated the steeple to Life Center Church of God in Christ. Ironically, the latter church was home to Pentecostal Holiness Church in the 1940s.

Shipman also owned—opposite his Chariot banquet facility on North Church Street and West Sixth Avenue—the Grace Lutheran Church (1924), which had been vacant since 1979, when the Lutherans moved into their new sanctuary at the corner of Blythe Street and U.S. 64 West. In 1999, Shipman donated the property to the Reformation Presbyterian Church (RPC), which purchased Shipman's former cafeteria next to it and outfitted the building for its Kirkside Hall. Members lovingly restored the old Lutheran church, which reopened as the RPC sanctuary in 2006.

Alfred A. McCall Family House

Within the Hendersonville city limits and across from Judsen Lane, the home of Alfred A. McCall (1888–1959) may be glimpsed at 941 Kanuga Street. Once comprising several acres, the estate has been whittled down to a little over one acre.

Erle G. Stillwell designed the early 1920s Craftsman Bungalow–style house with a broad front porch featuring stone piers, steps and porch surface; heart-pine floors and ten-foot ceilings on the ground level; and oak floors and nine-foot ceilings on the second story. Each bedroom includes a sink and transom windows over its door. Alfred McCall, a plumber, overrode Stillwell's plumbing designs and installed more elaborate bathroom fixtures.

The heavily landscaped property previously included the land under the town home developments flanking it, where previous owners Amos James Overton Sr. (1893–1970) and Effie Shipman Overton (1888–1976)—of Overton's Cash Wholesale Company in Hendersonville—planted a show-stopping display of azaleas and other specimen shrubs and trees during their tenure from the 1940s to 1980. The remaining McCall/Overton property still sports hydrangeas, hollies, ligustrum, Japanese aucuba, camellias and one hundred azalea bushes, as well as Chinese chestnut, magnolia and Japanese maple trees under a canopy of ancient oaks.

WEST HENDERSONVILLE BAPTIST CHURCH

On White and Yarborough Streets stands a white, weatherboarded, church-like building that houses MLH Paper & Party Supplies (slated to close in 2013). This was the first home of West Hendersonville Baptist Church, founded in 1934, when White Street was called Arcadia Street. The congregation began worshiping in a tent on this site during the World War I years and conducted Sunday school classes in a house owned by Joseph P. Hollingsworth (1886–

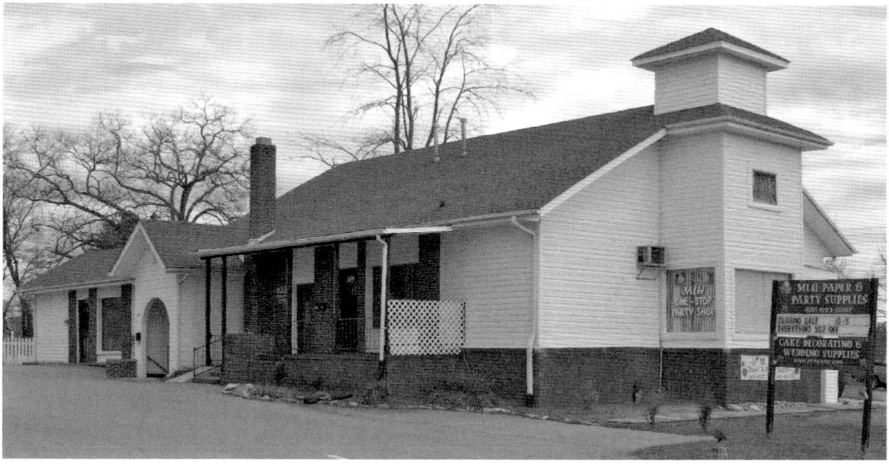

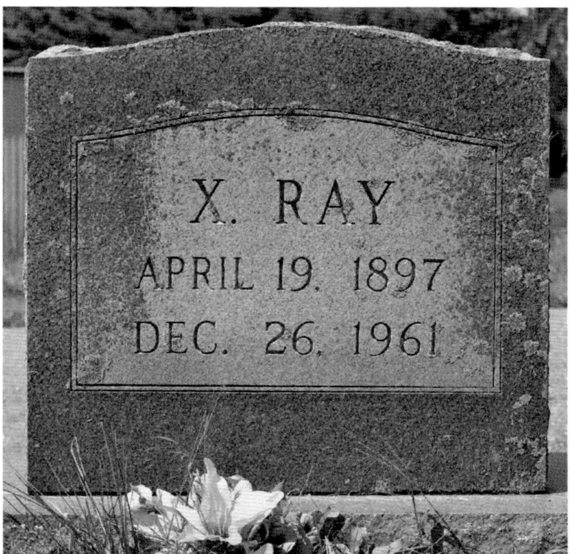

Above: The first sanctuary of West Hendersonville Baptist Church.

Right: X Ray's tombstone, Mills River Presbyterian Church. X Ray was the father of Lenoir Ray.

1952) on Yarborough Street. Next, the growing congregation rented Lyda's Store and used it for worship services while raising funds to build its own church. Members organized this church, Kanuga Street Mission, into a missionary Baptist church, with H.H. Mace (1883–1955) elected as first pastor, William L. Sentell (1856–1946) as deacon and X Ray (1897–1961) as first clerk. Members purchased the lot on White and Yarborough in 1936 and completed their new church that year. Having outgrown the wooden church, members built a brick sanctuary on Willow Road in 1972.

EDGEMONT SANATORIUM

During the late nineteenth and early twentieth centuries, tuberculosis led the top-ranked causes of death in the United States. A wide assortment of treatments claimed to soothe and even reverse the disease, the most popular and widely accepted of those cures involving the placement of the afflicted in an environment boasting clean air, low humidity, cool nights and abundant sunshine. By the late 1800s, sanitariums—or sanatoriums—designated for TB treatment were being built in various temperate locations throughout the country. Given its climate and pristine ozone, western North Carolina quickly emerged as one of the premier destinations for those suffering from the dreaded disease.

Several tuberculosis infirmaries sprang up in the Blue Ridge Mountains—a number of them grand facilities with open sleeping porches, ensuring patients the benefits of uncorrupted mountain air. With the coming of the railroad to Hendersonville in 1879, patients arrived in droves for a hopeful cure.

One such TB patient was Dr. William Redin Kirk (1870–1960), a surgeon in the United States Army throughout the Spanish-American War. Kirk arrived in Henderson County from Harrodsburg, Kentucky, in 1901. Once cured, he remained in Hendersonville, where he married Josephine Egerton (1880–1957), one of the daughters of Dr. James L. Egerton (1857–1933) and Martha Eliza "Mattie" Fletcher Egerton (1852–1892). Kirk opened the Edgemont Sanatorium at 515 Kanuga Street near the Southern Railway tracks, on the west side. The Kirks operated the facility, which offered—in addition to medical treatments—the entertainments of the Hendersonville Male Quartet. A listing in *Miller's Hendersonville Directory* 1926–27 listed Miss De Etta Quinn as superintendant. One can only wonder what all the smoke from the passing locomotives did to the rarified air.

The *French Broad Hustler* mentioned, in June 1907:

> *The Kirkwood Sanatorium is a new enterprise for Hendersonville, recently organized. The company has leased the Atkinson property and will open as a modern, carefully managed sanatorium. The officers are Dr. W.R. Kirk, president and treasurer; Miss Atkinson, vice-president; Mrs. Susie Allen, secretary. The reputation Dr. Kirk has achieved along this line is sufficient guarantee that the sanatorium will be successful from the start.*

The Kirkwood Sanatorium was apparently a precursor to Dr. Kirk's facility established on Kanuga Road in 1910—on a lot athwart what was then named Edgemont Street and now called Davis Street. Dr. Kirk purchased the land from Anna V. Atkinson in 1907, according to deed records. The recorder of the deed described the property as "beginning at a stake on the west side of the Transylvania R.R. and N.E. corner of a lot conveyed by J.H. Ripley to the Town of Hendersonville, known as the 'Quay lot.'"

By 1913, Kirk's sanatorium had caught on, according to an article in the *French Broad Hustler*: "In order to meet the demands upon the Edgemont, Dr. Kirk has begun the erection of an eight-room cottage next door to this institution. This building will be equipped with sleeping porches and many of the rooms will be supplied with private baths."

An ad in the *Journal of Outdoor Life* (1918) read:

> *Edgemont Sanatorium*
> *In the Land of the Sky*
> *Hendersonville, N.C.*
> *Established 1910*
> *Owned and conducted by Dr. William Redin Kirk for his tuberculous* [sic] *patients. A modern, up-to-date, private Institution, where the closest personal attention is given each patient. Completed laboratory and X-ray equipment for diagnosis. Rest, Open Air and Diet, Tuberculin and artificial pneumo-thorax treatment given as indicated. All buildings are steam heated, have electric lights, call bells and private sleeping-out porches.*
> *Rates from $18.00 a week up, which includes medical attention and nursing.*
> *Mrs. A.H. Williams, Matron*

A mover and shaker, Dr. Kirk became known as one of Henderson County's leading physicians. As one of a fifteen-member committee of financiers and businessmen of Hendersonville, he worked for street improvements in the burgeoning town. In 1912, he pushed for a hospital to be built in Hendersonville, resulting in the establishment of Patton Memorial Hospital. A November 1906 brief in the *French Broad Hustler* mentioned, "Dr. Kirk was a delegate to the tenth district medical society, held in Asheville. Dr. Kirk was elected vice-president of the society and will endeavor to have the next meeting held in Hendersonville."

In 1926, Dr. Kirk, who as president of Hendersonville's Cooperative Community Building Corporation, announced plans for a ten-story office building to be constructed on Church Street and Fifth Avenue. Erle Stillwell had drawn up the plans for this proposed chamber of commerce building, which would feature eighty offices, two elevators and a grand lobby. A concrete foundation was poured, but the 1929 crash that led to the Great Depression halted construction of the building. Today, Four Seasons Florist and buildings to the south of it rest on the foundations of the proposed tower. A keystone on the one-story building reads, "KEITH 1963."

Dr. Kirk commissioned Stillwell to design a brick structure on Hendersonville's Main Street and Fifth Avenue East, a building that housed retail businesses on the street level with apartments above. Tenants have included Branstetter Shoes, Holley-Swofford Shoes, Emory's Dad & Lad

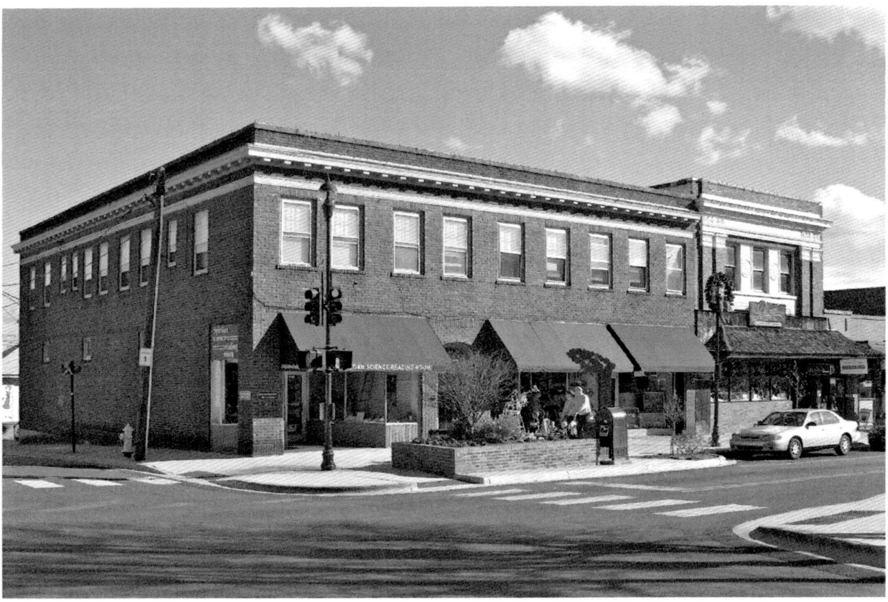

In the foreground: the Kirk Building. The frame building behind it housed Dr. W.R. Kirk's medical offices.

Shop and local philanthropist Bert Boyd, who kept an apartment upstairs for more than seventeen years. The Christian Science Reading Room currently occupies the street-level space. Dr. Kirk operated his medical practice from a wood-frame building at 118 Fifth Avenue East and the Edwards Street alleyway, behind the brick structure on Main Street named for him.

Kirk became hospital chief of staff at Patton Memorial Hospital, was a member of the Hendersonville City Library Committee and, with four other members, chartered the Golden Valley Mines, Inc., in 1927. He also served briefly as Henderson County sheriff in 1907 and was a county coroner.

Dr. and Mrs. Kirk lived at one time at 213 Fleming Street and Third Avenue West, and a January 1907 issue of the *French Broad Hustler* made mention of the couples' moving into their new home, Belleview, opposite the Methodist church. They had a daughter, Louise. The Kirks are buried at Calvary Episcopal Churchyard Cemetery in Fletcher, North Carolina.

ROUNDING THE BEND

Looming above the western side of Kanuga Street, alongside what locals refer to as the "Busy Bend," two contemporary houses stand on Toms Hill, a site formerly owned by business leader and Confederate veteran Captain Marion Columbus Toms. Toms's home, a stately Victorian he named Oklawaha, sported views through downtown Hendersonville to the ridges beyond. Below the hill, on the site of the present Whitmire Activity Building at Lily Pond Lane and West Allen Street, Toms installed lily ponds where locals enjoyed drifting in small, flat-bottomed boats. This was known as Toms Park, donated by Captain Toms to the City of Hendersonville in 1917.

When Toms moved to an English-style house on South Main Street in 1898, he gave his hilltop estate to his son Charles French Toms, who convinced his friend Colonel Sylvester Thomas Everett (1838–1922) to appeal to his colleague Andrew Carnegie (1835–1919) for a $10,000 grant to fund a library to be built in Hendersonville—making Hendersonville the only town with a population under ten thousand to have a Carnegie Free Library. In 1911, Captain Toms gave a lot at the southeast corner of King Street and Fourth Avenue, and Carnegie's funding built the library, which opened in 1914. The elder Toms, a former Hendersonville commissioner and North Carolina senator, owned considerable real estate, including apple and peach orchards on Echo Mountain and the Toms Building on the southeast corner of Main Street and Third Avenue, currently home to Hannah Flanagan's Pub.

At the base of Toms Hill, the Mug & Brush Barbershop occupies a strip center featuring three classic Koken chairs in mint condition. In the 1980s, the shop's owner acquired the chairs from the old Skyland Barbershop in the Skyland Hotel on Main Street. At the other end of the center, in what is now an antique consignment shop, famous heavyweight twin Benny McCrary operated his pawn and auction business.

BLACK BOTTOM

The real estate bounded by Kanuga, Barnwell and South Church Streets once hosted "Black Bottom," a hamlet of stilt houses occupied by members of Hendersonville's African American townspeople. The houses, mostly built in the 1940s, were razed when the Department of Housing and Urban Development moved many of the families to housing projects in the 1970s. The Hendersonville Chamber of Commerce offices and the Hot Dog World restaurant also occupy a fringe of what was Black Bottom. Nearby stood a two-story boardinghouse run by Estelle Ballard, and a general store called Mace's stood on the bend of Kanuga Street at the site of the Dal-Dawa Cycle Center.

"They called it Black Bottom because the neighborhood consisted mostly of blacks and it was at the bottom of Hendersonville," said Donald R. "Donnie" Parks (1955–), who, with his 10 siblings, began his life there. Parks, son of Pearson Parks (1923–1956) and Gussie Beasley Parks (1936–2011), became Hendersonville's first African American chief of police in 1987, serving until 2007—the city's third-longest-serving police chief. Donnie and his twin brother, Ronnie, remember when Frank and Virginia McCrary and their twin sons, Benny and Billy, lived in one of the small frame houses that stood on the southwest corner of Barnwell and South Church Streets before the McCrarys built a new house on Kanuga Road. Parks now teaches leadership development, budgeting and general courses for aspiring police commanders at the North Carolina Justice Academy, Edneyville.

According to Parks, Black Bottom was a poor, albeit well-maintained, blue-collar community, "invisible because we kept to ourselves and through a watch program we governed and policed our neighborhood to keep down crime and other potential problems." Migrant workers, mostly from Florida, counted among the seasonal residents in the neighborhood. Other African

American neighborhoods in Hendersonville—still existing, although reduced in size due to redevelopment—include Peacock Town between Allen Street and First and Second Avenues and bounded by Whitted and Church Streets; "Old Brooklyn"/Green Meadows, near the historic railway station, between Fifth Avenue East, North Grove Street, Ray Avenue and Duncan Hill Road; and West End, near Oakdale Cemetery between Oak, Adams, Blythe and Valley Streets to Ninth Avenue, with Highway 64 West running through the center of it. Residents of Peacock Town say it was possibly named for landowner Samuel Peacock (1914–1980), who owned lots in that part of Hendersonville and also owned a café and store there. Melinda Lowrance added that residents of the neighborhood "walked proudly like peacocks."

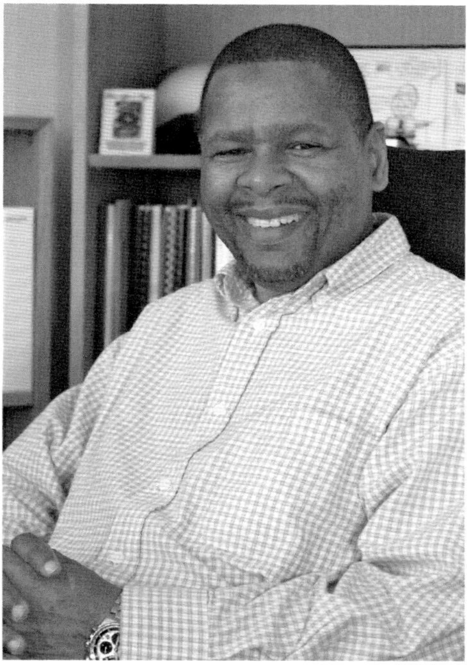

Donnie Parks.

Parks well remembers the infamous, unsolved triple murder case of 1966. Two of the victims, Vernon James Shipman (1923–1966) and Charles W. Glass (1929–1966), frequented Black Bottom, where some of their customers lived. Shipman and Glass owned and managed Hendersonville's Tempo Music in the record store's early locations in downtown Hendersonville. The third victim was Louise Davis Shumate (1904–1966) of Asheville. Locals maintained theories of why someone murdered the threesome, and Parks believes the motive had something to do with drugs or the voodoo practices in which the three colleagues were known to dabble.

Commercial buildings and tarmacs now occupy the former neighborhood where children played in the creek and where the adults kept law and order in place—and Black Bottom, like so much else, has faded into the recesses of time.

Afterword

Not unlike detective work or archaeology, historical research involves boundless investigation, site visits and interviews, the poring through the slapdash of sometimes nearly illegible records and checking, then rechecking facts. At times, the path seems clear until it steers the researcher down a sidetrack—or chasing rabbits, as some might describe the process. Much of history has receded into the shadows of time—lost to fire, floods or carelessness—and a good deal of information has gone to the graves of folks in the know, while some of the documents lay forgotten in attics, cellars and sheds or tucked within family Bibles.

Handed-down accounts verge on exaggeration, with a tendency to mire facts in folklore. Conflicting birth and death dates appear betwixt the genealogical websites, family histories and even in tombstone inscriptions, and oral accounts change with each person who recounts them. It requires enormous patience to study the past, and accordingly, it is up to those of us blessed—or is it cursed?—with inquiring minds to fill in the missing pieces of the puzzles. Nevertheless, we fervently attempt to hold local memory in place.

It is selfish to forget
and worthy to remember.

Bibliography

Agudas Israel Congregation. "Simhat Dor L'Dor: Celebrating Generations, 87th Anniversary Celebration." 2009.

Bailey, Louise Howe. *Generations of Excellence. History of Pardee Hospital.* Alexander, NC: WorldComm, 1999.

———. *Remembering Henderson County: A Legacy of Lore*. Charleston, SC: The History Press, 2005.

———. *Saint John in the Wilderness. The Oldest Episcopal Church in Western North Carolina, 1836–* . Asheville, NC: Biltmore Press, 1995.

Bailey, Louise Howe, and Jody Barber. *Hendersonville and Henderson County. A Pictorial History*. Norfolk, VA: Donning Company Publishers, 1995.

Black History Research Committee of Henderson County, with Gary Franklin Greene. *A Brief History of the Black Presence in Henderson County*. Asheville, NC: Biltmore Press, 1996.

Blazey, Frank. "A History of Sugar Hollow Farm, Henderson County, North Carolina." Unpublished paper, 2005.

Bray, Mary, and Genon Hickerson Neblett. *Chosen Exile*. Nashville, TN: Rutledge Hill Press, 1980.

Edney, Kermit. *The Kermit Edney Weather Book*. Hendersonville, NC: Golden Glow Publishing Co., 1986.

———. *Where Fitz Left Off.* Alexander, NC: WorldComm, 1979.

Fain, James T., Jr. *A Partial History of Henderson County*. New York: Arno Press, 1980.

Finlay, Catherine "Bee." *Early Kanuga Memories*. Columbia, SC: State Printing Company, 1976.

FitzSimons, Frank L., Sr. *From the Banks of the Oklawaha*, Vols. 1–3. Hendersonville, NC: Golden Glow Publishing Co., 1976, 1977, 1979.

Garren, Terrell T. *Measured in Blood: The Role of Henderson County, North Carolina, in the American Civil War*. Asheville, NC: Daniels Graphics, 2012.

Giles, Jennifer "Jennie" Jones. *Jacob Hix Jones Family*. Asheville, NC: self-published, 2012.

Gooch, Albert S., Jr., and Robert M. Smith (Robin) Jr. *There's a Sweet, Sweet Spirit in This Place*. Asheville, NC: Blue Ridge Printing and Kanuga Conferences, Inc., 2000.

Hammer, Sue. "Woodhaven History." Hendersonville, NC: Woodhaven POA, 2004.

Henderson County Genealogical and Historical Society. *Henderson County, North Carolina Cemeteries*. Spartanburg, SC: The Reprint Company, 1995.

Jenkins, Reverend Mark. *Calvary Episcopal Church. First 100 Years*. Fletcher, NC: Calvary Parish, 1959.

Jones, Frederick B. *Darkness Comes in the Morning*. Henderson County, NC: self-published, 2012.

Jones, George Alexander ThM, PhD. *The Heritage of Henderson County, North Carolina*. Vols. 1 and 2. Spartanburg, SC: The Reprint Company, Publishers, 1988/2003.

Kephart, Horace. *Our Southern Highlanders*. Alexander, NC: Land of the Sky Books, 1913.

Marsh, Kenneth, and Blanche Marsh. *Historic Flat Rock*. Asheville, NC: Biltmore Press, 1961.

McIntire, William J. *The Pioneer Log House in Kentucky*. Frankfurt, KY: Kentucky Heritage Council, State Historic Preservation Office, 1998.

Mitchell, William. *Buildings as History: The Architecture of Erle Stillwell*. Hendersonville, NC: Friends of the Henderson County Public Library, 2006.

Morgan, Larry G. *Mountain Born, Mountain Molded*. Boone, NC: Parkway Publishers, Inc., 2002.

Patterson, Cecil L. *Kanuga—Story of a Welcoming Place—A Beginning Made*. Hendersonville, NC: Kanuga Conferences, Inc., 1998.

Patton, Sadie Smathers. *A Condensed History of Flat Rock*. Asheville, NC: Church Printing Co., ca. 1950.

———. *The Story of Henderson County*. Asheville, NC: Miller Printing Co., 1947.

Perry, Jim, and Betsy White. *Le's Whittle Awhile*. Greenville, NC: Era Press, 1976.

Phillips, Laura A.W., and Deborah Thompson. *Transylvania: The Architectural History of a Mountain County*. Raleigh, NC: Transylvania County Joint Historic Preservation Commission in association with Marblehead Publishing, 1998.

Ray, Lenoir. *Postmarks: A History of* Henderson *County, North Carolina, 1787–1968*. Chicago: Adams Press, 1970.

Reak, Jack. *Kanuga: Story of a Gathering Place*. Hendersonville, NC: Kanuga Conferences, Inc., 1993.

Rhodes, Raymond R., and Virginia W. Thompson, eds. *Minutes of the Henderson County, North Carolina Court of Pleas and Quarter Sessions: 1839–1849*. Vol. 1. Spartanburg, SC: The Reprint Company, 2010.

Rockoff, Dr. Stuart. *Encyclopedia of Southern Jewish Communities*. Online history archive, 2006.

Talley, Norman W. *Where Is Penrose?* Shelby, NC: Westmoreland Printers, Inc., 2009.

United States Department of the Interior, National Park Service. National Register of Historic Places Continuation Sheets. "Kanuga Lake Historic District," 1995; "Bryn Avon," 1999.

———. National Register of Historic Places Multiple Property Documentation Form. "The Evan and Catherine Talley House," 1993.

Wood, Dorothy (Kelly) MacDowell. *Gleanings from the* French Broad Hustler, *Hendersonville, North Carolina*. Vols. 1–4. Hendersonville, NC, 1991, 1996.

Index

C

D

M

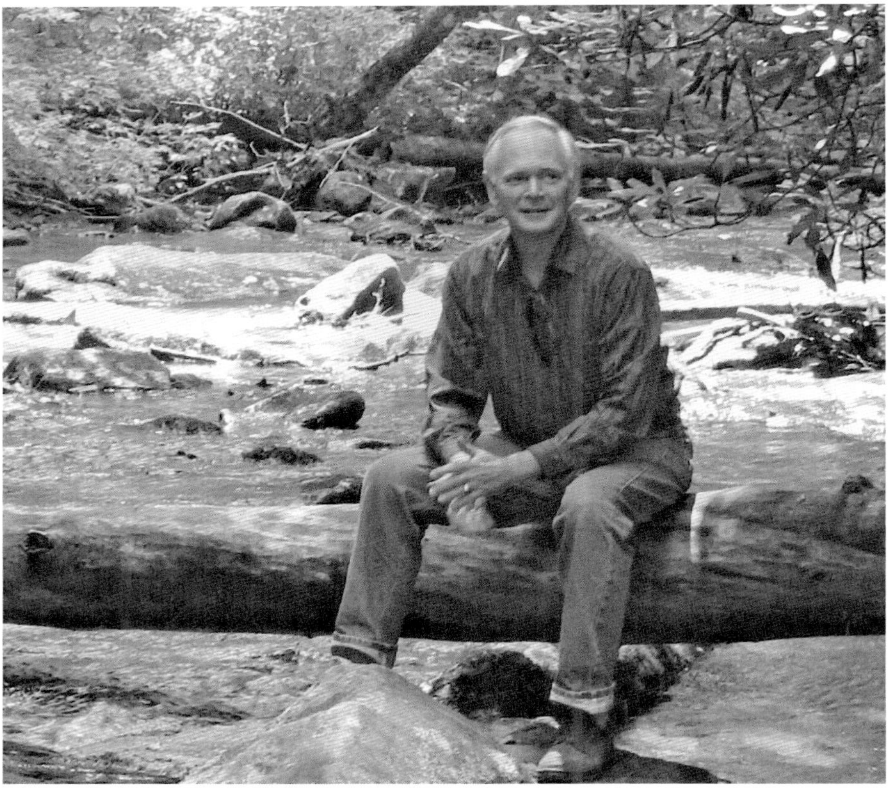

Photo by Beverly Halvorson.

About the Author

Terry Ruscin, an author, photographer, researcher and retired advertising executive, is a member of the Henderson County Genealogical and Historical Society, Inc.; Historic Flat Rock, Inc.; and DRAC (Design Review Advisory Committee overseeing the city's historic districts for the Hendersonville Historic Preservation Commission), as well as a commissioner with HRC (Henderson County Historic Resources Commission). Ruscin has served on the boards of the Henderson County Heritage Museum and the California Missions Foundation.

Ruscin wrote the books *Hendersonville & Flat Rock: An Intimate Tour*; *Mission Memoirs* (a Benjamin Franklin Award winner in 2000); *Dining & Whining*; and the travelogues *Los Duendes: A Nostalgic Journey through Spain*, and *Taste for Travel* (about England, France and Italy). Ruscin and Louise H. Bailey's son Joseph Bailey Jr. finished Louise's tenth book, *Historic Henderson County: Tales from Along the Ridges*, published posthumously in 2010. He has also collaborated on other books on history and travel.

A graduate of Wayne State University in Detroit, Ruscin owned and served as creative director for Ruscin Advertising, Inc., in San Diego, California, before retiring to Hendersonville, North Carolina, in 2004. In addition to writing and research, Ruscin enjoys photographing architecture and the wonders of nature in western North Carolina.

Also by Terry Ruscin

Dining & Whining: Commiseration and Celebration for Gastro-Snobs

Hendersonville & Flat Rock: An Intimate Tour

Los Duendes: A Nostalgic Journey through Spain

Mission Memoirs: A Collection of Photographs, Illustrations, and Late Twentieth-Century Reflections on California's Past

Taste for Travel: A Trilogy of Gastronomic Adventures: Great Britain, France, Italy

Terry Ruscin also collaborated in *An Uncommon Mission* with Father Jerome Tupa and coauthored and edited Louise Howe Bailey's last book, *Historic Henderson County: Tales from Along the Ridges*